Historicizing Race

MARIUS TURDA AND
MARIA SOPHIA QUINE

Bloomsbury Academic
An imprint of Bloomsbury Publishing Plc

B L O O M S B U R Y
LONDON · OXFORD · NEW YORK · NEW DELHI · SYDNEY

Bloomsbury Academic

An imprint of Bloomsbury Publishing Plc

50 Bedford Square	1385 Broadway
London	New York
WC1B 3DP	NY 10018
UK	USA

www.bloomsbury.com

BLOOMSBURY and the Diana logo are trademarks of Bloomsbury Publishing Plc

First published 2018

© Marius Turda and Maria Sophia Quine

British Library Cataloguing-in-Publication Data
A catalogue record for this book is available from the British Library.

ISBN:	HB:	978-1-4411-8424-5
	PB:	978-1-4411-4367-9
	ePDF:	978-1-4411-8016-2
	eBook:	978-1-4411-5824-6

Library of Congress Cataloging-in-Publication Data
Names: Turda, Marius, author. | Quine, Maria Sophia, author.
Title: Historicizing race / Marius Turda and Maria Sophia Quine.
Description: London; New York : Bloomsbury Academic, 2018. |
Includes bibliographical references and index.
Identifiers: LCCN 2017032614 (print) | LCCN 2017049175 (ebook) |
ISBN 9781441158246 (ePUB) | ISBN 9781441180162 (ePDF) |
ISBN 9781441184245 (hardback) | ISBN 9781441143679 (paperback)
Subjects: LCSH: Race–History. | BISAC: HISTORY / Modern / General.
Classification: LCC HT1507 (ebook) | LCC HT1507 .T87 2018 (print) | DDC 305.8009–dc23
LC record available at https://lccn.loc.gov/2017032614

Cover design: Adriana Brioso
Cover image: Our Goddess of Liberty. United States, 1870.
(Courtesy of the Library of Congress, LC-USZ62–136241)

Typeset by RefineCatch Limited, Bungay, Suffolk

Printed and bound in Great Britain

To find out more about our authors and books visit ww.bloomsbury.com. Here you
will find extracts, author interviews, details of forthcoming events and the option to sign up
for our newsletters.

Historicizing Race

CONTENTS

ACKNOWLEDGEMENTS

This project originates in a separate, but shared interest in the history of race and racism. For much of the 1990s and first decade of the twenty-first century, Maria Sophia Quine taught an undergraduate course on evolutionary science and race at Queen Mary, University of London, both alone and occasionally, and much more enjoyably, with Daniel Pick. One of the core aims of that course was to introduce students to new and interesting historical examples and case-studies. In England, most university courses on race and racism focus on Britain, France, and Germany alone; it seemed then and seems still today very important to try to broaden and deepen understanding of the entirety of the European and international experience of race and racism. Another intention was to bring new life into the field of political science which is called "nationalism studies" by exploring the connections between constructions of race and nation in new ways.

In the autumn of 2014, Marius Turda began teaching an undergraduate course at Oxford Brookes University on the history of race and racism. His concern has been to introduce students to the vast historical, sociological, philosophical, and anthropological material that has characterized the development of the idea of race in the modern world. The shape and contents of this book reflect the desire of the co-authors to redress some of the shortcomings in the historical literature and current syllabi. We would like to move away from highly specialized debates, found in such segregated fields as the history of anthropology, the history of science, the history of ideas and nationalism studies, and be more interdisciplinary and integrative in our approach. We hope to present the material in such a way that is attractive to a student who is interested as much in history as in philosophy, science, and politics. At the same time, we have consciously chosen not to limit our gaze to the past alone. Though we are both historians, we have tried to pose important questions about the continuing and perplexing presence of ideas of race in our lives.

The book itself began before the co-authorship started. Marius had been ruminating about writing a book "On Race" for some time and would like to express his gratitude first to Claire Lipscomb, who has now left Bloomsbury, but who never gave up on the project. It is mainly due to her insistence, support, and patience that this book is published today.

Both Marius and Maria Sophia would like to thank Emma Goode, also at Bloomsbury, who was always tremendously helpful, generous, and understanding whenever we ran into difficulties and missed deadlines. We are grateful to Paul King, our copy editor, who has laboured diligently and efficiently over the entire book.

Marius is also very grateful to Mark Hardy, Thomas Loughlin, Lisa Pine, Patrícia Ferraz de Matos, Karim Murji, Chloe Hadjimatheou, Simon J. Wilson, Tudor Georgescu, and Mark Galt for their critical readings of the manuscript and their attentive comments. Maria Sophia would like to express her most heartfelt thanks to Deirdre Storey, Lucy Blake, Rachel Long, Sarah Gelpke, and Shirin Syed, all wild and wise "wimmin," who persistently enquired for over a year about the progress of the book and courageously awaited and endured her sometimes despairing replies. We are blessed to have such good friends. Authorship is never an easy process; co-authorship can be impossible at times. Nonetheless, we are both aware of the special gift that is intellectual partnership and feel that this book is a true melding of ideas and styles, rather than the single-authored chapters that we had initially discussed. That our friendship is still intact is also testament to its strengths and to our tenacity.

This book benefitted from the intellectual environment provided by the School of History, Philosophy, and Culture at Oxford Brookes University. Marius shared his thoughts and ideas with colleagues across the university, including Roger Griffin, Tom Crook, Mariama Sheriff, Graham van Wyk, Christiana Payne, and Joanne Begiato. Marius thanks them all for their encouragement and support. Social anthropologist Jeremy MacClancy convened a seminar on anthropology in the spring of 2015 and he was generous enough to invite Marius to discuss the first draft of the book. Marius extends his very warm thanks to him. Now ensconced as Senior Research Fellow in the Centre for Medical Humanities at Oxford Brookes, Maria Sophia also benefits from the community and conviviality found there.

Personal bonds are just as sustaining as scholarly ones. Last but not least, Marius would like to express his deepest thanks to his family and his parents. They have always been there for him and, particularly so, during the last stages of this book. Maria Sophia would like to dedicate this endeavour to Sam Quine-Church and Luke Haughton, in thanks for their many words of encouragement and acts of kindness during the course of writing this book. The occasional cocktail and glass of Gavi helped too.

London and Norwich
July 2017

Introduction

Plus ça change, plus c'est la même chose.[1]

The definition of race has been the subject of a prolonged debate for which, perhaps, there is no satisfactory solution. As recently noted by sociologists Karim Murji and John Solomos "what is interesting about much of the literature about race and racism is the absence of commonly agreed conceptual tools or even a common framework about the general parameters of races and racism as fields of study."[2] Nothing in this area of research, then, is clearly defined or securely labelled. Such imprecision, it has to be recognized, further complicates the attempt to explain why people continue to believe that races are real, notwithstanding the overwhelming evidence to the contrary which is provided by evolutionary biologists, population geneticists, and other scientists working in disparate fields today. When encountered in daily conversations, race predominately refers to a group of people who share common descent and genealogy and whose biological and social realities have been shaped by culture and environment. A standard description of race therefore includes both biological and cultural determinants.

Perhaps more than any other idea in the history of human culture, race is imbued with a great deal of responsibility. It is not just another abstract concept with little social and political impact outside academia or the university. During the time of its ascendancy as an organizational principle of society, throughout the nineteenth and twentieth centuries, the idea of race has fundamentally changed the history of many countries, individuals, and communities across the world. It was a source of both national self-esteem and national disgrace, particularly during the Second World War. Many peoples have been oppressed, marginalized, and killed for not belonging to the "right" race. Notwithstanding this painful history, racial stereotypes continue to exist in contemporary society and various representations of race still inhabit and invade our lives in disturbing ways.

It is as if race, though now viewed as an obsolete and anachronistic concept, has become ossified in the very foundation of our culture and public consciousness, serving as a permanent source of indurated ideas, influencing thought and behaviour, both personal and public.

A crucially important feature of race is its endurance through stealth and wiliness. The idea of race as we know it in the twenty-first century has not changed significantly by comparison to the sixteenth or seventeenth centuries, when it first emerged as a way to classify and explain human difference. Certainly, there are noteworthy changes and heterogeneity in racial thought and practice within and between different historical contexts and periods, but there is also a remarkable continuity in conceptions of racial self-identity and racial otherness. This is not to suggest, however, that the idea of race is absolute. Contrary to what many continue to believe, race is a product not of nature, but rather of the human mind. It is moulded by what people think and as such it requires human understanding, even if it seems preposterous, foolish, and offensive.

Race, as a marker of individual and group identity, arose from both a fascination and a struggle with accepting human difference not only in terms of perceived physical and psychological abilities but also in terms of cultural achievements and scientific progress. For centuries now, the idea of race has been endowed with cultural, religious, and scientific meanings, and has defined relations amongst individuals and between communities across the world. From today's perspective, many of these meanings may seem unacceptable. Yet if we merely discard them as irrelevant or as expressions of a retrograde past, we will never understand race's constant appeal in the present. Certainly, we have come a long way in fighting racial inequality and injustice and many of us consider ourselves to be enlightened and open-minded but we should try to understand past and present ideas of race within their own time and context, no matter how distorted and untrue they may seem to us.

Although scholars have tried to identify the birthplace of the idea of race, there is no single origin and no author can claim exclusive ownership of the term. Since the great geographical explorations and scientific discoveries of the sixteenth and seventeenth centuries, and especially after the advances of human knowledge during the Enlightenment, philosophers and biologists, explorers and anthropologists, socialists and feminists, fascists and liberals, have all used race in equal measure, albeit for different reasons. Not surprisingly, race grew steadily in importance and scope, covering a remarkably wide spectrum of opinion, though not without facing severe criticism along the way. By the time of the great revolutions of the eighteenth century—in North America and France—the concept of race had attracted its own cultural, scientific, and political supporters amongst disparate, and sometimes surprising, sections of society. Some embraced it wholeheartedly, others reluctantly so. Even those who rejected it, such as the French philosopher Charles de Secondat, Baron de Montesquieu [1689–1755], had to accept its growing influence amongst their contemporaries, most notably the Scottish philosopher David Hume [1711–1776] and the German philosopher Immanuel Kant [1724–1804]. Influenced by the political upheavals following the French Revolution and the Napoleonic wars in Europe, and by the birth of nation-states and nationalism, the idea of race had begun to permeate all aspects of modern, Western culture and civilization. It influenced the humanities and the social sciences, and also political practices, religious beliefs, and cultural tastes.[3]

New academic disciplines, such as anthropology and comparative linguistics, also contributed to an understanding of human variety and diversity in all its complexity. By the time the French zoologist Georges Cuvier [1769–1832] suggested in the early 1800s that racial differences were permanent, the acceptance of different human races had exceeded the realms of natural science.[4] The modern idea of race merged with ideology and politics, and was often used to assert ideas of cultural superiority, as it did so clearly in the case of Cuvier and many of his contemporaries who viewed black Africans as inferior. It is important to note, however, that it was not only the Europeans who portrayed the black peoples of Africa in negative terms. Arab authors, for instance, often described the indigenous populations they encountered in Africa in disparaging terms.[5]

Considering then its continued importance in our society and the wealth of scholarship it has produced over the past decade alone, where can one hope to place a new book on race? This is certainly not an easy task but it is one worth undertaking. As the sociologist Tanya Golash-Boza noted, there is a continuous need for "a sound theoretical approach to the study of race and racism."[6] As will be argued in this book, more is needed in terms of both historical exegesis and philosophical reflection on the meaning and place of the idea and practice of race in our lives, institutions, and societies. Beliefs in the veracity and influential role of racial ideas do not exist only in some countries, such as the USA, Britain, France, or South Africa. Such beliefs are deeply entrenched across the world, as a stratum and residuum of popular ideas, superstitions, and prejudices about "us" and "them," foreigners, strangers, and outsiders. These beliefs continue to be derived from the importance of lineage, family, genealogy, and "blood ties."[7] For most people, a fixed biological identity is an attribute imbibed from infancy, safeguarded by family and community. Most of us, in fact, accept this biological identity as a universal principle of nature, which may explain the widespread need to use racial belonging in many diverse social, cultural, and political contexts. The historian Laura Tabili fittingly captured this aspect when she suggested that "race is a relationship not a thing."[8]

This book on race is thus written consciously from the perspective of the present.[9] The occurrence of certain recent events—especially the rise of nativist, right-wing populism in Europe and the USA, home-grown terrorism, the rise of Islamophobia, anti-immigration campaigns and Brexit, and the challenges posed by the current war in Syria—bear particular scholarly significance for us—as it does, surely, for many readers. One of the less-desired outcomes of these events is a situation in which cultural and political discourses about the future of the West, in both Europe and the USA, have been able to retain the concept of race and attach new meanings to it. To be sure, few politicians, if any, would come forward and declare themselves to be racists, although their speeches and public statements are unmistakably suffused with racial tropes.[10] Can there be, to quote the sociologist Eduardo Bonilla-Silva, "racism without racists"?[11] Furthermore, how can we interpret those racist ideas and statements, which are formulated, as so many are today, without any explicit reference to race?[12]

We may observe, along with the literary philosopher Hayden White, that when we seek to make sense of problematic topics such as race, people "never say precisely what we wish to say or mean precisely what we say."[13] Shunned by decades of public opprobrium, current racism is less explicit; yet the consequences could be no less damaging than previous forms of overt racism, which we experienced in the nineteenth and twentieth centuries. Together with populism and ethnic nationalism, this new form of racism works insidiously to erode commitment to liberal-democratic values. Grassroots groups and political organizations use it to condemn established political parties for their failure to protect the nation from the current economic and social decline. It is also used to blame "foreigners" and "immigrants" for all existing problems. In some cases, such as Italy and Greece, the use of racism also reflects collective nostalgia for past dictatorships or authoritarian regimes.[14]

This book argues that in order to understand what the purpose and the meaning of race is we must accept that there are people around us for whom race and racial differences are real and are relevant. To combat the use of race and of racist interpretations of human relations, we should not avoid the term but rather try to understand its meaning and sense, across time and place. In this book, therefore, we emphasize not only the performativity of race—namely that all individuals become racialized[15] similarly to the way in which they become gendered[16]—but, more importantly, its historicity, namely the ways in which the racial past influences the present.[17] It is the latter aspect that is the main contribution of this book.

By historicizing race in this way and by locating its historical trajectory concretely, we can also review the claim of the biological sciences that race can be dealt with objectively, so its use is somehow justified.[18] According to the anthropologists Michael Kent and Peter Wade "racialised constructs persistently re-appear in biological science" because scientists continue to think of "populations as simultaneously social and biological entities," ultimately leading to "a constant slippage between the two aspects, thus potentially underwriting social categories with an explanatory, predictive biology."[19] This inability to overcome conceptual ambiguity is disappointing, as noted by the cultural theorist Paul Gilroy.[20] The underwriting of the social by the biological occurs not only in science but also in public and political realms. It is, therefore, more difficult to prevent it. As made clear by the Report of the Commission on the Future of Multi-Ethnic Britain, published in 2000, "expunging the traces of an imperial mentality in the national culture, particularly those who see the White British as a superior race, [remains] a much more difficult task. This mentality [had] penetrated everyday life, popular culture and consciousness."[21]

To recognize the growing popularity of race, therefore, we must attend to its historical and scientific traditions, and to ideas of national belonging which have ensured its continuing survival to this day. As the sociologist Michael Skey reminds us, most people in Britain continue to believe that "the world is (and should be) divided into identifiable nations, that each person should belong to a nation, that an individual's nationality has some influence on how they think and behave and also leads to certain responsibilities and entitlements."[22] The referendum on Britain's membership of the European Union, held on 23 June 2016, confirmed Skey's summative evaluation of British selfhood, and the convergence of that sentiment of national belonging with a generalized blame on others (immigrants, European bureaucrats, and so on), which itself is based on a form of scapegoating and a pronounced disenchantment with the collectivizing European project, a supra-national organization, which, the argument goes, undermined the sovereignty of the nation-state.[23] Consider, for instance, Hungary's Prime Minister, Viktor Orbán, who in a speech given in September 2015 highlighted the fact that the desperate refugees passing through Hungary on their way to Germany and Northern Europe "represent a radically different culture. Most of them are not Christians, but Muslims." In so saying, he clearly reproduced one of the main tenets of Eurocentrism, namely Christianity. "Europe and European identity is rooted in Christianity," he remarked, echoing the view of many politicians in other countries as well.[24] Orbán favoured descriptions such as these as they resonate strongly with Hungarian nationalism, old and new. By invoking Europe's (and thus Hungary's) Christian tradition, Orbán unequivocally defined what it meant to be European (and, in effect, Hungarian).[25] Oncoming Muslim refugees, similar to existing European citizens of Arab descent, are perceived as a threat![26] Politicians on the right such as Marine Le Pen of France's Front National or Geert Wilders, the leader of the Party for Freedom in the Netherlands, similarly oppose cultural and religious customs brought from beyond Europe.

Racism, the ordering and understanding of the world with reference to race, continues to exist across the world. It manifests itself in Orthodox Christian countries such as Greece, or in Shintö/Buddhist countries such as Japan; it flourishes in advanced, secularized, social democracies such as Sweden and in post-communist countries such as Hungary, Slovakia, and Russia. It endures in the former colonial powers, such as Britain, the Netherlands, Portugal, and France, and in countries whose past regimes were openly racist, such as Germany and South Africa; last but not least, it remains a painful, daily occurrence in the USA, as President Barack Obama's farewell address reminded us.[27]

These countries are particularly important case studies in this discussion, not only as the birth places of modern racism but, equally importantly, as the places where, after 1945, considerable efforts have been made to expunge race from public and political arenas, and from social institutions, such as schools and universities.[28] To some extent, these concerted efforts to de-historicize race have had unintended consequences, namely that new generations of Europeans are often left unaware of their countries' own racial traditions. The historian Fatima El-Tayeb did not exaggerate when she declared that any reference to the long history of European racism "violates the powerful narrative of Europe as a colour-blind continent, largely untouched by the devastating ideology it exported all over the world."[29] The assumption that Europeans and Westerners, more generally, are more "enlightened" today than in the past, needs revision as much as any other triumphalist interpretation of the world's history through the prism of Western ideas of progress and democracy.

As this book will show, Europe and the West not only invented the modern idea of race but through the pre-eminent place these concepts and constructs occupied in culture and science during the eighteenth and nineteenth centuries, consolidated and exported a racist worldview which placed white Europeans above all others.[30] This is not to marginalize local traditions of race which had existed and continue to exist outside of Europe.[31] To be sure, there is an established racial tradition in countries which are neither white nor European such as Japan and China; and various ideas of race circulated in the Muslim-ruled Middle East and Africa before the Europeans established their presence in those parts of the world. This demonstrates, once again, that the conditions for race and racism to emerge lay not so much in pronouncements of different biological and physical factors, such as the colour of the skin, but often in claims of superior cultural and historical achievements. Such claims are often completely internalized as constitutive elements of personal and collective identity.

To understand how the "racialization of the globe"[32] occurred, therefore, this book draws attention to the interaction between various European and non-European traditions of race. New connections between race and the historical, cultural, scientific, and political contexts within which it circulates are emerging, and they are anything but straightforward. In this sense, at least, we are compelled to recognize the persistence of race in contemporary society. Racism, too, has repeatedly resurfaced, and recent political events in both Europe and the USA confirm that the trend is towards exclusion not inclusion, and towards social autarky, not an open society. The new era of economic nationalism and political isolationism, signalled by events such as Brexit in the UK and the election of Donald Trump in the United States, has provided a stimulus for these forces. New political agendas are now put forward in the name of European and American ways of life and the related claim that there are unbridgeable cultural and religious differences between "us" and "them" has gained many adherents. In its current personification, the idea of race is expressed in a political vocabulary that utilizes strategies of coping with an identity which, allegedly, is under threat by "enemies" without and within the nation. The articulation of a "patriotic" political vision also seems to confirm the return to more aggressive forms of whiteness, highlighting further the radicalization and polarization of the public debate on race.[33]

Following the succession of recent terrorist events, and confronted with a daily influx of refugees from Syria and other war-torn countries, many European governments have become worried about their citizens' personal security, their social stability, and their economic prosperity. In response to an ever-increasing sense of crisis, some of them have adopted a xenophobic language and posture that is boldly set against the image of a harmoniously multicultural and multi-ethnic society which has been in place since the 1980s. Others have responded by tightening border controls and increasing the monitoring of certain ethnic and religious groups.[34] Such measures prompted the political writer Arun Kundnani to suggest that current Islamophobia in the West is "a form of structural racism directed at Muslims."[35]

There is, of course, rich material to be explored in race's enduring appeal to contemporary sensibilities, not only in the USA, but also in France, Greece, and Hungary. In Britain, for instance, since the Brexit vote, new factors have become important, highlighting a broader crisis of individual and collective identity which Britain and Europe at large are experiencing at the moment. In articulating such views, many amongst the general public, as well as the political class, assume that individuals and communities need to be protected against those who are different, although the ontological lines between "us" and "them" are always blurred and unstable.[36] Some authors even go so far as to suggest that European culture and European identity are destined not to survive these uncertain and frightening times of rising global terrorism, economic recessions, and mass movement of displaced peoples.[37]

Such pessimist scenarios of cultural erosion and vanishing civilization imitate classical narratives of decline and cyclical theories of history elaborated in previous centuries by such diverse authors as Arthur de Gobineau, Henry Adams, Max Nordau, and Oswald Spengler.[38] On the other hand, the connection between these narratives of civilizational decline and the idea of race is not incidental. In fact, it is fair to say that race is one of the most salient concepts in the entire history of European and Western theories of progress and decline. Its importance for understanding cultural phenomena, human relations and political arrangements cannot be understated. Its pervasiveness, and the inability of our societies to abandon it completely, highlights an unmitigated paradox, best summarized by the cultural theorist David Theo Goldberg: "Race is irrelevant, but all is race."[39]

To this effect, we must understand the development of race not only as a science and ideology (the literature abounds here) but, more importantly, as a cluster of arguments underpinning ideas of European and Western cultural superiority. In this way, a careful investigation of the relationship between race and culture is required. Admittedly, there is an impasse here which we must struggle with, because to an extent the idea of race bound up in theories of culture owes its compelling significance not only to literary practices (race as a metaphor for identity), but also to debates in social and natural sciences (race as a constitutive factor of reality). As a result, we must treat these disparate traditions of racial thought together, on the grounds that what makes race such a pervasive concept is the fact that since the Renaissance it has been embedded in a remarkably wide spectrum of theories about European culture, civilization, and science. For the authors of these theories, to write about culture and civilization was to write the history of a group of peoples whose authority and dominance over other cultures of the world was often questioned but never relinquished. Martin Bernal [1937–2013] has suggested that "the political purpose" of his book, *Black Athena*, was "to lessen European cultural arrogance."[40] By exploring the centrality of the human and social sciences to the development of modern ideas of race, this book similarly endeavours to demonstrate that cultural arrogance and race are inextricably linked, and so are scientific debates in different academic fields, such as history, philosophy, comparative linguistics, and physical anthropology.

In his acclaimed *Black Skins, White Masks*, Frantz Fanon [1925–1961], the Martinique-born philosopher, wrote that the life of a black person has "two dimensions. One with his fellow blacks, the other with the whites."[41] Fanon reflected upon the question of how could someone who is not black or does not have a so-called "mixed racial identity" or, indeed, someone who has no personal or family experience of colonial history at all possibly understand the concept of race? Or to put the question differently, as formulated by the American idealist philosopher Josiah Royce [1855–1916] at the beginning of the twentieth century, how can we appreciate those "who seem to us somehow very widely different from ourselves, in physical constitution, in temperament, in all their deeper nature, so that we are tempted to think of them as natural strangers to our souls, while nevertheless we find that they are stubbornly there in our world."[42]

This question is as much a challenge for philosophers of race as it is for historians of race and what is needed to answer it is a methodological strategy that fuses moral philosophy with phenomenology and intellectual history with anthropology.[43] To paraphrase the philosopher Immanuel Kant, the aim is to capture race's "universal communicability," its representation as a universal norm.[44] Cast in these terms, the issue of race requires that we consider it from the dual vantage point of its history, that is race as a historical and scientific category, and of its recurrent function as a social signifier.[45] To speak of race, therefore, is to speak of an experience which is both historical and social, real or imagined, but one that nevertheless connects the individual to a broader community whose members are bound together by a sense of purpose, mission, and identity.

To contest the relevance of race is to expose it, not only as ideologically flawed, but equally as historically contingent. An emphasis on history can help us to acquire a better knowledge of race, especially when the objective is to *identify*, *define*, and *understand* it.[46] Through empathy with various historical materials we may be able to propose a renewed criticism of race. For instance, acknowledging that race, within the biological and social sciences, as well as within political discourses, has been instrumental in shaping our modern culture and society, means to accept its conceptual fluidity and not to reify it as unchanging and permanent. It also means to disengage from the outdated strategy that sees race either as biologically defined or as exclusively constructed as a result of social imagining. What we are describing here is the way in which the idea of race is actively redefining what identity is, on the basis of its own social, cultural, historical, and political interests. In this respect, we aim to overcome the too rigidly drawn distinction between the concept of race as a "fact," when used by scientists to describe human groups, and its depiction as a "fiction," when applied to society.[47]

This methodological position might help us overcome the "facticity of race," described by Fanon above, which "presents itself differently to blacks than to whites."[48] We are, therefore, aware that when writing about race, one cannot and should not impose a *history* of race "based on the white experience" onto others (blacks, Asians, and so on), but we should not be afraid to try to historicize race within its ontological framework.[49] According to the philosopher Charles W. Mills, "race can be ontological without being biological, metaphysical without being physical, existential without being essential, shaping one's being without being in one's shape."[50]

Organization and Themes

This book is organized around broad central themes. The first of these is the historical reality of race. Chapters 1 and 2 discuss the assertion that, in order to understand the recurrent appeal of race, we should start by placing it in its appropriate intellectual traditions and currents of thought. In Europe and in the West, more generally, we continue to cling to a historical narrative about our culture, progress, and civilization that we had ostensibly banished long ago; yet, it lingers on. The fundamental argument centred on the nature and meaning of human diversity and, connected to it, on the difference between the so-called "primitive races" and the "superior European races." Stripped of its explicit racial content but still subtly Eurocentric, this historical narrative continues to provide powerful ideological sustenance in the twenty-first century, alongside a process of identification that is constantly reinvented to draw out the difference between "us" and "them." As current populist movements in many European countries draw much of their inspiration from theories of culture and civilization which were developed during the nineteenth and twentieth centuries, it is important to highlight these theories in order to understand the current revival of ideas of racial belonging and protection.

The second theme to be addressed in this book is the interaction between race and nation. Chapter 3 describes how the idea of the modern nation and its character evolved gradually from assumptions of cultural specificity and unique historical conditions to claims of autochthonous identity, defined as continuous and unbroken. Cultural myths of origin and historical purpose enshrined a people's sense of national belonging in inspirational, iconic, and instructive stories, codes, and symbols. The nation, moreover, needed not only to be affirmed, but also to be protected so that it could flourish. To this day, the modern nation seems to be constantly under threat from internal and external "enemies," be they ethnic minorities, "inferior races," "foreigners," and, more recently, "immigrants." Deeply essentialist notions about national character are often used to supply comfort and reassurance in difficult times and, in this respect, we need to understand the historical context of these ideas.

To be sure, current defenders of European and American "values," for all the effectiveness of their rhetoric, do not depend upon the objective existence of different races; nonetheless, the idea of race remains embedded in their conceptualization of their own country as "white" and Christian. Racial and national identities are thus conceived as a continuous nourishing process, for both the individual and the collective. The political rhetoric now claiming to defend European, British, and American national cultures may appear legitimate to many but it risks unleashing even more radical responses. To some, such demands to return a country's alleged tarnished sovereignty bring to mind calls for national revival of the 1990s[51] and they certainly characterize the ethnicist repertoire promoted at the moment by the populist right in the USA, Europe, and Russia.[52] To be sure, assertions that national identity is under threat reflect a growing apprehension amongst politicians and the general public across Europe, an apprehension, moreover, that feeds off the growing popularity of native nationalisms everywhere.[53] The exclusionary and rhetorically aggressive language one hears daily in Budapest, London, Stockholm, and Paris, critical of immigration and advocating a return to true national values, aims to re-historicize the responsibility towards one's ethnic community, deemed to have been devalued by the European project, encroaching globalization, and predatory forms of ethnic assimilation, unencumbered by the restraints of national values.

The third and final theme addressed in this book is the racial embeddedness of scientific practices, particularly in physical anthropology. Complementing various historical traditions of race is the interaction between the cultural perception of human difference and its codification by scientists and various academic disciplines. Chapter 4 focuses on racial genealogies such as the Aryan myth that were founded upon claims put forward by comparative linguistics, religion, and history. That these theories rested on imperfect readings of historical records and false assumptions about a scarcely documented past mattered little to those determined to find a connection between language and race, between history and religion.

Alongside this ideological tradition of race, and the cultural field to which it gave rise, existed another, already in full display of its potential during the nineteenth century: anthropological classifications of humans. Anthropologists looked to find ways to mobilize the passion of the people towards the scientific idea of race. As ideas of culture and civilization increasingly came to rely upon racial theories about the national community, its dominant physical type, and the preservation of its specific racial characteristics, anthropology attempted to furnish the necessary evidence for the notion that nations too were racially and hierarchically organized. In doing so, anthropology developed both scientifically and politically.

Chapter 5 considers in more detail the relationship between physical anthropology and race and the historical problem this interaction raised throughout the nineteenth and twentieth centuries. Anthropologists measured crania and then photographed individuals with a view to demonstrating how brain size and weight, the shape of the skull, and cerebral circumvolutions differed between men and women, and between the races. The central argument was that observable and measurable variations found in the bodies and brains of human beings revealed significant differences in the morality and intelligence of the races and of men and women.

Although anti-racism in science has been growing gradually since the 1930s, receiving a new impetus in the 1950s and 1960s, the concept of race remained in use in a number of academic disciplines and across geographical divisions. In the stereotypes which still have currency today, we are not a world away from the attitudes deeply imbedded in nineteenth-century racial anthropology. Categories to describe racial and ethnic identity are highly ambiguous and misleading. All are reliant, moreover, upon stereotypes, biases, and prejudices for an understanding and ordering of the world which distinguishes black peoples from white peoples (and so on) and divides humanity into distinct groups according to prevailing definitions of race and ethnicity.

This book, in short, examines certain episodes in the history of race in order to expose its complicated relationship with philosophy and history, theories of culture and civilization, science and politics. Delving into the labyrinthine meanings of these racial narratives will not only shed light on the worldview of certain influential authors, but also help us understand the current transformation of race in Europe, Britain, the USA, and elsewhere. What this book aims to do, simply, is to turn "the corrosive historicizing eye"[54] on the concept of race, so that we can unmask and discredit its discursive possibilities. This ambition is tied up with another, final claim.

The political philosopher Larry Siedentop recently remarked: "We [in the West] no longer have a persuasive story to tell ourselves about our origins and development."[55] This book seeks to show that a "persuasive story" does continue to exist and to inform our daily life, albeit one that has been for a long time chastised as immoral, unscientific, oppressive, and even genocidal. This is the story of race.

CHAPTER ONE

History

[I]n our calmer moments, we must acknowledge that human beings are divided into races.[1]

Like all political and cultural symbols, race has no regular or necessary connection with scientific or social reality; yet it feels *real*. For the sake of simplicity, one can certainly define race to be everything that is believed to be race by a particular group of people in a given historical context.[2] In this regard, it may be worth noting the work of the historian of religions Mircea Eliade [1907–1986]. According to Eliade, a myth "expresses the *absolute truth*, because it narrates a *sacred history*." As Eliade further notes, "Being *real* and *sacred*, the myth becomes exemplary, and consequently *repeatable*, for it serves as a model, and by the same token as a justification, for all human actions."[3] It is daunting, but far more rewarding intellectually, to attempt to understand race as a *real* political, cultural, and social signifier, one that has shaped our lives for centuries and continues to have an impact on both a personal and social level in most countries across the world. Put differently, there are many theories of race, but, ultimately, it is personal knowledge that dictates how one internalizes and experiences race in daily life.[4] As the social anthropologist Pierre L. van den Berghe put it: race matters "only if you think it does."[5]

It is, therefore, only appropriate that we ask whether and in what ways ideas of race found a fertile environment in the emergence of terms such as Western culture and civilization. To be sure, what is perceived as historically significant changes with the passage of time. In other words, in order to understand how race continues to have an impact upon our lives, we must explore it not only within its current social context (both real and fictitious), as prompted by philosophy, sociology, literary and cultural anthropology, but also within its own conceptual territory acquired progressively through the conquest of (geographical) space and (historical) time. Race is neither simply a natural entity based upon the sum of certain biological characteristics (as racial authors had argued for centuries), nor just the outcome of cultural and social imagination (as modern sociologists and cultural anthropologists would have it). It contains elements of both nature and culture, of both personal and collective history.

Some authors, however, afforded little importance to culture. In 1911, the English biometrician Karl Pearson [1857–1936], described "racial character" as "the product of many centuries of selection, one which passes from generation to generation, and one which is not fundamentally modified if a child be born to the race in India, Canada, or Australia."[6] Pearson's strong emphasis on the hereditarian nature of race did not exclude the role of cultural and environmental factors altogether. "In using the term *racial*, which signifies ultimately hereditary qualities," Pearson clarified, "we are not *a priori* refusing to consider how far nature and environment affect physical or mental characters."[7] Then as now, it proves difficult to confine race to one interpretation—be it cultural, biological, or a combination of both.

To complicate further an already complex picture, in some countries, such as Russia, which "had annexed, absorbed, and exterminated its others" and where "everyone was of one and the same colour," the idea of race was integrated into the notion of estate. According to the historian Alexander Etkind, in nineteenth-century Russia, estate, "like race [. . .], defined people's roles and regulated their relations; [. . .] it was inherited and from many practical purposes, unchangeable."[8] In Russia, the peasantry was often seen as a different "race" by ruling political elites, anxious about the preservation of their social status. The relationship between rich and poor was naturalized and emphasized as an essential biological and cultural constituent of society. The colour of the skin was replaced by social stratification, whilst legal and cultural barriers functioned as impenetrable demarcation lines.

One of the striking aspects of the study of race is that everyone *knows* or *thinks* he or she knows what race is but no one can easily define it. In many respects, the possibility of defining race appears limited, both because of an unavoidable looseness in its use and because terms such as these can only be defined by other concepts and definitions. Imagination also plays an important role, as argued by the historian Amos Morris-Reich.[9] When anthropological measurements and cultural categories of identification failed to demonstrate any significant differences between individuals, the answers were found in the realm of the imagination. For racists bent on more radical forms of group boundary maintenance, culture and, in particular, language did not create a sufficiently impermeable screening mechanism against the Others (languages could be learned, after all). Biological racism introduced a more absolute principle of closure: the Other could never, even with the greatest will, cross over the symbolic boundary line, since physical difference was indelibly stamped into the body.

Therefore, to some people race has an apparent physical reality that may appear to be permanent, static, and fixed, bound up with its historical instantiation. In view of this, any cultural engagement and criticism of race and racism acquires an overriding moral importance, not simply because *it is the right thing to do*, but equally because without it, we would fail to render it historically relevant. Connected to this is race's own historical genealogy. Some scholars consider that the concept of race and the ideas associated with racism began with the Ancient Greeks; others look to the crusades and the first religious wars between Christians and Muslims as the starting point; others believe they originated in the Renaissance or the Enlightenment.

Historicizing race is, however, not as difficult as it appears to be. To be sure, throughout time, the idea of race and thinking along racial lines have passed through many incarnations. The idea of race, therefore, appears so imprecise, fluid, and ambiguous as to have little meaning or use-value as a category of analysis. Conceptual clarity seems impossible because of the changing nature of understandings and representations of race. However, a good place to begin is by recognizing that race's primary purpose is to signify and explain differences between human beings and this impulse to divide people into quite distinct groups, though historically contingent, seems "essential" to human society and social organization. It is this apparent essentialism and universality which continue to confound and confuse the modern reader.

It is relevant, in order better to grasp the meaning and significance of the idea of race, to highlight a specific chronology and the context of racial thinking. In the first century, for instance, Pliny the Elder [23–79 CE] described the "monstrous races" of Africa, such as "the Androgini of Africa, Blemmyae of Libya (with their faces in their chests), the one-legged Sciopods and dog-headed Cynocephali of India."[10] Three centuries later, St Augustine, Bishop of Hippo [354–430 CE], added the authority of the Biblical narrative to question the existence of "those monstrous men that are mentioned in profane histories." As a believer in the racial unity of mankind, St Augustine concluded: "either the stories of such monsters are plain lies, or if they be such, they are either no men, or if they be men, they are the progeny of Adam."[11]

Yet such depictions of "human monstrosities" residing in the farthest, nether regions of the non-European world continued to inform later debates about what distinguished human beings (defined as white Europeans) from the barbarians (Others).[12] Before the Renaissance, awareness of human diversity and the meanings attached to it had primarily to do with kith and kin, lineage and inheritance; the stock, class, clan, family, or tribe to which one belonged signified the existence of a common origin and descent and shared characteristics, especially language and customs.[13] The term "race" itself entered usage in the early 1500s, and was probably a direct borrowing from the Italian term *razza*, which, before the modern period, denoted good character, lineage, and family and was used to distinguish the nobility from the lower orders.[14] The age of European exploration, imperialism, and colonization, as well as the age of European discovery and the scientific revolution of the seventeenth century, brought new understandings of race.[15]

At first, it was encounters between Europeans and non-European peoples that resulted in a search for the reasons behind human diversity and the meanings to be attached to anatomical differences. As a result, a new form of knowledge transfer and cultural entanglement developed between European countries and indigenous populations in their colonies. The French physician and explorer François Bernier [1620–1688] is often considered to be the very first thinker to promote a modern conceptualization of race, in which mental attributes are ascribed to observable physical differences and human diversity is incorporated into an entire taxonomical system of racial classification dividing all the peoples of the world into distinct groups. In his 1684 publication, "Nouvelle division de la terre par les différentes espèces ou races d'hommes qui l'habitent" ("A New Division of the Earth according to the Different Species or Races of Men which Inhabit It"), which was based upon his travels, he separated between "four or five species or races of men in particular whose difference is so remarkable that it may properly be used as the foundation for a new division of the earth."[16] The countries of Europe were one "species"; Africa was comprised of another. The third one included the Japanese, the Vietnamese, and the Thai people, but also the Russians, the Tartars, and the Turks. The Lapps, or the Sami, were identified as the fourth "species"; finally, Native Americans represented the fifth one.

A similar emphasis on innate physical differences between humans was put forward by the English physician Charles White [1728–1813] in his *An Account of the Regular Gradation in Man*, read to the Literary and Philosophical Society of Manchester in 1795 but published in 1799.[17] If Bernier stressed the importance of colour, for White it was the hair that symbolized racial difference. "The hair of the negro's head," White remarked, "seems to be a different species from the European hair, and not a variety occasioned by any difference of climate, or from any peculiar mode of living, dependent on their want of civilization."[18] Predictably, White's physiological account of human variation led to the claim that the "white European" was "the most beautiful of the human race," whose "superiority in intellectual powers" placed him above "every other man."[19] The French conservative writer Victor Courtet de l'Isle [1813–1867] agreed with this assessment. In his *Tableau ethnographique du genre humain* (*Ethnographic Portrait of the Human Race*), published in 1849, Courtet too equated physical beauty with progress and culture: "the more beautiful the type of a race, the more advanced the civilization of this race; the uglier the representative, the more imperfect the civilization."[20]

These works helped introduce a new paradigm of race that was conceived around notions of physical differences, especially skin colour and body shapes, cultural superiority, and the inviolability of racial difference.[21] In the following centuries, the concept of race became an important explanatory framework for representations of the history and development of humanity. Racial classification as the new foundation for a division of the world which sought to identify and describe "inferior" and "superior" races began to replace Classical and Renaissance cosmography, which saw the world in terms of membership in clans and tribes. Gradually, the concept of race evolved from a genealogical attribute to a notion with which scientists explained the natural world, and through which certain communities developed conceptions of their physical attributes (race as species and subspecies), then to a concept that embodied the features of a specific religious or ethnic group (race as nation), and most recently to linguistic codes and patterns of behaviour (race as language).[22]

Whereas, during the seventeenth and eighteenth centuries, emphasis had been placed on the supposed innate differences between Europeans and non-Europeans, during the nineteenth and, especially, during the twentieth century biological differences within the same country became a focus of attention. A new semantic field gradually formed that gave priority to the biology and nature over culture and education in shaping individual and collective character.[23] Under the guidance of generations of philosophers, linguists, anthropologists, ethnologists, biologists, and physicians, the idea of race was gradually channelled in new directions. It left the domain of science and embedded itself deeply within an emergent Western culture eager to conquer new worlds, destroy the old order, build empires, forge nations, promote industry, and serve progress.[24] The idea of race attached itself to the great enterprise of constructing modernity in all its immense complexity and all its multiform aspects.

Far from being a universal or innate phenomenon common to all societies, past and present, and to all humankind as a whole, racism as an ideology is a relatively recent phenomenon. The argument that human beings are subdivided into distinct groups which have different characteristics has a long history, but the idea of race as biology and destiny does not. Something approximating it, however, did exist in the form of xenophobia in the ancient world, as the works of Herodotus [c.484–c.425 BCE] illustrate.[25] To be sure, Ancient Greeks were contemptuous of the so-called "barbarians," but there was no "colour prejudice" of any kind in Greece or Rome.[26] For example, the Greek philosopher Aristotle [384–322 BCE] saw slavery as necessary and expedient, but his ideas did not derive from colour prejudice. His dictum that "From the hour of their birth, some men are marked out for subjection, others for rule" appears to define slavery as a consequence of the differing inborn qualities of human beings, but Aristotle's views were complex.[27] In his *Politics*, he depicted the two types of slavery as "slavery by law," in which those captured during war became enslaved, regardless of their abilities for self-governance, and "slavery by nature," in which those lacking, from birth, the capacity for self-determination needed to be governed by others. Aristotle believed that non-Greeks, though not entirely devoid of reason and virtue, and, therefore, not wholly inferior, like animals, lacked many of the higher characteristics of natural-born masters; they were more like children than adults, and were, therefore, natural-born slaves.[28]

Following the Christian crusades of the eleventh century, fear and loathing of Arabs and indeed black people, began to grow in the West, but scholars have found no racialized conceptualization of human diversity, race-based form of discrimination, or real racial belief system before the fourteenth century.[29] Not until laws to protect blood purity or *limpieza de sangre* (Spanish), *limpeza de sangue* (Portuguese), *neteja de sang* (Catalan) emerged in the Iberian peninsula after the so-called *Reconquista* (Christian Reconquest), and the collapse of al-Andalus, the last Muslim kingdom, in 1492, did race become a politico-biological concept used to explain human diversity, defend a mind-set with racial ranking at its core and to legitimate discriminatory practices.[30]

In the centuries which followed human and social sciences began to play a major part in the emergence of racial identification as an organizing principle in society. In the early modern period, natural history and ethnology became singularly focused upon classifying human beings by race and assigning them a role as "inferior" or "superior" types. This process of ordering human beings into a hierarchy of races was continued by their successor, the ascendant and increasingly influential anthropology, which became the pre-eminent race science in the nineteenth century. By then, the idea of race was finally "consolidated as a central pillar of Western thought and, above, all, science."[31]

To include questions concerning the scientific validity of race is not to exaggerate the importance of racial thought in Western society and history, but to recognize the historical variability of race as well as the often disjointed juxtaposition of diverse traditions of racial thought both within and outside Europe. This is not to suggest that race stands above or outside of history; rather it is to acknowledge its longevity and durability, without falling into the trap of reductionism. We ought to avoid being "bewitched" by "the subject of race" and to resist "the same philogenetic fantasies and teleological visions that underwrite racial ideologies themselves."[32] As appropriately described by the philosopher George Yancy "the reality of race is indexed to the fabric of our historicity, which makes its reality historically specific."[33] Thus, interrogating certain significant texts of European culture makes it imperative to understand not only the discursive nature of race, but, more importantly, for our purpose here, its historical embodiment.

The idea of race (similar to gender, religion, and language) gives meaning to one's identity and its surrounding cultural, social, and political realms (group, community, society, or nation).[34] As seen, to some, race is a matter of culture; to others it is a matter of nature. The German biologist Hermann W. Siemens [1891–1969], for example, offered a two-pronged definition of race. There was a "system race: a subdivision of a species in a natural-science system" and a "vital race: the super-individual unit of continuing life, which is represented by a circle of similar individuals who live in sexual commerce with one another; the body of the people continuously living on."[35] This definition illustrates the proclivity amongst some early twentieth-century biologists to retain a description of race based on the transmission of biological heritage from generation to generation.

The pervasiveness and persistence of a pattern of thinking which depicts humanity as divided into distinct races—sometimes called ethnic groups, in a seemingly neutral way—is deeply entrenched within Western culture and, in some cases such as the USA, within their immigration policies. For instance, aware of the difficulty distinguishing between members of different ethnic European groups arriving in the early twentieth century, the US Congress established an Immigration Commission in 1907 and appointed Republican Senator William P. Dillingham [1843–1923] as Chair. The Commission completed its work in 1911, having submitted a total of 42 reports on as diverse issues as "Emigration Conditions in Europe," "Immigrants in Cities," and "The Children of Immigrants in Schools." One of its reports, published in 1911, was entitled *Dictionary of Races of Peoples*. It aimed to provide immigration officials with an instruction manual to enable them to identify new arrivals and, more importantly, to which ethnic group and races they belonged. The *Dictionary* divided immigrants into "races," such as "Caucasian" and "Mongolian"; "stocks," such as "Aryan" and "Semitic"; "groups," including "Teutonic," "Slavonic," "Italic," and "Hellenic"; and, finally, "peoples," such as the English, the Portuguese, the Finnish, or the Chinese.[36]

Anxieties concerning immigration were substantiated with information provided by statistical records. Thus, according to the Bureau of Immigration and Naturalization between 1898 and 1910, almost 2 million of southern Italians emigrated to the United States, followed by 1 million Jews. There were still a significant number of Germans (754,375), Irish (439,724), and English (408,614) arriving, but the number of Eastern Europeans was also on the rise: Slovaks (377, 527), Hungarians (338,151), Croats and Slovenes (335,543).[37] Increased immigration of the latter ethnic groups compounded concerns over the decline of "traditional American values" which these groups allegedly did not respect or care for.[38] Partly driven by statistical data demonstrating the demographic growth of "undesired peoples," the racial dimension of American anti-immigration policies during the 1910s and 1920s strongly invoked the image of the "Anglo-Saxon" Protestant citizen and his or her cultural superiority. Such concerns continue to be expressed by supporters of anti-immigration policies in the United States to this day.

Race, of course, is not the only concept used to classify, demarcate, and divide human groups. Class, gender, sex, and education are also significant markers of difference. To be sure, the widespread tendency to see racial differences everywhere, and to assign value to them, has not gone unchallenged. Current public opinion in the West, for instance, accepts that physical differences between individuals are not culturally and socially significant. Yet, that we continue to see the category of *difference* as being relevant at all is significant, and within this mental framework race continues to be an important component of daily human interaction, especially for those, such as African-Americans in the United States or North Africans in France, for whom it continues to be a limiting and determining feature of existence.

One may see the continuous presence of race in our public life as an expression of our civic failure to embrace the liberal-democratic ideal of cultural tolerance and ethnic diversity. Has civil society so deteriorated in the twenty-first century that we can feel no sense of empathy or compassion for the sufferers of the world or any moral responsibility towards each other? The ambitious goal of the creation of a world where all nations and peoples are recognized as part of one human family was already articulated at the First Universal Races Congress held in London in July 1911. Amongst the participants there were luminaries such as anthropologists Felix von Luschan [1854–1924], Giuseppe Sergi [1841–1936], and Franz Boas [1858–1942]; sociologists Ferdinand Tönnies [1855–1936] and W. E. B. du Bois [1868–1963]; and philosophers Alfred Fouillée [1838–1912] and Brajendra Nath Seal [1864–1938]. The Congress displayed a generally optimistic disposition regarding the future of race. As the editor of the proceedings and humanitarian writer Gustav Spiller [1864–1940] proudly concluded there was "a remarkable agreement on almost every vital problem with which the Congress [was] concerned" and that all participants supported "a view which must be very encouraging to those in every land who see a brother and an equal, at least potentially, in every human being, whatever the colour of his skin."[39]

It took, however, two world wars, the experience of Nazism and the Holocaust, decolonization in Africa and Asia, the civil rights movement in the USA and the end of the Apartheid regime in South Africa, for such an "agreement" to become reality. The fallacy of race was, of course, compellingly promoted as the official political and scientific norm in the West after the Second World War. The broad condemnation of the Nazi crimes, the Nuremberg Trials, and the international recognition of the Holocaust, all highlighted the salient role played by ideas of racial superiority and purity, alongside a worldview depicting nations and peoples according to their biological value. As early as 1949, the United Nations Educational, Scientific and Cultural Organization (UNESCO) mobilized experts across a number of disciplines, hoping to provide new guidelines for the academic thinking on race.[40] The outcome, published in July 1950, became known as the first UNESCO statement on race.[41] Thinking in terms of "superior" and "inferior" races was declared "unscientific," for all races had similar mental capacities. Moreover, it was stated that ethnic mixing did not contribute to biological degeneration. Most controversially of all, perhaps, the statement separated race "as a biological fact" from race as "a social myth."[42] The anthropologist Ashley Montagu [1905–1999], one of the main contributors to the statement, also suggested that *race*, as a term, should be removed entirely from the scientific literature and replaced with *ethnic group*. He pointedly denied the relevance of the idea of race for science.

As with many other anti-racist pronouncements, this first statement on race and the one that followed in 1951 did not persuade many scientists to abandon the use of race. In fact, some of them, such as those who established the International Association for the Advancement of Ethnology and Eugenics in 1959 and its journal *The Mankind Quarterly*, continued to endorse various forms of scientific racism well into the 1960s.[43] By then, however, new geopolitical and ideological divisions dictated by the onset of the Cold War and the expansion of the Soviet Union into East-Central Europe, alongside the growing importance of genetics and molecular biology, contributed significantly to a gradual demise of the biological concept of race. The civil rights movement in the USA, followed by broader campaigns for social, cultural, and sexual liberation, also played an important role in this process. In Western Europe, new immigrant policies were enacted during the 1950s and 1960s, contributing to widespread concerns about the ethnic and cultural divisions in society. The "race riots" of 1958 in Britain are but one example of how race continued to shape post-war politics.[44]

The 1964 Civil Rights Act and the 1965 Voting Rights Act formally ended the post-Civil War racial apartheid system in the United States. However, pronounced racial inequalities in education, housing, and employment remain. Whilst the entrenched racism of white supremacists of all varieties continues to be challenged, new sociological research seems to suggest that African-Americans and other ethnic minorities face damaging and life-limiting discrimination on a daily basis more because of the effects of cognitive biases embedded by racial and ethnic stereotypes than by overt and politically-motivated racial prejudice. The unconscious and everyday workings of racial stereotyping, and their detrimental impact upon those denied access to equal opportunities in all areas of social and economic life, can, however, be reinforced by institutional forms of discrimination such as racial profiling. Furthermore, unconscious biases and overt racism are reinforced by such objectionable practices as racially biased policing.

Historicity

As many geneticists, sociologists, and anthropologists would readily agree, race cannot be thought of in hermetic isolation. On the contrary, race is experienced through a perceptual framework derived from inherited traditions of biologized sociability (family, community, nation) and which is transformed continually by personal and collective experiences of belonging.[45] Hence a new investigation into what race is and what it does requires a twofold, albeit contradictory, approach: on the one hand, we continue to challenge race's scientific credibility; whilst on the other, we acknowledge that for some people race does, in fact, have a biological foundation. In other words, we need to rethink the assumption that race is "an entirely social and cultural construction"[46] in order to unveil its anchorage in reality.

Hence, it is hardly surprising that racial authors often stumbled and failed to maintain a prolonged consensus on human diversity. A much-needed endorsement came from philosophy.[47] By the seventeenth century, debates on human nature, prompted by development of rationalism and empiricism, began to harness race with a new vocabulary whilst, at the same time, informing the drawing of the political map of the world with wide-reaching cultural, social, and economic consequences. This underlines one salient aspect of modern philosophy, namely that it also served to justify Europe's historical achievements, creating in fact, "the European-centred conception of humanity."[48]

Connected to this conception is the appropriation of ethno-cultural identities, based upon a sense of belonging to a certain community. In Britain, for instance, it took centuries for the idea of race as one of the constitutive elements of English culture to be established, through a historical process of appropriation and transfer of knowledge that was constantly resisted and often rejected.[49] At the end of the nineteenth century, moreover, race infused not only dreams of an expanding British empire, but also an Occidentalist narrative, defined by the literary critic Saree Makdisi as "a set of discourses articulating the process that made England Western."[50] This interpretation is particularly relevant, as it substantiates the argument that, in order to understand race as a constitutive element of modern culture and civilization, we must also acknowledge its ontological metamorphosis at the juncture between particularity and universality.

According to Makdisi, at the beginning of the nineteenth century, England "was not what would today be called a Western country, nor was it possible to neatly and cleanly distinguish it as a metropolitan space from the various colonial sites—both near and far—over which it sought to project political, economic, and cultural power."[51] Within a century, however, Britain's imperial geography became much clearer, with England emerging both as the metropolitan centre of empire and the centre of its culture and civilization. Augmented by its nationalist insularity, an idiosyncratic and elastic racial worldview gradually came into existence, alongside an imperial culture.[52] But how can we disentangle the overlapping concepts inherent in ideas of cultural superiority projected by the European empires, at home and abroad?

The idea of race is one of the cultural categories that thrived under the protection of empire. This is a view that many authors writing on colonialism share. The East (this time the Far East, the Orient, and so on) is not simply an "invention" of the West, but is also a heteronymous condition, simultaneously shaping the West and the rest of the world. Thus, imperialism embraces European racism, providing it with cultural credibility and the civilizational authority needed to dominate over both *external* (the Orient, the colonies, and so on) and *internal* representations of itself as superior. According to the philosopher of culture Edward Said [1935–2003] this is how "Orientalism as a discourse" produced "the Orient politically, sociologically, militarily, ideologically, scientifically and imaginatively during the post-Enlightenment period."[53]

Suffusing the entire cultural edifice of the nineteenth and early twentieth centuries was a confident faith in science and a readiness to believe that the alleged qualities of the white Europeans such as inventiveness, purposefulness, and rationality were admired and imitated across the world. It is worth mentioning here again Karl Pearson. Pearson devised the widely-used multivariate statistic, the so-called "Coefficient of Racial Likeness" or CRL, in order to measure even minute differences between races.[54] Pearson was a founder of modern statistics, which he defined as an exact science, because it was based on mathematics. His influence can still be felt today with the neo-Pearsonians who believe, like him, that the anthropometric approach is preferable to any other because it has the potential to identify patterns of variance over a large geographic area and between large population groups or samples.[55] Pearson was very fond of converting algebraic results into precise-looking and impressive tables which commanded respect and authority because numbers appear, by their very nature, more factual than words. Like members of the so-called "American school" of physical anthropology before him, who used measurements of brain sizes to argue that black people had inherently low intelligence, Pearson utilized numbers, curves, tables, and graphs as the basis for an underlying ranking system with racial intent. He brought a new statistical sophistication to an old system of racial thinking and classification which sought to divide human beings into separate, distinct, and even opposing groups.

Modern European ideas of superiority emerged not only as a process of political, legal, and institutional control over distant territories, but also as an imagined community of scholars whose identity was based on the knowledge which they produced.[56] European science reinforced ideas of a superior culture and civilization, depending not only upon a colonial "Other," but also on an indigenous Self, in constant need of affirmation and protection. Seen in this way any form of racism must specify itself within a set of discrete boundaries which it recognizes as its own, within an exclusive historical context. What this presupposes is the indigenization of culture, as new means of expressing a collective identity were needed. It also requires the representation of the world according to certain subjective criteria of ethnic differentiation and classification.

How are we, then, to historicize the argument about the need to reinstitute the biological validity of race? This is a crucially important point, as it directly challenges the constructivism of race,[57] which had for decades dominated social and cultural studies. It also dovetails with claims put forward by the new "genomic racial experts," according to whom "race is meaningful socially *and* biologically."[58] The matter is complex and increasingly discussed by social scientists as well. As the sociologist Rogers Brubaker has admitted in his book *Grounds for Difference* "the largely uncontested jurisdictional monopoly over race that the social sciences enjoyed in the last decades of the twentieth century"[59] is now seriously challenged. He further believes that, due to recent discoveries in genetics and biomedicine, we are witnessing "the return of biology"[60] to the field of social sciences.

Is this true only of social sciences? How about history and the writing of history? Historical material can provide a salutary warning against the resurgent influence of race in contemporary societies and we may learn something from understanding how certain historical moments allowed race to acquire its importance as one of the integral elements of Western culture.[61] Race is embedded in history as much as it is in culture and science, and as such it must be studied in relationship with the historical specificity of its past.

The Writing of History

The ability of race to acquire new meanings, according to cultural and political contexts, was at the core of nineteenth-century human sciences. It was not only the natural sciences but also the humanities that have been involved in the maintenance of race as both subject and object of theorizing about human differences.[62] The possibility of creating scientific *evidence* about race was appealing not only to the anthropologist or the biologist, but to the historian as well.

For example, the first book by the Protestant conservative historian Leopold von Ranke [1795–1886], considered to be the founder of scientific historical writing, was *Geschichten der romanischen und germanischen Völker von 1494 bis 1514 (History of the Latin and Teutonic Peoples from 1494 to 1514)*, which was published in 1824. The work opened with Ranke's vision of a reborn Visigoth kingdom merging the old Germanic tribes with the Roman world. "Ataülf, King of the Visigoths," Ranke began, "conceived the idea of gothicizing the Roman world, and making himself the Caesar of all."[63] Not surprisingly, twentieth-century followers, such as Wolfgang J. Mommsen [1930–2004], viewed Ranke as a Romantic and recognized his importance as a *cultural historian* who tried, above all, to understand what constituted the very best of the German nation and all its creative endeavours.[64] Committed to the idea of Europe as home to the greatest cultural achievements ever known, Ranke sought to show in this work how the "Teutonic" nations of Scandinavia, England, and Germany, along with the "Latin" nations of Italy, Spain, and France, were all bound together by a unity of purpose and attainment. Individually and collectively, these nations had been engaged for centuries in an enterprise of cultural advancement with immense benefit for all.

Ranke was one of the founders of the German historicist tradition and, like his successors, when writing about Germany, he focused on the importance of the Reformation and Counter-Reformation, and religion in general, in the development of the traits which he and others associated with the "Germanic" character (which sometimes meant the "Prussian" character) and "Germanic" principles, such as a strong state, the rule of law, social solidarity, economic progress, and shared values, such as education, discipline, and hard work.[65] Historians and philosophers working in the German "school" of history included Heinrich von Treitschke [1834–1896], Adolf von Harnack [1851–1930], and Ernst Troeltsch [1865–1923], who devoted their attention to exploring the positive role of Protestantism in grand narratives documenting the origins and evolution of the nation as well as of the superior "German spirit."[66]

In Italy, the *Risorgimento* (Rebirth or Regeneration) movement similarly gave rise to nationalistic outpourings linking the achievement of national unity with Italy's glorious past, chiefly in the Roman Empire and the Florentine Renaissance. A proliferation of historical works flourished alongside a growing literature on the "Italic" race being developed by ethnologists and anthropologists. They explored the qualities and attributes of Italian nationality, from the Etruscans to the Romans and beyond, which had resulted in Italy assuming the role of the inheritor of Classical Greece, the Prometheus of the cultural and political reality of Europe and the originator of all that Western civilization represented.

The historian Ettore Rota [1883–1953] favoured this nationalistic approach in historical writing and was actively involved in the project to establish the foundational basis for the writing and appreciation of national history. Rota was concerned to show in his writings that the *Risorgimento* movement, leading to the liberation and unification of Italy, was the product of the invincible Italian spirit.[67] He divorced the wars of national liberation (1848–1859), the so-called National Revolution, from foreign revolutions, such as, most importantly, the American and French Revolutions.[68] The "Great Idea of Italy" lived in the hearts and minds of all Italians, he proclaimed, and emanated directly from the "ancient seeds" implanted many centuries in the past. Rota traced Italy's history backwards in time in order to display a continuous and unbroken line linking monarchy, nation, and people.[69]

Other European historians shared the zeal with which self-styled Italian patriots served the cause of the liberal enterprise to plant firm roots for Italian nationhood by "nationalising the past" and promoting national civic values and virtues.[70] In 1877, just as the Great Oriental Crisis was unfolding in Europe, the English historian Edward Augustus Freeman [1823–1892], wrote an article "Race and Language," in which he endeavoured to understand the growing appeal of "a distinct doctrine of race, and of sympathies founded on race, distinct from the feeling of community of religion, and distinct from the feeling of nationality in the narrower sense."[71]

Freeman remarked upon the artificiality of such a doctrine, acknowledging, however, its growing political importance and emotive force. He also aimed to explain the connection between race and language, both thought as indelible markers of identity by the relatively compact nations across Europe. "Language," Freeman argued, was "no certain test of race." He hastened to add, however, that "though language is not a test of race, it is, in the absence of evidence to the contrary, a presumption of race—that, though it is not a test of race, yet it is a test of something which, for many practical purposes, is the same as race."[72] The use of the same language was no indication of common lineage and undoubtedly "no certain test of community of blood," Freeman insisted. The lack of any common origins was, however, no demise of the idea of race, as Freeman suggested; instead, the adoption of "language, manners, institutions, anything but physical conformation, as the distinguishing marks of races and families."[73]

What distinguished Freeman's proposal from other nineteenth-century writings on race was the elasticity of its scope. Rigid interpretations of race relied heavily on biological definitions of the human types and of anatomical classifications. Since the Enlightenment, such interpretations were instrumental in codifying race, reducing it to a sum of physical and mental characteristics and, also, standardizing identifiable markers of race to produce ideal types of the different varieties. Freeman deemed all discussions about the physicality of race imperfect. Whilst anthropology produced a visually persuasive description of race, history had arguably the greatest potential to demonstrate its existence, Freeman believed. To this effect he placed the principles of "moral proof" and "legal fiction" at the foundation of modern theories of race. Seen this way, it mattered less whether race was detectable in people; it existed nevertheless, Freeman argued:

> If then we do not ask for scientific, for what we may call physical, accuracy, but if we are satisfied with the kind of proof which is all that we can ever get in the historical sciences—if we are satisfied to speak in a way which is true for popular and practical purposes—then we may say that language has a great deal to do with race, as race is commonly understood, and that race has a great deal to do with community of blood.[74]

If race was to be acknowledged at all, it had to be revealed not through a succession of biological types but through a process of cultural reasoning and acculturation. There was "no such thing as purity of race at all," Freeman reiterated. It was pointless to attempt to "define with any philosophical precision the exact distinction between race and race, [and] between nation and nation. Nor can we undertake to define with the like precision in what way the distinctions between race and race, [and] between nation and nation, began."[75]

The fact that biological differences between races were fictional produced not just a powerful critique of the reification of physical attributes of various nations but also a paradigm shift in ways of thinking about race itself. Freeman criticized the idea of racial purity but, similar to Gobineau, he did not deny the fact that certain achievements were due to superior elements within the race. "While there is not in any nation, in any race, any such thing as strict purity of blood, yet there is in each nation, in each race, a dominant element—something which is the true essence of the race or nation, something which sets its standard and determines its character, something which draws to itself and assimilates to itself all other elements."[76]

In highlighting the centrality of certain racial elements in producing culture and civilization, and indeed their capacity for adaptation, Freeman, in fact, endorsed a racial interpretation of history. Yet there is a caveat to his strategy. According to Freeman, races which were accepted by the general public and racial authors alike, such as the Celtic, Teutonic, and Slavonic, had from "a strictly physiological point of view, [...] no existence at all"; yet, he pointed out, these races "have a real existence from the more practical point of view of history and politics."[77] In this context, history (as a scientific discipline) played a dual role: to narrate the nation's continuous cultural development and, in so doing, to inspire other nations into pursuing similar achievements.

Greek nationalists were amongst the first to connect race, culture, and civilization to the project of a national state. For instance, one of the leaders of the Greek War of Independence, Alexandros Ypsilantis [1725–1805], invoked ancient Hellenism as the model to guide his compatriots in their revolt against the Ottoman Empire: "Let us then once again, O brave and magnanimous Hellenes, invite liberty to the classical land of Greece! Let us hold a battle between Marathon and Thermopylae! Let us fight on the tombs of our fathers, who, in order to keep us free, fought and died there!"[78]

Such claims had clear consequences in shaping national identity in the nascent state, particularly as the Greek idea of historical permanence in the region of Athens and its environs was met with scepticism and even refuted, most notably, by the Austrian historian Jakob Philipp Fallmerayer [1790–1861].[79] By denying any racial and cultural continuity between ancient and modern Greeks, Fallmerayer articulated an idealized image of ancient Greece that was, in fact, already widely shared amongst the cultured elites in Europe by the mid-eighteenth century, but which, under the guidance of such art historians and archaeologists as Johann Joachim Winckelmann [1717–1768], reached its most elaborated form in Germany.[80] As the historian Suzanne L. Marchand remarked, "the Germans wished to see themselves as rediscoverers of a lost Arcadia and pioneers of a new kind of pedagogy."[81]

Defying this Romantic nostalgia for the perfect ancient Greek culture, the historian Konstantinos Paparrigopoulos [1815–1891] proposed an alternative model of national belonging, which was at the same time a response to the fundamental premises of those theories of race reflecting the superior historical and cultural achievements of Western and Nordic Europeans. This alternative model centred, in short, on historical continuity and the construction of new ways of defining modern Greeks, not as "Albanians" and "Asiatic" as Gobineau and others suggested.[82] Paparrigopoulos saw the modern Greeks as heirs to the successive Hellenic traditions originating in antiquity. As the cultural philosopher Stathis Gourgouris has argued, Paparrigopoulos's six-volume Ιστορία Του Ελληνικού Έθνους (*History of the Hellenic Nation*, 1860–1877), offered "a historical demonstration of cultural integrity," whose aim was to demonstrate "the physiologically undemonstrable case of racial integrity."[83] A few decades later, in the highly nationalistic context of the 1920s, following the exchange of population between Greece and Turkey, ideas of racial continuity were combined with the ambition to forge a monocultural and monoreligious ethnic community.

At a time when Europe experienced a resurgence of imperialism, hostilities between nations intensified, and national boundaries were re-drawn, anthropology was in flux and characterized by the same intensifying nationalist rivalries which permeated the political arena.[84] Many anthropologists became committed nationalists, notably by generously defending the ideological foundations of official propaganda, which, in the years leading up to the outbreak of the First World War became increasingly racist, even in liberal-democratic countries such as Britain and France. It is thus all the more important to reiterate that the politicization of anthropology was not a fortuitous ideological construct, but the logical culmination of a series of reflections about the nature of race, on the one hand, and about the role of science in serving the nation, on the other.

In some countries, anthropology was viewed as a practical instrument to decipher a complicated ethnic microcosm, as in the newly created Kingdom of Serbs, Croats, and Slovenes. In his *La Péninsule Balkanique*, published in 1918, the Serbian geographer Jovan Cvijić [1865–1927] had classified the population of the region into four physical types: Dinaric (groups of the Dinaric mountains); Central (groups from the Southern Morava valley, the Vardar valley, and the Šopi in western Bulgaria); Balkan Oriental (the Bulgarians); and, finally, Pannonic (Slavic groups of the Great Pannonian plain and the surrounding mountains). Using "direct observation," namely his own travels and ethnographic research, Cvijić argued that the Dinaric type—to which most of the Serbs belonged—was intellectually the most gifted, the most heroic, and the most loyal of all the Yugoslav physical types.[85] These ideas of racial synthesis were combined with theories of geographical and racial determinism elaborated by geographers such as Friedrich Ratzel [1844–1904] in Germany and Paul Vidal de la Blache [1845–1918] in France which became very influential during the early twentieth century, validating not only the specifically biological nexus between race and culture, but also the notion of national space and its corresponding human geography.[86]

Anthropologists in East-Central Europe were, in fact, rather late in producing racial narratives of belonging, and when produced during the early 1920s these attempts to re-interpret the national past along ethno-biological lines borrowed unhesitatingly from the latest developments in racial sciences. The multi-ethnic character of the region also played a role, and may explain the popularity the newly emerging sub-field of serology enjoyed particularly in Poland, Hungary, and Romania.[87] It was assumed that blood groups could offer more accurate means for classifying human races as well as insights into the ethnic composition of various modern nations.[88] The numerous articles published on this subject reflected the growing influence of bio-anthropological knowledge and racial literature, alongside the persistent animosity amongst the successor states in East-Central Europe. As the Hungarian racial scientist Lajos Méhely [1862–1953] put it in 1934, blood group research was necessary for "the strict protection of [our] racial borders."[89]

Territory, therefore, was central to racial theories of national history, as well as to ideas of long-enduring continuity. As the Romanian historian Petre P. Panaitescu [1900–1967] declared: "We are not only the sons of the earth, but we belong to a great race, a race which is perpetuated in us, the Dacian race."[90] Like many on the political right, Panaitescu located the fascist rebirth of the Romanian nation in the resurrection of the Dacian past.[91] A new interpretation of history was thus proposed, one that strove to enunciate an organic connection between the dominant ethnic group and its ontological and geographical development.[92]

Romanian anthropologists, for instance, argued for the existence of an autochthonous racial type, located in the Carpathian Mountains. Their views confirmed what other Romanian nationalists proclaimed with respect to the country's ethnogenesis: only a race superior in its qualities and perfectly adapted to its environment could have survived centuries of dislocation and foreign domination. As what specifically constituted this race remained unclear, as neither Romanian nor foreign commentators could agree whether it was Pelasgian, Roman, Dacian-Roman, Dacian, or Dacian-Roman-Slavic.[93] If for the Serbs it was the "Dinaric racial type," for the Romanian anthropologists it was the "Dacian racial type" that they deemed as theirs, and which gave them the right to rule over territories where descendants from that race had lived, in both the past and the present.[94]

After the Second World War, the theory of racial continuity was forcefully endorsed by the anthropologist Ioannis Koumaris [1879–1970], who postulated the permanence of a "Greek race," one composed of "almost uniform characteristics, physical and psychical, inherited in its descendants; it has all the principal characteristics of the basic elements, which are all Greek and indigenous in spite of the variety of types."[95] The notion of historical continuity carried forward its own cultural epistemology and attendant historiography, providing a new discourse on race, one which endowed the Greek nation with the superiority of a natural, biological entity. The racial quality of the nation, and the ways it shaped the community, depended upon a wide range of elements, including a characteristic racial geography, historical continuity, and a specific national topography. According to Koumaris: "The Greek race was formed under the Acropolis

Rock, and it is impossible for any other to keep the keys of the sacred rock, to which the Greek soul is indissolubly linked."[96]

Ideas about national biology involving notions of racial differentiation, cycles of growth and decay, genetic genealogies, the interconnectedness of nurture and nature, and so on, continued to characterize the collective anthropological investigations published in communist countries in Eastern Europe during the late 1950s and the 1960s. This was the very period in which a new narrative on ethnogenesis was expounded in Bulgaria, Romania, and Hungary, allowing anthropologists to reposition autochthonous ideas within their discipline. The biological codes of the interwar period were brought back in a nuanced form. The 1960s and 1970s were characterized, as the cultural geographer Mark Bassin has argued, by attempts to "develop new perspectives on the nature of ethnos and ethnicity in the decades following Stalin's death."[97]

Permeated with ethnogenesis themes, ideas of race and ethnicity have been made to accord with the technical examination of physical anthropological types. Race and biology were the central elements of this re-defined physical anthropology, a relationship reaffirmed in the general acceptance of racial classification amongst anthropologists in these countries. The same sites of anthropological knowledge, which narratives of ethnic homogeneity and historical continuity occupied during the 1930s and 1940s, were reinvested with meaning and proposed to the general public during the 1970s and 1908s. Once again, the anthropological language of ethnicity, initially the privileged property of experts, was increasingly adopted by various authorities of cultural and political life as well as by nationalist propagandists. The anthropologists' ambition to engage with debates on national identity echoed precisely what the communist regime aimed to achieve more broadly, namely the advancement of scientific knowledge in the nation's service.

Anthropologists, like professionals in other disciplines, were not deterred in their attempts to synchronize interwar racial narratives with communist nationalist principles. In Romania, for example, a further change occurred with the accession of Nicolae Ceauşescu [1918–1989] to power in 1965. After Ceauşescu delivered his "July theses" in 1971, the "cultural revolution" commenced and autochthonism became the norm. Some topics, such as the Dacian-Roman continuity, became ubiquitous in the official discourse, generating a veritable "Dacomania" amongst intellectuals and Party officials alike.[98] Bulgaria experienced a similar form of historical megalomania, which connected the modern Bulgarians to the ancient Thracians,[99] whilst some Hungarian anthropologists laboured intensely to establish the contribution of the "steppe peoples," such as the Avars, to Hungarian ethnogenesis.[100] This anthropological manoeuvring of traditional strategies of national identification based on language and archaeological findings constantly and actively reinvented the national past, whilst subsuming the idea of race to the theory of historical continuity.[101]

The actual ideological meaning of such theories was nonetheless in constant flux. These nationalist claims about the existence of indigenous racial types competed with other interpretative frameworks offering a cultural interpretation of race and of the nation's physiological and intellectual qualities.[102] Anthropologists, as other professionals, embraced the nationalist instrumentalization of the past, stressing its abiding ethos. In that endeavour, they produced new narratives of national belonging. Such a practice, as we shall see in the next chapters, was neither new nor specifically Romanian, Bulgarian, or Hungarian. It characterized all modern nations.

CHAPTER TWO

Culture

Europe remember, you will reign over nations.[1]

In 1877, whilst still a student at the University of Oxford, the future mining magnate Cecil Rhodes [1853–1902] sketched some of his ideas about empire, leadership, and colonial management in a somewhat sermonizing text entitled "Confession of Faith." Most important amongst his assertions was the conviction that the English people represented the embodiment of Europe's racial dynamism and its most excellent and accomplished exemplar: "I contend that we are the finest race in the world and that the more of the world we inhabit the better it is for the human race. Just fancy those parts that are at present inhabited by the most despicable specimens of human beings what an alteration there would be if they were brought under Anglo-Saxon influence."[2]

Similar statements are abundant in the political literature of the time. Certainly, Rhodes was not the only one to believe that the English people were the pinnacle of human evolution and, as such, the most adaptive and successful of all races; nor was he the originator of racial Anglo-Saxonism in Great Britain.[3] The Labour politician, Sir Charles Dilke [1843–1911], also eulogized the superior capacity of the English people to colonize and thus improve the world, in his travelogue about his journey across the English-speaking countries of the world. Published in 1869 under the rather ostentatious title, *Greater Britain*,[4] it was a book that celebrated the imperial ambitions and achievements of his country. Having surveyed the cultural, political, economic, and linguistic influence of the English people throughout the globe, including such diverse and distant places as the USA, Canada, New Zealand, and India, Dilke remained confident that his countrymen would successfully prevail over the increased weakening of racial boundaries which he believed was diluting the very best from the biological stock of some peoples. "The result of our survey," he noted, "is such as to give us reason for the belief that race distinction will long continue, that miscegenation will go but little way toward blending races; [. . .] that Saxondom will rise triumphant from the doubtful struggle."[5] Dilke's confidence is a revealing confirmation of the rational-didactic nature of English expansionism during the nineteenth century, based on ideas of political and cultural progress, alongside shared economic interests between the metropolis and its self-governing colonies.[6] This was an age of industry and empire, and belief in progress and the civilizing mission of the English race.[7]

Dilke's work is significant because it endorsed the governance of race in history. He imbued his own nation with special characteristics, which gave it an indisputable and unrivalled ascendancy in world history. In Dilke's opinion, this ascendant universality rested upon the unequalled capacity of the English to impress upon other nations and peoples the overwhelming superiority of their language, culture, and civilization.[8] But there were others, such as the Regius Professor of Modern History at the University of Cambridge, Sir John R. Seeley [1834–1895], who in his *The Expansion of England (*1883), subverted this view by describing the growth of the British Empire in the eighteenth century as having failed to generate a patriotic attachment towards England's territorial aggrandizement. As he put it: "There is something very characteristic in the indifference which we show towards this mighty phenomenon of the diffusion of our race and the expansion of our state. We seem, as it were, to have conquered and peopled half the world in a fit of absence of mind."[9] This notion of *indifference* provides Seeley's history project with an epistemic framework that accounts for his intention to refashion the boundaries of English patriotism, not just metaphorically, but politically too, as an act of reaffirming its civic virtues.[10]

Were these believers in empire and in the supremacy of British culture "absent-minded imperialists," to use Bernard Porter's coinage, rarely, if at all, displaying the proclivities of an imperial master race?[11] Some were, some were not. Either way, the vision of the imperial and civilizing mission of the English presented one dominant model for heralding the dissemination of ideas of cultural superiority to a wide audience, both home and abroad. These ideas also permeated the schoolbooks and the curricula, familiarizing generations of young people with the importance of empire and national efficiency.[12]

Authors in other countries adopted and adapted to reflect their own national specificities and nationalistic inclinations.[13] For instance, the Italian liberal philosopher Giovanni Bovio [1837–1903], offered a related model of racial domination, the goal of which was the intellectual betterment of the "inferior" races in Africa by means of European colonization. Culture and civilization, he argued, were intimately intertwined. He had no doubt that progress was inevitable and that "immense, black Africa" will eventually "open up," by force if necessary, to that superior form of European culture, which was rational thinking.[14] Similarly, in his 1910 *Domination et colonisation*, Jules Harmand [1845–1921], the French physician and explorer, insisted that the dominance enjoyed by the European races was the outcome of both their advanced civilization and their "moral superiority."

The French belonged to a "superior race and civilization," he posited, and this status in the world was equally a tremendous source of national pride and an overwhelming responsibility towards other races.[15] At the end of the nineteenth century, the "civilizing mission" (*mission civilisatrice*) enabled the French to exhibit their superior culture, whilst at the same time presuming, as the historian Alice L. Conklin has shown, that they were "particularly suited, by temperament and by virtue of both their revolutionary past and their current industrial strength, to carry out this task."[16] This seeming innate capacity for ruling and domination also characterized the Portuguese colonial experience in Africa. This was described as "a distant and inhospitable world to which the Portuguese, with their courage and good intentions, brought civilization."[17]

But it was not only European elites who believed in their superior culture and civilization, both seen as prerequisites for colonial expansion. At the end of the nineteenth century, the Japanese too used similar arguments to colonize the island of Hokkaido and to rule over the indigenous Ainu population, deemed to be "barbarian" and "inferior."[18] The Ainu, the anthropologist Koganei Yoshikiyo [1859–1944] claimed, "are not capable of acquiring civilization, the same as the world's ordinary barbarian races."[19] A more nuanced, albeit conspicuously racist, language was also used after Japan acquired its first formal colony, Taiwan, following the victory in the Sino-Japanese War (1894–1895). Another Japanese anthropologist Torii Ryūzō [1870–1953], who studied Taiwan's native populations between 1896 and 1899, described them as "savage tribes [. . .] who have completely turned their backs on civilization." And, further, "From the point of view of civilization and human solidarity, they are in an unhappy state that merits our pity."[20]

These examples illustrate how, at the end of the nineteenth century, European and Japanese racial superiority was defined in terms of empire, culture, and what was called, often anachronistically, "civilization." The mastery of Europe over much of the globe was lauded as a noble, ennobling, and moral duty leading to the advancement of primitive races. No one put it better than the English theologian John Henry Newman [1801–1890] for whom European civilization, "together with the society which is its creation and its home" was "so distinctive and luminous in its character, so imperial in its extent, so imposing in its duration, and so utterly without rival upon the face of the earth, that the association may fitly assume to itself the title of 'Human Society' and its civilization the abstract term 'Civilization'."[21]

This vision of a superior European culture and civilization also reaffirmed the historical meaning of such contested terms as the "superior White race" (English, French, Italian, and so on). As the American anthropologist James M. Blaut [1927–2000] expressively described it: "Europe, eternally, is Inside. Non-Europe is Outside."[22] To think about race, culture, and civilization is— and has always been—to think of an ideal European community whose members prefer themselves over others, and of a situation in which the putative boundaries between "us" and "them" restrict and limit who is inside this community, who is outside, and why. Moreover, this envisioning of Europe and its relation to the rest of the world involves thinking about power, domination, and control by Western nations over non-European cultures. It was a generalized belief that the white European race was the "one race [that] has consistently earned the right to be considered the race whose main mission is to expand beyond its own domain."[23]

There is another reading of the modern history of race that emerges out of the complicated relationship between culture and science, one that markedly influenced the development of academic disciplines such as anthropology. This reading reveals how ideas about race were used as a means of understanding not only human diversity but also cultural value, according to which certain peoples were propelled forward by their racial inheritance, and were, more than others, predisposed to intellectual activity, science, and the arts. In Germany, during the second half of the nineteenth century, anthropologists and philosophers of culture such as Gustav Klemm [1802–1867], Adolf Bastian [1826–1905], Theodor Waitz [1821–1864], and Alfred Vierkandt [1867–1953] spoke of "passive and active races" and "natural peoples" (Naturvölker) and "cultured peoples" (Kulturvölker), respectively.[24]

Their interpretation was based upon geographical diffusionism and the acceptance of racial differences as the basis of universalism and monogenesis. These authors also provided new foundations for the development of specific theories of culture, including the one put forward, most famously, by the Oxford anthropologist, Edward B. Taylor [1832–1917], in his 1871 The Primitive Culture[25] and, indeed, by the celebrated German-American anthropologist Franz Boas during the 1930s and 1940s.[26] Such authors enlarged the relationship between race, culture, and civilization in a crucially different direction, to include a positive vision of universalism in which physical and mental differences were not deemed to be essential in shaping the evolution and progress of society. They also refuted ideas of racial superiority and inferiority.[27]

We refer to these authors only in passing, as historians of anthropology have already provided ample discussions of their arguments, and there is no need to repeat them here.[28] The impact of ethnography and anthropology, as well as philosophy and history, on the development of ideas of race was to amplify greatly the interconnectedness of culture and civilization. Equally importantly, these scientific disciplines aimed to transform the popular version of the view of progress which was defined as an entirely white European project and as such perceived as one inherently superior to the presumed racial destinies of non-European peoples and nations.

Connections between ideas of race, culture, and civilization were enhanced after the Enlightenment by a conviction in the existence of intellectual hierarchies between different peoples, which by the mid-nineteenth century had begun to function as traditions of thought used to legitimate and rationalize cultural imperialism, both within and outside Europe. In directing our attention to theories of culture, we are, in fact, highlighting the central role of race in the functioning of European conceptualization of theories of progress and civilization. In so doing we should delve beneath political arrangements and ideological constructs and aim to reveal those racial ideas that loom large in European culture and whose impact continues to be far-reaching. Inspired by the historian of Victorian racism Douglas Lorimer, we should aim to reconsider the current "narrative of the ideology of race." This narrative "misconstrues the relationship between nineteenth-century science, race and culture, [and] it overlooks the Victorian language of race relations which constitutes the most substantial legacy of the nineteenth century for the racism of the present."[29]

Most contemporary commentators were aware of the racial foundation upon which the idea of a superior European civilization was based although, of course, not everyone welcomed such interpretations about the role of race in history and the supremacy of white Europe. The German philosopher Johann Gottfried Herder [1744–1803] did not hesitate to call "European culture" a "mere abstraction" and an "empty concept," considering that "only a real misanthrope could regard European culture as the universal condition of our species."[30]

Yet, to many nineteenth-century European authors the connections between cultures, civilization, and race were essential parts of their worldview, which was universalistic and expansionist. By 1900, peoples all over the world were, in one way or another, affected by these ideas, as they were put into practice in multiple forms of cultural, social, economic, and political imperialism.[31] As noted by Edward Said, this "Eurocentric culture relentlessly codified and observed everything about the non-European or peripheral world, and so thoroughly and in so detailed a manner as to leave few items untouched, few cultures unstudied, few peoples and spots of land unclaimed."[32] To this set of cultural values, scholars added European jurisprudence and law. As the social scientist Olindo de Napoli has fittingly pointed out, during the 1930s it "was the jurists who emphasized that Italy's mission was above all one of *juridical* civilization: it lay in the exportation of the superior juridical civilization derived from Roman law, of which Italians were the natural heirs."[33]

As seen, it was not only interwar Italian scientists who promoted such arguments concerning the presumed pre-eminence of their cultural inheritance and mission in the world. Precedents provided by the past were a constant source of inspiration for most European authors who were engaged in developing ideas about race as a signifier and carrier of culture, knowledge, institutions, and law. Ancient and medieval Greece, Rome, and Japan, for instance, provided European and Japanese scholars with a triumphant pedigree and heritage and left an indelible mark on modern ideas of nation, empire, and race. It also suffused the emerging Eurocentrism and Japanism, with an unprecedented influx of racial tropes. Indeed, old ideas about Europe's and Japan's place at the centre of the world were now rewritten to include a justification for racial superiority.[34]

It is not a surprise, therefore, that any global expansion entailed strongly reified notions of race, culture, and civilization. In Europe, these interlocked notions had been embedded in the production of social sciences and the humanities since at least the seventeenth century.[35] From the birth of the European colonial empires, the very purpose of the scientific knowledge of the world was, as noted by the philosopher Denise Ferreira da Silva, to produce race within its global "ontoepistemological context."[36] The layered interconnectedness of race, culture, and civilization dominated both the emergence of the "science of man" during the Enlightenment and the codification of its intellectual foundations as European and thus superior.[37]

Increasingly, scholars across scientific disciplines and particularly in countries such as Germany, Britain, and France began to formulate the production of a European culture and civilization, which presupposed, as Martin Bernal has noted, "that the greatest 'race' in world history was the European or Aryan one."[38] The rapid growth of sciences in these countries and, indeed, elsewhere in Europe, more generally, from the eighteenth century onwards, can thus be seen as leading to the formulation of a specific European racial science whose aim was to "confront intellectually, describe systematically and analyze critically other cultures beyond Europe."[39]

The belief in the cultural superiority of the European races was long in the making, and intensified during the nineteenth century, particularly after the 1870s when Africa became the focus of the European, and of other, colonial projects.[40] The relationship that Europe had with other non-European cultures was never uniform, however. Observers such as John A. Hobson [1858–1940] have recognized the need to differentiate between "countries inhabited by what appear to be definitely low-types, unprogressive races, countries whose people manifest capacity of rapid progress from present low conditions, and countries like India and China, where an old civilization of a high type, widely different from that of European nations, exist."[41] Although critical of ideas of racial superiority, Hobson admitted that entrenched ideas of a highly developed European culture influenced imperialism enormously. To this effect, the European self-image as the most superior race was the medium through which the identity of other races was filtered.[42]

At the end of the nineteenth century, it was assumed that large parts of Africa were inhabited by the so-called "low-types, unprogressive races," notwithstanding centuries of economic, social, and religious (particularly Muslim) exchanges, which affected many parts of the continent.[43] Even authors who rejected the idea of biological races such as the influential social psychologist Gustave Le Bon [1841–1931] spoke of the superior "historical races" such as the "Indo-European" in contrast to inferior ones such as "the Negroes."[44] It was in reference to this cultural and historical context that the German ethnographer Leo Frobenius [1873–1938], declared "the idea of the 'barbarous Negro' ['Nègre barbare']" to be, unashamedly, "a European invention."[45] With growing racism in Europe during the 1930s, Frobenius had wanted to unmask the racial fabrication propagated by the West's canonical thinking about the ineluctable superiority of white Europeans and the inferiority of the "black races,"[46] but decades earlier, in the 1890s, there was little questioning by Europeans of the notion of Europe's cultural hegemony and pre-eminence.[47]

The Allure of Race

"All is race; there is no other truth!"[48] This categorical statement comes from Sidonia, a character in Benjamin Disraeli [1804–1881]'s novel *Tancred*, published in 1847. Most nineteenth-century authors viewed European culture through racial history.[49] The so-called "Anglo-Saxons" and the "Teutons" were assigned the highest position, whilst the other races, the Celts or the Slavs, were allocated lower positions within an increasingly inclusive interpretation of the identity and culture. The "Teutonic races" were, according to the English educator, Thomas Arnold [1795–1842], "the regenerating element" in modern Europe,[50] a view of history that many authors would embrace with resolute conviction in the following decades.

Other authors preferred terms such as the "Caucasian," which the great naturalists Johann Friedrich Blumenbach [1752–1840] and Georges Cuvier used to describe the superior European race, originating "in that group of mountains situated between the Caspian and the Black seas." Cuvier described the "Caucasian" according to the "beauty of the oval formed by its head, varying in complexion and the colour of the hair." Not surprisingly, he believed that "to this variety, the most highly civilized nations, and those which have generally held all others in subjugation, are indebted for their origin."[51] Politicians such as the afore-mentioned Benjamin Disraeli in England, also found the term appealing, albeit, in this specific case, to express the superiority and the purity of the Jewish race.

Finally, there were those who dismissed the "Caucasian," but retained the usage of the concept of an "Anglo-Saxon race." This was the case with Robert Knox [1791–1862], a lecturer in anatomy at the University of Edinburgh, who spoke of the "Scandinavian race" instead. In 1850, in a book entitled *The Races of Men*, Knox articulated the opinion of many in the world of politics, including Disraeli, when he declared that "Race is everything: literature, science, art, in a word, civilization, depend on it."[52] From such conviction emerged the idea of the permanency of race and the theory of the biological basis of cultural and intellectual differences between races. This set of ideas could apply to questions of anthropological research into the origins of different races and indeed it markedly influenced the ongoing debate between the monogenists and polygenists about whether humanity was one family of races sharing the same origins and evolution or a disparate group of races with separate histories and destinies.[53] It also had an impact upon discussions of more cultural issues such as "the progress of civilization" and its corollary, the superiority of Western (white) civilization.[54] Though a far more prominent figure in the history of anatomy, Knox was also a compelling commentator on broader issues of race[55] and an influence upon the young Charles Darwin [1809–1882] who spent time in Edinburgh in the 1820s.[56]

Knox produced a lucid and informed essay on what he called austerely "the Zoological history" of man, which put forward a biological theory of history premised on two straightforward arguments. Firstly, he propounded that "Men are of various Races; call them Species, if you will; call them permanent Varieties; it matters not. The fact, the simple fact, remains just as it was: men are of different races."[57] Deriving from this conviction, which was the springboard of the polygenic viewpoint, was Knox's second argument, namely: "The results of the physical and mental qualities of a race are naturally manifested in its civilization, for every race has its own form of civilization."[58] The "amalgamation of races" seemed to him to be harmful to a country's cultural welfare, as it introduced "inferior" blood and elements into the racial stock. Knox supported the cause of racial polygenism and separatism. As an advocate of the protection of the "Saxon race," Knox described its ethnic mixing with the Celts and others, as disharmonious, acting imperiously towards the weakening of the former. Each race needed to protect its civilizational potential, alongside that assemblage of physical and cultural traits deemed its own. Not surprisingly then, Knox scoffed at those who formulated theories of a homogeneous white ("Caucasian") race, and of a corresponding "European civilization."[59]

For polygenists such as Knox the most useful way of facilitating the flourishing of one race, its culture and its civilization, was to condemn any racial mixture. To this effect, Knox offered an important and influential contribution to the extensive interpretation of human history as the parallel biographies of competing races, some successful, others less so. His rejection of racial miscegenation had a wide impact in many countries, most notably in the United States, where its prominent supporters included physicians Samuel Morton [1799–1851], author of *Crania Americana* (1839), and Josiah C. Nott [1804–1851], author (together with Egyptologist George Gliddon) of *Types of Mankind* (1854). The wide appeal of Knox's ideas could be seen most clearly not only when they appear interwoven with "extinction" narratives of history[60] and with the emerging theories of survival of the fittest,[61] but also as they re-emerge in the widely distributed theories of Western culture and civilization informing Europe's troublesome period, following the 1848 revolutions. Furthermore, what is important for our purpose is not the relationship between race and colonial rule,[62] which was in ascendancy after the 1850s, but rather another tradition, constructed upon theories of race propounded by a very diverse group of writers, historians, and literary critics. Of particular interest herein are those theories whose use of race was justified not on the basis of physical differences (colour of skin, facial structure, head shapes, and so on) between human groups, but on a complex system of intellectual and moral abilities enabling these groups to create their own culture and civilization.

"Our liberty is neither Greek nor Roman; but essentially English."[63] This view, expressed by the English poet Henry Neele [1798–1828] shortly before his death, chimed with the widespread perception of cultural distinctiveness that had been growing steadily in England since the beginning of the nineteenth century. Neele, too, acknowledged that this form of particularism reflected "our manners and [. . .] our insular situation. It has a language, too, of its own, and a language singularly idiomatic, full of meaning to ourselves, scarcely intelligible to strangers."[64] Such descriptions blend together various forms of cultural rootedness that cement the idea of exceptionalism and along with it, ethnic solidarity and cohesion. It also substantiated claims for England's historical role in terms of its mission to spread ideas of culture and civilization to the rest of the world.

According to the political historian Reginald Horsman "the middle years of the nineteenth century, the idea of a superior Anglo-Saxon race regenerating a world of lesser races, was firmly ingrained in English thinking."[65] Tellingly, and perhaps more worryingly, it provided the foundation upon which American colonists formulated their vision of a manifest destiny, organically fixed on white elite-dominated institutions and cultural norms. As will be discussed in the next chapter, the North Americans of the eighteenth century believed they were "a chosen people." As such, they had articulated a composite interpretation of their own cultural superiority which included such notions as "the Anglo-Saxons had always been peculiarly gifted in the arts of government" or that "they were of a distinct Caucasian race, innately endowed with abilities that placed them above other races."[66]

Such confidence in the racial strength of the Anglo-Saxons was, as Robert Knox pointed out, waning. Other authors, too, began to lament the gradual degeneration of the "white race" and of its varied subdivisions, producing a wealth of literature about the rise and fall of civilizations throughout history. In the late nineteenth century, the most influential such theory was the *Essai sur l'inégalité des races humains* (*The Inequality of Human Races*), by the French aristocrat Arthur de Gobineau [1816–1882]. Published in two volumes in 1853 and 1855, this treatise on race might have remained a scholarly curiosity, of interest only to those concerned with France's decaying nobility, had it not aimed at something more universal: it was a history of the world which identified race as the primary factor of historical change. Race, for Gobineau, was the reason behind the rise and fall of civilizations. As Gobineau remarked at the outset: "The fall of civilizations the most striking and, at the same time, the darkest of all phenomena of history."[67] Such a significant occurrence as the collapse of a civilization was, however, due neither to political abandonment, nor to the lack of social progress, or the corruption of morals: the sole cause was the gradual degeneration of the "blood" within the race. "The word *degenerate*," Gobineau explained,

> when applied to a people, means (as it ought to mean) that the people has no longer the same intrinsic value as it had before, because it has no longer the same blood in its veins, continual adulterations having gradually affected the quality of that blood. In other words, though the nation bears the name given by its founders, the name no longer connotes the same race.[68]

Pre-Lombrosian notions of biological degeneracy were re-modelled by Gobineau to make a persuasive theory of cultural decline caused by the disappearance of the superior racial elements within the nation. And similar to Knox, Gobineau condemned racial mixing, as it contributed significantly to the waning of "racial blood." Yet contrary to Knox, Gobineau was less impressed by biology, and his understanding of "blood" was premised not simply on physiology but, more importantly, on a sense of historical destiny that a superior race once possessed.[69] In addition, not only did he use the generic term "white race" but he placed it at the top of a racial hierarchy, above the "yellow and the black races." Significantly, he glorified the Aryans as the finest racial types that ever existed. No less disillusioned with modern times, Gobineau expended his impressive literary fluency to denounce the end of an Aryan civilization that was living out its last moments in the personification of the "Germanic races" in Europe.

Gobineau's discussion of racial decline, as aptly noted by the literary philosopher Tzvetan Todorov [1939–2017], is certainly idiosyncratic,[70] but it did not make it less influential, either in Europe, the USA, or Latin America.[71] Concerns with decadence and degeneration alongside technological and cultural progress, grew in intensity from the 1850s onwards.[72] Indeed, like many others at the time, Gobineau was not immune to the social disturbances and dynastic ruptures characterizing Europe after the French Revolution of 1789 and the Napoleonic wars of 1803–1815.[73] In the United States the first volume of Gobineau's three-volume work was published in translation almost immediately, in 1856, under the motivating title *The Moral and Intellectual Diversity of Races*. Promisingly, the editor and translator Henry Hotze [1833–1887] dedicated it to the "statesmen of America."[74] In Brazil, on the other hand, Gobineau's condemnation of miscegenation was used to strengthen the importance of the white European race and its aura of cultural superiority.[75] As in other Latin American countries, such as Cuba and Chile, whitening "was cultural as well as racial."[76]

The focus on the decline of European civilization was warranted, Gobineau noted, at the same time as a warning against persistent ethnic mixture and as an appreciation of the white/Aryan race's former historic glory. There was something new about the vehemence with which Gobineau prophesized racial doom and his verdicts echoed widely. His constant admirers were, as the political scientist Alexis de Tocqueville [1805–1859] predicted, soon to be found amongst German nationalists.[77] Indeed authors such as Paul de Lagarde [1827–1891], Theodor Fritsch [1852–1933], and Karl Ludwig Schemann [1852–1938], adopted many of Gobineau's ideas,[78] adding significantly to the country's growing discussion of race and to the emerging German anti-Semitism.[79]

The years between 1850 and 1890 constituted a period of intense creativity in the cultural history of race, as well as one of profound changes in the political landscape of Europe, with the unification of Italy (1861) and Germany (1871) amongst the most important. The interaction between race and culture appealed to the prevailing fascination with national "rebirth" and renewal, and the taste for the *Gesamtkunstwerk* (total work of art), most dramatically expressed in Richard Wagner's [1813–1883] operas and in Friedrich Nietzsche's [1844–1900] vision of a vital culture, detailed in *The Birth of Tragedy* (1872) and *On the Genealogy of Morality* (1887).[80]

In Germany, the nexus between race, culture (*Kultur*), and civilization (*Zivilisation*)[81] became reflected in the transmission of a certain body of knowledge, explicitly confined within the epistemological boundaries already delineated by the German philosophers of the eighteenth century, most notably Immanuel Kant. Long admired for this philosophical system, Kant is now also recognized as one of main contributors to the formulation of a modern, systematized, and scientific theory of race.[82] Kant engaged with the topic in his 1775 (revised in 1777) text "Von den verschiedenen Racen der Menschen" ("Of the Different Human Races"), in which he endorsed the superiority of the white race whilst, at the same time, opposing the mixing of races. Yet Kant was no polygenist. He believed in the unity of mankind. He defined races as "deviations that are constantly preserved over many generations and come about as a consequence of migration (dislocation to other regions) or through interbreeding with other deviations of the same line of descent, which always produces half-breed offspring."[83]

For some scholars, such views alone suffice to make Kant an "unfamiliar source of racism" and likewise the most suitable candidate to stand for the originator of the modern idea of race.[84] Indeed, it would be easy to exaggerate the extent of Kant's contribution to the rise of European racism.[85] Here, however, we want to discuss less whether his views on human difference were intrinsically racist, and more the influence his philosophy had on late nineteenth-century racial authors, most notably Houston Stewart Chamberlain [1855–1927].

Although mostly known for his 1899 *Die Grundlagen des neunzehnten Jahrhunderts* (*Foundations of the Nineteenth Century*), Chamberlain also published on German music and philosophy, including the works of Richard Wagner[86] and Immanuel Kant. According to Lord Redesdale [1837–1916], who wrote the introduction to the English edition of *Die Grundlagen*, Chamberlain considered his study on Kant to be the most important of his works.[87] Not only was Kant deemed to be the greatest of the German philosophers but the entire "unfolding of our Teutonic culture," Chamberlain asserted, "has found in this man a specially pure, comprehensive and venerable expression." Such praise may seem excessive, but it reflected Chamberlain's understanding of Kant's philosophical system as the highest expression of the Teutonic race.

Viewing the grand sweep of Europe's racial history, Chamberlain ascribed Kant an epochal role. He was "the first perfect pattern of the absolutely independent Teuton who has put aside every trace of Roman absolutism, dogmatism and anti-individualism."[88] The motivation behind this appropriation of Kant's philosophical system went beyond the mere attempt to bestow a lustre of credibility to his racial theories. The aim was to testify most convincingly to the argument that culture and civilization in the West were predicated upon the inherent superiority of certain races. Chamberlain's view of the German philosopher was thus commensurate with the main aim of the book, which was to demonstrate that "our whole civilization and culture" were "the work of one definite race of men, the Teutonic."[89]

At the beginning of the thirteenth century, according to Chamberlain, the Teutons (*die Germanen*)—by which he meant, "the various portions of the one great North European race"[90]—had experienced their racial awakening. Since then, the Teutons, by means of their ingenuity, industry, creativity, and genius, which were unequalled, provided the superior racial matrix that generated the achievements of European culture. In a different form, as seen already, other authors, including Robert Knox and Arthur de Gobineau, had put forward the same idea in the nineteenth century. What makes Chamberlain's racial philosophy worth mentioning here, however, is not his identification of the Teutons as the superior European race (this has been duly pointed out by others), but his intuitive, almost spiritual, definition of race. "Nothing is so convincing as the consciousness of the possession of Race," he argued. For Chamberlain, "The man who belongs to a distinct, pure race, never loses the sense of it." And further, "Race lifts a man above himself: it endows him with extraordinary—I might almost say supernatural—powers."[91]

Chamberlain appears to be viewing race not as an objective reality, the dynamic factor in history, as Gobineau did. For him, race was a subjective and higher entity, internal to the human mind and within people, which shaped their impressions and actions. In this sense, he seems to be operating within a tradition valued not only by idealist philosophers, such as George Berkeley [1685–1753], Friedrich Schelling [1775–1854], and, of course, Kant, but also by mystics through the ages. Race for him was immaterial but real. It comprised those higher human intuitions and experiences, propelled individuals to greatness, and elevated human beings to transcendental heights, close to the gods of any religion. Chamberlain's race was the soul of a people.

Seen in this way, the idea of race signified a specific intellectual receptivity, identified by Chamberlain strictly with the Teutonic peoples. As he put it, "all those who from the sixth century onwards appear as genuine shapers of the destinies of mankind, whether as builders of States or as discoverers of new thoughts and of original art, belong to the Teutonic race."[92] As is known, Chamberlain's obsession with the Teutons was later appropriated by Nazi ideology,[93] but during the *fin-de-siècle* period his was a characteristically modernist idealization of race that went beyond biological racism. In this respect, Chamberlain's theory of race revealed a philosophical affinity for intuition and imagination as methods to comprehend the reality of race, although he endowed it with a rationality and historicity of its own.

With Chamberlain, perhaps more than with any other authors mentioned already, the nexus between race and culture belies the superficiality of modern civilization (one without a "soul"). As far as the progress of European civilizations (here he considered Ancient Greece and Rome, as well as Christianity and Judaism) was concerned, Chamberlain only appreciated it when "it led to an increasingly intensive intellectual and artistic shaping of life and to an inner moral enlightenment."[94] This is as much a consequence of Chamberlain's negative appreciation of other cultures (Arabic, Semitic, and so on), as it is of his conviction that any canonical classification of the human races reflected archetypical cultural characteristics of certain individuals. The superior Teutonic race and the culture which it created succeed in dominating other races and cultures mainly because there had been individuals in history who "proved their Teutonic individuality by their civilizing activity"[95] and were aware of their critical role as "creators of great imaginative power."[96]

In this way, Chamberlain privileged the racial awareness of the individual over that of the collective, which is inextricably interwoven with his assertion that the racial configuration of culture demands a process of self-discovery. As the historian Michael Biddiss pertinently noted, Chamberlain's "discourse is not of a racial perfection already attained, but of a process of perfectibility as yet unfinished—a process of *Volkwerdung* (or ethnic fulfilment), echoing the paradoxical Nietzschean imperative that men must become what they are."[97] In other words, it is within the race that the individual finds completeness; or, as noted by the Romanian philosopher Constantin Rădulescu-Motru [1868–1957]: "the individual lives for a second; the race is infinite."[98]

Chamberlain did not promote ideas of racial purity, arguing instead that the mixing of races could have both negative and positive consequences. This was even a necessary historical process, since it contributed to the augmentation of superior racial qualities. Tellingly, he used Charles Darwin's laws on the obliteration of racial characters by crossbreeding under controlled conditions to assert that a race originated as a result of the specific combination of geographical and historical conditions. According to him, inbreeding and artificial selection "ennobled" the race.[99] Chamberlain highlighted the concepts of "crossing" and "breeding" as the two most important factors in determining the character of race. Yet uncontrolled racial mixing—especially between races of different origin—would jeopardize the qualities of the superior race, Chamberlain believed.

Chamberlain established five interlocked strategies meant to protect the superior race from degeneration or, as he put it, from "the prostitution of the noble in the arms of the ignoble." The first one applied to the superior "quality of the material" in a race, which could only be assured by two other methods, "inbreeding" and "artificial selection." The fourth method was "racial crossing" but under certain conditions. Chamberlain insisted on "the necessity of strictly limiting these crossings both in respect of choice and time" (the fifth method).[100] The race that successfully combined these five methods was destined for survival and great historical achievement. Chamberlain thought that, in modern times, only the Teutons ("die Germanen") were such a race, and many race theorists across Europe, from Romania to Sweden, shared his conviction.[101]

Chamberlain's philosophy of race included Aryanism, Social Darwinism and the recently developed doctrines of eugenics and anthropo-sociology.[102] To these theories he added anti-Semitism and German nationalism.[103] By portraying the "negative" and "destructive" effects that the Jews had on Western culture, and by weaving Jewish inferiority into a system that seemingly embraced all of human history, Chamberlain harnessed common anti-Jewish prejudices of the late nineteenth century to a philosophical theory of race.

At the same time Chamberlain connected modern anti-Semitism to its religious roots: the Judeo-Christian conflict. While other anti-Semites at this time, most prominently the German political activist Wilhelm Marr [1819–1904],[104] relied on the dichotomy between "inferior" Jews and "superior" Aryans, Chamberlain developed a more sophisticated, if equally intolerant, approach. According to Chamberlain, positive and negative qualities of the race were the consequence of miscegenation. In some cases, mixing races with similar virtues led to cultural progress and intellectual achievements, as was the case with the Germanic peoples. The reverse phenomenon happened when the Jews were assimilated, as such a process had disastrous effects on them as well as for the nation into which they integrated.[105]

Chamberlain's racial arguments popularized cultural knowledge about the Germanic people but other authors used them to substantiate theories of national uniqueness and superiority. The central tenets of this Eurocentric, nationalistic, race-centred thinking and discourse—a growing sense of cultural distinctiveness and a closer identification of modern Europeans with "glorious" peoples of the past, such as the Ancient Greeks or Romans, and certainly the Teutons—absorbed the imagination of historians across Europe. What late nineteenth- and early twentieth-century historical narratives articulated, what their legacy entailed, was the epistemology of race described above, premised on ideas of culture and civilization whose superiority centred not only on the domination of non-European cultures, but also on an intra-European racism.

Before and after the First World War, academic tensions were heightened by rival interpretations of national boundaries, and European states became deeply entangled in struggles over contested territories. The Germans and the French clashed over Alsace-Lorraine, the Hungarians and the Romanians conflicted over Transylvania, the Bulgarians and the Greeks over Macedonia, whilst some Croatian nationalists maintained that Bosnia-Herzegovina was historically Croat.[106] These rival nationalisms generated a tremendous amount of historical, ethnographic, political, and linguistic literature. Most of it worked with changing notions of nation and race, promoting an ethnic mythology of belonging and a glorious historical genealogy. Influenced by Chamberlain and other Nordicists, the nationalist priest Kerubin Šegvić [1867–1945], for instance, suggested that the Croats, unlike the Serbs, were not of Slavic, but of German origin.[107] Of course, to assert that the Croats were non-Slavic in origin, supposedly hailing from the Germanic tribes, had a particular political meaning during the late 1930s and the early 1940s.[108] By then, however, the Nordic ideology of race was highly praised in most countries in East-Central Europe which came under the influence of Nazi Germany during the Second World War.[109]

Political realities often highlighted the importance of racial metaphors of national identity but the local traditions of racial thought should not be neglected. In Romania, the Orthodox writer Nichifor Crainic [1889–1972] criticized German racism for its anti-Christian overtones whilst painting a future Romanian national community united by race and religion.[110] Orthodoxy for Cranic and other Romanian racial authors was endowed with its specific autochthonous culture and civilization.[111] Historical genealogies had dynamics of their own, as we have seen, but they shared an identifiable narrative of ethnogenesis. In some cases this narrative also became increasingly protochronist. The Bulgarian cultural historian Nayden Sheytanov [1890–1970], for instance, attempted to connect modern Bulgarians to the ancient Thracians. Emulating Nietzsche's argument that the myth of Dionysus was central to the birth of civilization, Sheytanov described Orphism and its Thracian followers as the forefathers of Bulgarian culture in the Balkans. As he put it in 1939: "here, in the Balkans, things are being built on a huge, almost continental scale. World-makers and demiurges are born and perform their miracles here. [. . .] there are titans, and their deed is a Balkano-Bulgarian titanism."[112] Self-aggrandizing aside, Sheytanov attempted to resurrect Bulgaria's Thracian past, projecting onto it his hopes for racial renewal.

These Greek, Romanian, Croat, and Bulgarian authors, similar to their counterparts in Western Europe and the USA, turned to compelling racial metaphors to interpret their theories of national culture and the need for universal recognition.[113] These broad tendencies, as argued here, are attributable to the claim made by European philosophers, scientists, men of letters, and travellers since the Enlightenment, namely that scientific and intellectual progress reflected their superior culture and civilization.[114] Amongst the ideological results of this process of transference and adaptation, from West to East, was the strengthening of theories of national character and cultural superiority, which had noticeable consequences at every level of political thought and cultural politics during the interwar period. Tellingly, as early as 1928, in his *Das Spectrum Europas* (translated into English as *Europe*), the German philosopher Hermann Keyserling [1880–1946] reprimanded those nations which "exalt[ed] themselves above others," considering that "their boastfulness really indicat[ed] an inferiority complex."[115]

Keyserling's criticism of cultural superiority was not heeded, however, and the ever-widening relationship which the term race had with ideas of a superior culture and civilization would continue well into the interwar period, and beyond. To be sure, this intellectual tradition existed in parallel with sciences of race (anthropology, anthropometry, craniometry, serology, and so on), feeding into modern societies' obsessive concerns with human typologies, taxonomies, and classifications. But before we discuss the racial theories put forward by anthropologists there is need for another chapter, connecting race to the idea of nation. The next chapter takes the discussion further into the world of racialized narratives of national character; these conflate the easy binary divide, between a presumed biological configuration of race and a cultural understanding of nation, which is upheld in so many orthodox interpretations of nationalism.

CHAPTER THREE

Nation

Every people has or ought to have a national character, and if it lacks one it would be necessary to begin by giving it one.[1]

Myths are the foundations of our societies. The earliest examples, such as the Sumerian Epic of Gilgamesh (written c.2150–1400 BCE), are religious accounts of how the gods who command the cosmos, and preside over terrestrial temples, created the earth and all living things under human stewardship. All recorded civilizations possess sacred texts or oral traditions about the creation of the world and the people who inhabit it.[2] After the American and the French Revolutions, it was the myth of the nation that took on and adapted many of the narrative structures and features of religious myths. Although disputed and sometimes rejected, national myths or symbolic narratives about the origins and destiny of nations and peoples continue to shape our perception of history and culture.[3] As the sociologist Gérard Bouchard summarized, national myths "are enduring, deeply rooted, inclusive representations that suffuse a nation's past, present, and future with a set of values, ideals, and beliefs expressed in an identity and a memory."[4]

A national myth is a collection of multiple narratives that "dramatizes the historical sense of a people and culture, reducing centuries of experience into a constellation of compelling metaphors." The narrative "recapitulates that people's experience," "rehearses their visions of that experience," and "reduces both experience and vision to a paradigm." A national myth that fails to evoke a sense of "total identification and collective participation" ceases to function as a foundation narrative. According to the cultural historian Richard Slotkin myths must possess "evocative power." He termed those narratives that exhibit "this kind of power persistently in many cultures over long periods of time [. . .] *universal archetypes*," whilst those which function largely within a single culture he defined as "*cultural archetypes*" and "*cultural myths*."[5] Whether one considers Romania, Turkey, or the United States, there is a long tradition of asserting the public importance of cultural myths of origins and historical destiny.[6] For instance, in the eighteenth century the Transylvanian Romanian Samuil Micu [1745–1806] put forward the doctrine of Daco-Roman continuity in Transylvania, aiming to demonstrate the direct descent of the Romanians of the eighteenth century from the Romans who had settled in the province of Dacia (as the territory of Transylvania was known in antiquity) in the second century CE.[7] It has proven to be the single most important myth of Romanian nationalism and has endured to this day. Its power has derived from the fact that the theory of historical continuity embodied what Micu saw as the constitutive elements that defined his people's distinctive character and identity. A highly idiosyncratic interpretation of the past and a loyalty to the idea of the nation assured the success of the theory of historical continuity in modern Romania.

Seemingly flawless and objective "facts" and incontrovertible "truths" about the existence of biologically-determined racial hierarchies, could be used persuasively by nationalists keen to disseminate ideals of patriotic sentiment and bravery through narratives and myths about national origins. For instance, one of the first anthropological and craniological surveys of Romanians was attempted by the physician Mihail Obedenaru [1839–1885], who in 1874 presented three skulls to the *Société d'Anthropologie de Paris*, one of which, he asserted, was "Dacian," as it "resembled the Dacian figures represented on the Column of Trajan" in Rome.[8] Obedenaru's incipient craniological research was further developed in his 1876 *La Roumanie (Romania)*, where he suggested that the Romanians were "brachycephalic" (short-headed). It was no accident that one of the first Romanian anthropologists readily adjusted his craniological research to reflect the then national preoccupation with ethnogenesis and historical continuity. Under these political circumstances, anthropology proved critical in defining national territories and guiding linguists, geographers, and ethnographers towards asserting nationalist claims. The anthropologists' ambition to engage in debates on race and national identity echoed precisely what scientists in all disciplines aimed at achieving, namely scientific knowledge in the service of the nation.[9]

A similar attempt to trace the ethnic roots of the nation can be seen during the last decades of the Ottoman Empire and then in early republican Turkey. In this case, to translate a sense of imperial identity into an ethnic one required not only the experience of history but also the experience of religion, in this case Islam. The political movement of the Young Turks (1908–1918) accentuated this move towards the creation of a Turkish ethnic nationalism.[10] It was often Muslims from outside the Ottoman Empire such as Yusuf Akçura [1876–1935], who promoted a new vision of Turkish history and identity based on ethnicity and race.[11] This interpretation of the ethnic Turkish nation re-wrote not only the Ottoman past but also the meaning of the Islamic community ("ummah"). Within this new political and cultural geography, Anatolia was portrayed as the birthplace of the Turkish race, untainted by the corrosive effects of ethnic mixing. "It is there," wrote the Turkish anthropologist Nurettin Ali Berkol [1881–1955], "that [the race] continues to run its purest blood, far from the contacts that could debase [it]."[12]

In the United States, on the other hand, the focus of the myth-making of the nation was not on ancestors and religion but on descendants and secularism. The pilgrims' preservation of political virtues and religious liberties underpinned the emerging American identity, as Michel-Guillaume Jean de Crèvecoeur [1735–1813], noted in his *Letters from an American Farmer* (1782).[13] The point was not to stress historical continuity but to establish a new genealogy and with it a new identity. This strong sense of self-determination was further augmented by another myth, that of the frontier, which the historian Frederick J. Turner [1861–1932] codified in his 1894 study "The Significance of the Frontier in American History." Ideas of liberty and unrestrained expansion gradually became the cherished features of American national character, embedded in heroic stories of stoicism, endurance, and success. As the founder of American cultural history William R. Taylor [1922–2014] wrote, beginning with the 1820s, Americans were repeatedly told "parables and cautionary tales" and were thus "instructed in the traits which would weaken them as individuals and as a nation, and in those which would make them strong."[14]

The mythical, distorted, idealized aspects in these wilfully constructed shared memories of the national past are what inspire people to action and hold nations together. But, as will emerge, these foundational narratives also responded to a variety of racial impulses; in the nineteenth century, the myth of the nation and the myth of race were, in fact, intertwined, in sometimes complex, but always significant ways. Both provided complex social, cultural, historical, and political narratives that sought to create inherent similarities and differences amongst individuals and communities. Even countries with a remarkably long documented history such as China developed traditions of thinking about national character which emphasized not Confucian ecumenism but the "Yellow Emperor, the founder of a nation" and the patriarch of the Han "race."[15]

Racial theories of the nation reflected perceptions about the historical uniqueness of the national territory, advocating a system of national identification within which the nexus between race and nation was paramount. Once endowed with a noble historical genealogy, the nation was assigned a natural territory and fixed physical characteristics; racial miscegenation was either denied as a biological blunder or seen as a source of racial degeneration. Forms of racial thinking, moreover, were intrinsically connected to a reading of the nation and culture centring on the notion that race was the main bearer and conveyer of "true" culture. Nationalists often manoeuvred myths and historical narratives of cultural experience towards the idea of national uniqueness. A new interpretation of the nation was, therefore, proposed, one that strove to enunciate an organic connection between a native race and its ontological and geographical space.

A Secular Religion

A feature of the modern period, national myth-making is a process by which nationalists use "traditional metaphors" to address "ultimate questions" about the existence of a nation.[16] As the historian George L. Mosse [1918–1999] observed decades ago, the nationalist belief systems which arose in modern Europe were based upon myths and symbols of nationhood which were intended to inspire and to motivate patriotic sentiment. These were the essential building-blocks of the "political liturgy" and the "sacralization of politics" which Mosse argued were a central element of modern nationalism.[17]

The "artful moderns" who established nationalist traditions of writing and thinking, just like earlier religious myth-makers, used the same techniques found in ancient storytelling in order consciously "to recapture the unsophisticated, passionate, believing spirit of the primitive 'natural' man."[18] Mythologies are a fundamental component of the ideology and politics of modern nation-states. That is so largely because, after the French Revolution, the nation became an object of worship, and nationalism a form of secular religion, as the historian Carlton J. H. Hayes [1882–1964] observed as early as 1926. According to Hayes, not only was the French Revolution a pivotal moment in human history but an equally important "landmark in the development of nationalism as a religion."[19] The Declaration of the Rights of Man and of the Citizen, adopted by the National Constituent Assembly in August 1789, became the doctrinal centrepiece of the new "national catechism." The secular worship of the nation, and the newly erected "altars to *la Patrie*," became the "symbols of the new faith" of nationalism.[20] Not only the French people but the entire human race were to be transformed by this unprecedented revolutionary ethos of nation worship.[21] A new, secular myth of the nation and an entire system of national idolatry were thus born, and, in many ways, these were more gripping and more demanding than their religious counterparts.

Beginning with France, the modern secular religion of nationalism began to write a new history of Europe, as it gradually swept away the old empires, before spreading outwards globally. This history reverberates today in the micro-nationalisms which threaten to tear even long-standing nations asunder. Many scholars over the years have depicted successive generations of poets, linguists, writers, and painters as the main participants in debates about how to define nationhood and, even, how to forge nations and a national consciousness amongst newly-unified peoples. The entire history of the Italian *Risorgimento* and that of national "awakening" in East-Central Europe, for example, has been written and rewritten in this fashion.[22] The history of nationalism has been conceived largely as a project exploring the imagery of the nation and "imaginings" about the nation found in cultural representations, such as paintings, poetry, and monuments. This depiction colours the disciplines of history and political philosophy, which have contributed the most to the important literature on modern nation and race.

The dominant tendency within writings on the nation, at least, has been bolstered in the last decade or so by the growing influence of so-called "culturalism." This approach, which gives primacy to the study of cultural artefacts such as literary texts or artistic works, views culture as the chief explanatory and causative agent in historical development.[23] Within this firmly rooted and prevailing model, cultural constructions of nation and race have been perceived as the chief objects of study in order to discover the political culture of previous periods.

Narratives about the myth of origins of peoples and nations continue to be relevant; they remain essential to the core values, belief systems, and self-identities of contemporary cultures. Such stories about the "birth" of peoples and nations are committed to the collective memory and transmitted from one generation to the next by the written word through such varied sources as constitutions, anthems, and literature. Moreover, they are depicted in the images and iconography of paintings, re-enacted in the pageantry of national festivals, memorialized in the grandeur of historical buildings and monuments, and ultimately used for political ends.[24] Impressive works of nationalist art were commissioned in the nineteenth century such as the Statues of the Seven Chieftains in the Heroes' Square in Budapest or the Victor Emmanuel II Monument, known as the Altar of the Nation (*Altare della Patria*) in Rome, and the Battle of the Nations (*Völkerschlachtdenkmal*) in Leipzig, to amplify the public impact of mythologies of national origin and to instil national pride. The nation's possibilities were idealized as never before. In *Le Peuple* (The People), published in 1846, the French historian Jules Michelet [1798–1874], for instance, encouraged his compatriots to love France above all else: "Un peuple! une patrie! une France!"[25]

Nationalism as a secular religion could jointly channel the passions and emotions of elites and the masses. Such devotion to one's nation, however, was bound to open up chasms between countries. The nineteenth and twentieth centuries abound with examples of national aggression, as nationalists often became violent in their self-appointed mission to protect the people. As remarked by the English writer George Orwell [1903–1950] in his "Notes on Nationalism," written immediately after the end of the Second World War: "A nationalist is one who thinks solely, or mainly, in terms of competitive prestige. He may be a positive or a negative nationalist—that is, he may use his mental energy either in boosting or denigrating—but at any rate his thoughts always turn on victories, defeats, triumphs, and humiliations."[26]

To the most intractable supporters of the nation, such a succession of events seemed perfectly in tune with the indoctrination required to turn "peasants into Frenchmen."[27] Every modern state has a national pedagogy, a guiding "theology" and a creationist mythology. According to Hayes this is "a more or less systematized body of official doctrines which have been deduced from the precepts of the 'Fathers' and from the admonitions of the national scriptures and which reflect the 'genius of the people' and constitute a guide to national behaviour."[28] In the United States, for example, numerous learned and popular tracts, as well as accounts in the press, on television, and in classic films from the 1940s and 1950s, have all produced a historical narrative of the American people and nation as being invested by God and Destiny with a special mandate in history.[29] In many ways, this mission derives its sustenance from historical events, such as the Boston Tea Party of 1774, the battles at Concord and Lexington, Massachusetts of 1775, and, of course, the Revolution of 1776. This highly constructed and deeply felt self-perception of Americans as the guardians of liberty and democracy was consecrated by a group of individuals known solemnly as the Founding Fathers and, perhaps, exemplified best by Thomas Jefferson [1743–1826], the third President of the United States [1801–1809].

As "Father of the Nation," Jefferson enshrined these ideals in the Declaration of Independence and other public writings. Of particular importance here is *Notes on the States of Virginia*, which he wrote and first published (in French translation) in 1781, before an English translation was published in London in 1787.[30] This is, of course, a fundamental work in American political history. Here, it bears a second significance in terms of the topics discussed in this book, such as the role of science and anthropology in the shaping of discussions on human difference. As many of his contemporaries did, Jefferson adhered to the main premises of the Biblical model of a Great Chain of Being, with its prearranged historical function, and to ideas derived from natural history such as, most importantly, Linnaean anthropology, which allowed for intra-species hierarchy and the existence of several varieties within groups, including the human race. Therefore, it is perhaps not entirely surprising that although he denounced slavery in his early writings and career, Jefferson continued to believe in the idea of the "natural" inferiority of the blacks. In an oft-quoted paragraph in *Notes on the State of Virginia*, he suggested that "the blacks, whether originally a distinct race, or made distinct by time and circumstances, are inferior to the whites in the endowments both of body and mind."[31]

This was also the view put forward by David Hume in his study "Of National Characters," published in 1748. Although relegated to a footnote, Hume's description is no less poignant: "I am apt to suspect the negroes to be naturally inferior to the whites."[32] In one crucial aspect it seems, Jefferson's vision of the American nation, as with Hume's theory of national character, failed to dismantle the idea of white cultural superiority. To understand human difference, one had to place it back into nature, Hume contended. The emerging American democracy and the debate about who belonged to the new American nation was, thus, altered from the beginning by Jefferson's inability to eliminate racial inequality. To some extent, as is often pointed out, Jefferson's endorsement of racial boundaries in North America reflected the Enlightenment conception of the superiority of the white Europeans.[33] It also linked to a national mythology that depicted the providential role of the new country and which gradually would become embedded in the definition of American nationhood.[34]

One of the essential claims put forward by Jefferson and other modern revolutionaries was the universality of their national ideals. As embodied in the aspirations of the French Republic and the American Revolution, the principles of liberty, equality, fraternity, and democracy have crystallized into a dogma to which is ascribed applicability not just to the French and American peoples, but also to the whole of humanity. Yet ethnic and racial distinctions were not renounced. As the historian Ibram X. Kendi noted recently, Jefferson "did not pick sides between polygenesists and monogenesists, between segregationists and assimilationists, between slavery and freedom. But he did pick the side of racism."[35] With the creation of the modern nation-states, disputes about human diversity and inequality only grew in intensity. Testifying to their overflowing energies and beliefs, modern nationalists created new cultural connections amongst the members of their community but also retained the need for biological identification. Both history and biology were emphasized as essential elements of the new nations. As Hayes fittingly put it, modern nationalism "repudiates the revolutionary message of St. Paul and proclaims anew the primitive doctrine that there shall be Jew and Greek, only that now there shall be Jew and Greek more quintessentially than ever."[36]

Individuality

Hayes drew attention to the inherently autochthonous and exclusivist nature of nationalism, and so would many others in the subsequent decades.[37] Following conservative thinkers, such as the Irish political theorist Edmund Burke [1729–1797] and the French philosopher Joseph de Maistre [1753–1821], many nationalists in the late nineteenth and early twentieth centuries decried the popular democratization unleashed by the French Revolution. They argued that the French Revolution had destroyed the cultural traditions and organic links between people, as well as the social relations that represented the real sense of duty and responsibility through which individuals created and maintained their national community.[38]

Sometimes defined as "reactionaries," nationalists of this persuasion also lamented the fact that the French Revolution favoured the emergence of a modern democracy that made the masses uncontrollable and prone to political manipulation. Some of them, such as the Romanian Aurel C. Popovici [1863–1917] and the Greek Ion Dragoumis [1878–1920], adhered to a more organic understanding of the nation, as a unique, natural entity, "defined in relation to, and against, other nations."[39] This commitment to organicism, tradition, and collective cohesion was first formulated in the late eighteenth century by two philosophers: Jean-Jacques Rousseau [1712–1778] and Johann Gottfried Herder. Both authors added to the growing debate on race and nation a new vocabulary centred on cultural and national character.[40] Equally important for our discussion here, they drew on their firmly held convictions about cultural essentialism sanctified in separate historical traditions. These traditions were later used to justify claims of ethnic difference. According to the political scientist Zeev Sternhell, "It was Herder who gave Europe a view of history as consisting of cultures that, even when not cut off from each other, regarded foreign contributions as threatening their authenticity."[41]

A poet, critic, theologian, and philosopher, Herder defined the nation as an organic entity, regulated by natural law; nationality was the product of an irresistible natural force that was always at work, shaping the members of a group into a compact national community. Nationality was the "language of God in nature" and a part of the divine plan in history. Each individual people, Herder urged, had to rediscover their own native traditions and, above all, their national language, which was their true spirit and essence. Such was his commitment to this belief that he coined the term *Nationalismus* (nationalism) and described it as a moral imperative.[42]

In this way, Herder prepared the way for later theorists of the autarky of culture and civilization, whilst at the same time codifying the idea of ethnic authenticity that many nationalists found appealing. A new form of nationalism emerged from these arguments, characterized by an obsession with unique racial characteristics that allegedly distinguished one nation from another. According to this view, the nation was increasingly perceived as a biological community, one held together by ties of blood and with its own peculiar racial character and historical destiny. This view resonates with the argument put forward by Carl Ritter [1779–1859], who along with Alexander von Humboldt [1769–1859] is considered one of the founders of modern geography. "Character," he claimed, was "not something a people can give to itself; just as it is not something an individual can give to himself [. . .]. Character itself, however, emanates from a power higher than that of man in all its insignificance."[43] Geographical location (and all that it entailed) was essential in building character, and Ritter understood that nature shaped personality no less profoundly than culture did.

In keeping with this transformation of individual and collective character, the way race influenced national culture was reinstated. As noted by the Hungarian literary historian Zsolt Beöthy [1848–1922] in his 1896 *A magyar irodalom kis-tükre* (*The Small Mirror of Hungarian Literature*): "The present Hungarian nation has been shaped throughout the course of history; yet it has been shaped by the Hungarian race and shaped in its own resemblance. It was this race that guided and set up the objectives of its history; indeed, the race created it, and strove to assert itself in it."[44] Beöthy was not the only literary historian to highlight the importance of race in shaping national character and specificity.

By the end of the nineteenth century, other similar interpretations were put forward, most notably by the French literary critic Hippolyte A. Taine [1828–1893]. In his multi-volume *Histoire de la littérature anglaise* (*History of English Literature*), Taine articulated the argument that any national literature was the outcome of "race, milieu and moment."[45] National character did not displace race. However, it did suggest a new understanding of what was specific about each nation or group of nations.[46] Attention was turned towards both nature and nurture; it was geography and the environment as much as race and culture that were invoked as determinants of national character. And, to some such as the German geographer Friedrich Ratzel [1844–1904], the nation needed not only personality but with it an adequate territory to grow and expand.[47]

The modern state impelled by the need to generate a powerful sense of cohesion and shared identity amongst its citizens frequently underpinned nationalism through appeals to ethnic character. Thus were created essentially cultural and biological manifestations of national belonging that included shared religion, language, traditions, and history. Not surprisingly, then, historians of nationalism and ethnicity are keen to point out that Herder did not divide humanity into races and did not endorse ideas of superior European civilization.[48] Yet his pronouncements on national character are notoriously based on the laws of nature and not on those of culture. Here is one example: "Nature raises families; the most natural state is therefore also *one* people, with one national character. Through the millennia, this national character is maintained within a people and can be developed most naturally [. . .], for a people is as much a plant of nature as a family, only with more branches."[49] Indeed, Herder did not use race to explain the individuality of culture, but his idea of national character was not strikingly different. As Sternhell pointed out "In the context of the period, this term [national character] had more or less the role that 'race' had in the nineteenth century."[50]

In a different cultural context, the intellectual historian Stefan Collini, citing a nineteenth-century entry in the Oxford English Dictionary, pointed out that for Victorian authors "character" was about "the mental and moral qualities which distinguished an individual or [a] race viewed as a homogeneous whole."[51] Whatever the definition, it was assumed that national character unlocked the complexities of cultural formation, leaving an indelible mark on society. As remarked by the English philosopher John Stuart Mill [1806–1873]: "Every form of polity, every condition of society, whatever else it had done, had formed its type of national character."[52]

Certainly, whilst the ideological formulations of nineteenth-century nationalism frequently found expression through national character and race, it is important not to conflate the two terms so that any differentiation becomes meaningless. Mill, for instance, who was expressly interested in the English national character did not abandon the term race completely, but the fact that he and others used to speak about national character instead of race induced many historians who discuss modern nationalism and ethnic specificity to marginalize or overlook the importance of race. Of course, sometimes nation, national character, and race signified the same thing, but using only the category of national character to explain ethnic belonging invites confusion between what people considered to be their race and nation in the past and what is today assumed about these concepts.[53] In fact, the idea of race has existed within the interstices of collective and individual identities, originating from the same intellectual traditions that had formed and re-formed political and national cultures since 1789. More importantly, there were times, when ethnic difference did not immediately amount to a distinct national character. Gradually however, and particularly during the period from the 1870s to the 1930s, different views about nation and race were proposed, and it is important to restore some of these views to their proper historical context.

In much of the literature dealing with national and ethnic characteristics produced in Europe, "people," "nation," "tribe," and "race" constantly overlapped. Scholars and public alike spoke of the "German race and nation," the "Hungarian race and nation," and so on without providing clear definitions. Some authors did, however, try to explain the difference between the concept of race and that of nation. The Hungarian neo-thomist philosopher Gyula Kozáry [1887–1925], for instance, separated "people/nation" from "race," suggesting that the former was "a larger concept characterized by the unity of language," consisting of "individuals belonging to several races." By contrast, race meant "ancient, externally recognizable ties of blood."[54] In many situations, these two terms, race and nation, were conceptually interchangeable. Race, a biological term, and nation, a cultural term were often used synonymously, and not only in Western or East-Central Europe, but also in Russia, Turkey, and Japan.[55]

Despite elaborate anthropological argumentation, as will be seen in the next chapter, racial philosophies of belonging evaded accuracy of thought. Asked to define exactly what was meant by the expression "Anglo-Saxon race," "Teutonic," or "Turanic race," few high-spirited nationalists in Britain, Germany, or Hungary could have given an explicit answer. At the end of the nineteenth century however, a separation of the two terms can be detected, a procedure that became widespread with the advancement of nationalism and debates on national specificity.

In this changed historical context, the discussion about the relationship between race and nation received a new impetus, as attempts were made to define the ethnic community in both cultural and biological terms.[56] The new political climate during the 1920s promoted an abundant literature on national character and the national community. Far from being marginalized, race continued to provided sustenance to a variety of identity building projects. In early republican Turkey, for instance, representations of race became increasingly central to official efforts to formulate a cohesive state ideology. This was, as the sociologist Murat Ergin argued, "a historically oriented project to discover Turkish roots in a timeless past, and a future-oriented project of protecting racial essenses against threats of degeneration."[57]

Similarly, the newly established countries of Southern and East-Central Europe embraced nationalism as official politics; nation, rather than society, was the ultimate object of study and research.[58] With respect to Romania, for instance, "there was scarcely a politician, regardless of party, and scarcely a thinker, whether in economics, psychology, sociology, ethnography, philosophy, literature or art, who did not directly or indirectly have something to say about Romanians' essential character."[59] At the same time, however, a renewed emphasis was placed upon race and its connection to specific mechanisms of national identification and classification. More explicitly than before, philosophers, writers, and literary critics employed racial typologies and racial arguments in their definitions of the nation. In the context of generalized political radicalism, interwar racial theories became associated with all the other processes intrinsic to discussions about identity, culture, and history.[60] And to engage in discussions about nation and race during the interwar period was also to focus on physical descriptions, and consequently on the nation as a physical entity—as an object—existing in and through its exchanges with other nations and races.[61]

Yet, and to reiterate an argument made earlier, this transformation of national mythologies to include ethnogenesis and racial history did not supplant the other intellectual tradition originating with Jean-Jacques Rousseau and others in the eighteenth century that highlighted the people's capacity of good judgement and self-consciousness. In this regard, it is important to remember that this tradition, although altered significantly during the twentieth century, continues to provide guidance to debates on the nation and national character to this day.

The People as Nation

In *Du contrat social ou principes du droit politique* (known in English as *The Social Contract*), published in 1762, Jean-Jacques Rousseau outlined how the modern state could claim political legitimacy of rule and of law only when it succeeded at representing the general will of the people and encouraging the active consent of its citizens.[62] These ideas ran contrary to the founding principles of autocracy, which Enlightenment philosophers viewed as an outdated polity; as already mentioned, the new political thinking advanced the radical proposition that the ultimate authority of government should reside with the people. As the historian of nationalism Hans Kohn [1891–1971] observed over half a century ago, Rousseau was the "first great writer who did not share the belief that the aristocratic and rationalist civilization of his century represented the highest program so far achieved in man's development."[63] The reigning principle of government under absolutism was the idea of *regis voluntas suprema lex* (the king's will is the highest law). Rousseau wished to replace the sovereignty of the Prince, whose will was the state, with a new sovereign: the People.[64]

The revolutionary and utopian ideal of popular sovereignty propounded by Rousseau and other philosophers before him such as Thomas Hobbes

[1588–1679] and John Locke [1632–1704], was founded upon the opinion that modern liberal-democratic republics and constitutional monarchies were the best political systems, because they alone were capable of working towards a common good that would benefit the whole of the nation. According to Rousseau, individuals possessed a natural passion for liberty that could express itself in struggles for national liberation from foreign occupation and colonization such as that of the Poles, for instance, who needed to free themselves, he argued, from the shackles of their centuries-old subjugation by their Russian oppressors.[65] Truly popular governments also inspired, by their noble deeds, the loyalty and virtue of their citizens, which, Rousseau stressed, were voluntary functions of citizenship; patriotism had to be earned by governments and freely given by those whose interests were truly represented by their rulers.[66]

This liberal-democratic definition of nationalism has been influential for centuries now, although often repudiated, as during the interwar period, and again today, for example. As seen, it had a huge impact upon the American revolutionaries of 1776, most notably Thomas Jefferson, as evidenced in his famous preamble to the Declaration of Independence. This eminently Rousseauian document set out a grand design for a noble and good Republic founded upon a respect for the common people and individual liberty, and leading intellectuals in Britain, such as Jeremy Bentham [1748–1832] and John Stuart Mill, drew inspiration from it. Since the nineteenth century, the liberationist elements within this school of philosophy have influenced nationalists in emergent nations, such as Greece, Italy, and Germany, the nascent nations of East-Central Europe, and many in much of the African, South American, and Asian continents seeking an end to European colonial rule. It is usually associated with the conviction that long-established and newly-emergent nation-states had to cultivate a strong sense of social cohesion and national identity amongst their populations.[67]

It bears repetition that this form of civic nationalism did not see any moral incompatibility between nationalistic values and liberal ideals because it was premised upon the utopian idea, born out of the Enlightenment, that the fundamental duty of the state was to serve its people. In turn, it was assumed that the nation could develop, grow, and ultimately fulfil its historical destiny only in a state of its own. As the Catholic historian Lord Acton [1834–1902] put it: "If the nation could exist without the State, subject only to the instinct of self-preservation, it would be incapable of denying, controlling, or sacrificing itself."[68] Not surprisingly, many nationalists who propounded a concept of the nation that transcended the physical boundaries of the state distinguished between the two. The Greek nationalist Ion Dragoumis, mentioned earlier, offered the exemplary version of the debate between different visions of the nation and the state. Essentially, he distinguished between the "natural borders of the Hellenic nation" and the "artificial boundaries of the Helladic state," namely the Greek state at the beginning of the twentieth century.[69]

Drawing a clear distinction between state and nation, Dragoumis based his nationalism upon a belief in the unsurpassed cultural superiority of the Greeks, which, for him, dated from the Classical Age of the First Hellenic Civilization, when philosophy, art, literature, and science flourished from around 510 BCE until Alexander the Great's death in 323 BCE. Like many of his contemporaries, Dragoumis was an anti-irredentist nationalist, but he did not dream of expanding the territorial frontiers of Greece eastwards, reclaiming Constantinople for a Greater Greece, and, through military conquest, provoking the demise of the Ottoman Empire. Rather, before his political assassination in 1920, Dragoumis speculated about a future in which a Greek-Ottoman Empire would be founded; in this new *Hellenic empire*, Greeks would be the elite ruling class and the Ottomans their political servants. For him, Greece was a nation that did not need a state in order to survive and flourish.[70]

During the nineteenth century, civic-national states, such as France, Britain, and the USA, adopted the notion of *jus soli* (law of the soil), according to which all persons born within the integral territory of the nation-state were considered citizens, regardless of the place of birth of their parents, in contrast with the principle of *jus sanguinis* (law of the blood) that was prevalent in Germany and East-Central Europe, in which citizenship was inherited through family and descent.[71] For most nationalists, however, allegiance to the common values of the national community is paramount. For instance, in his "Europe: its Condition and Prospects," first published in 1852, Giuseppe Mazzini [1805–1872], a leading figure of European liberal-democratic nationalism, described the principle of nationality in terms of "natural" elements, such as territory, history, and ethnic origin, but moulded into the consciousness of the people by education.[72] This theory of the nation was based on the assumption that ethnic groups were intrinsic parts of nature, and hence combined two traditions: the Romantic idea of national character and racial origins, and the liberal notions of individual equality and universal unity.[73]

Mazzini was not the only nationalist in Europe depicting nationality along these lines. The liberal politician and one of the creators of modern Romania, Ion C. Brătianu [1821–1891], similarly insisted that the two principles, nationalism and liberalism, were complementary. Brătianu, and others like him in East-Central Europe, combined Michelet and Mazzini's views on the natural tendency of individuals to associate in larger groups, such as family, tribe, race, and nation, according to their interests and historical conditions, with the Romantic ideas about the permanence of cultural specificity. The rights of the nation derived, Brătianu claimed, from the rights of men that were by definition individual and universal. But these rights were also the creation of nature. Nations, he believed, were not only the result of cultural and political activity, but also communities of biological descent.

In highlighting the importance of heredity for collective identity, Brătianu echoed the views put forward by French romantic historians, most notably by Augustin Thierry [1795–1856], who in his discussion of national character argued that "the physical and moral constitution of peoples depends [. . .] on their ancestry and the primitive race to which they belong."[74] Robert Knox, in his already mentioned *The Races of Men*, endorsed this view. He too argued that "the human character, individual or national, is traceable solely to the nature of that race to which the individual or nation belongs."[75]

Brătianu was familiar not only with romantic historicism and republican themes that were discussed at length in revolutionary circles across Europe during the 1840s, but also with debates about racial types that characterized anthropology at the beginning of the nineteenth century. He was especially influenced by the theories of racial categorization of mankind proposed by Johann Friedrich Blumenbach, whose subdivision of races he followed. Nevertheless, and in keeping with his liberal convictions, Brătianu did not use the concept of race to justify ethnic exclusion, but rather to indicate the natural condition of a nation. Like Rousseau, he believed in the return to a primordial natural purity, but accented this with an awareness of one's ethnic destiny. According to Brătianu, racial belonging connected the individual "to the infinite," bestowing upon him a higher purpose. It ennobled him; it made him "immortal."[76] Yet the broader meaning of race for him, as for other mid-nineteenth-century nationalists, was thoroughly conditioned by an idealized awakening of the nation, which in effect functioned as a self-fulfilling prophecy.

Racial nationalism is embedded in the idea that members of a nation are related by birth and connected by ties of blood, as manifested by a community of language, religion, and customs. According to its fervent supporters, the nation has an inalienable right, bestowed by God, or by History, to growth and expansion.[77] Within that context, the idea of revitalizing the nation brought with it a new conceptualization of the importance of the idea of race. It increasingly conditioned cultural and social identification. This view was clearly expressed in 1910 by the racial biologist Alfred Ploetz [1860–1940] at the first meeting of the German Sociological Society. For Ploetz and for his followers, "the blooming of the race is a necessary foundation for the formation of the society."[78] By the beginning of the twentieth century, the link between race and nation underpinned a new form of constructing identity, one which has been described elsewhere as the biologization of national belonging.[79] In some countries, this process of appropriation of biological criteria for identity was more intense than in others.

Ethnic Nations

So-called ethnic nations such as Serbia, Romania, Germany, or Japan, historically, have defined their nationhood and nationality in terms of a presumed consanguinity and community of beliefs and interests. In the imagined and real entities, defined as ethnic nations, nationality is usually denied to anyone born outside of this community.[80] Nations and nationalism are all about drawing boundaries of inclusion and exclusion, and these can be elusive and shifting, as well as complex and contradictory. In the nineteenth century authors defined the nation by reference to a shared heritage and culture, which included a common language, faith, and ethnic ancestry; but the turbulent history of the twentieth century demonstrates that the solution to the problem of the nation is seldom so simple or straightforward.

Few worshipped the nation more than Mazzini, who founded the insurrectionary nationalist association *La Giovine Italia* (*Young Italy*) in 1831. "The Patria," he wrote in 1859, was "the life that link[ed] all the generations that have risen, acted, and passed on your land in a tradition of like tendencies and affections." In 1871, he added: "Language, territory, race are no more than signs of Nationality, insecure when not all entwined, and any event demanding confirmation in historical tradition, in the long development of a collective life designated by the same characteristics."[81] The nation was thus invested with an enormous force, whose profound power of seduction is felt to this day.

The worship of the nation, which was so prevalent in the nineteenth century, was epitomized in the political writings of Georg Wilhelm Friedrich Hegel [1770–1831], the German philosopher who believed that the "absolute final aim" of history was the coming together of people to form nations.[82] In the Hegelian view, as expressed in his monumental *Grundlinien der Philosophie des Rechts* (*Elements of the Philosophy of Right*, 1821), the nation was not a free union of individuals, as it was in the liberal conception of Rousseau, who spoke in terms of the "People-Nation" as a single entity. Rather, for Hegel, the nation was a super-personality, the source of all law and morality, and the expression of the Divine or Absolute Idea on Earth. Moreover, the nation was synonymous in his thinking with its political representation, the State, to whose will all citizens must submit and to which all people had a duty to obey unquestioningly.[83]

Hegel's admiration for the nation was premised upon the creation of a strong state with a "substantial will" and a "supreme right"; this state interpreted the "mind of the nation," behaved with "absolute rationality," and would serve the "ethical Idea" and its own higher morality: the national interest.[84] This powerful political entity was to be unfettered by any "Kantian categorical imperative" to limit its power in order to preserve individual freedoms and personal liberty.[85] Hegel's vision of the moral duty of blind obedience to the State was complemented by a heightened sense of ethnic preservation, articulated by another German philosopher, Johann Gottlieb Fichte [1762–1814].[86] Moved by the defeat of Prussia by Napoleon in 1807–1808, Fichte became a passionate German nationalist. In his *Reden an die deutsche Nation* (*Addresses to the German Nation*), a series of lectures delivered in the winter of 1807/08 in the Great Hall of the Academy of Sciences in Berlin, he invested the love of fatherland (*Vaterlandsliebe*) with additional meanings (both cultural and philosophical), derived from

Kant's transcendental idealism and, in particular, his moral philosophy.[87] At the time, a unitary German nation was more of vision than political reality so, perhaps not surprisingly, Fichte's message to his compatriots was both a homage to the German community and a plea for a new national pedagogy. "Love of fatherland, love for the whole people of the German nation," he declared, "had to reign supreme."

Fichte was, of course, not the only nationalist in Germany to proclaim the love of fatherland's "supreme, final, and absolute authority" over both the state and the individual.[88] As the nineteenth century progressed, he and Herder were embraced not only by the emerging German national movement but also by intellectuals in Southern and East-Central Europe who were determined to transform the destiny of their peoples and prepare them for the promised nationhood.[89] Communities were nationalized and nation-states envisioned within the great European empires of the Habsburgs and the Romanovs. A national language, which Herder deemed essential to collective identity, became not only the medium through which to communicate the new gospel of the nation but also a vigorously contested battleground. For example, the so-called "Slavic" or "Illyrian" language of the Serbs and the Croats (in the twentieth century, also called Serbo-Croat-Slovene, Bosnian-Croatian-Serbian, or Bosnian-Croatian-Montenegrin-Serbian, depending upon the observer's point of view) was codified by the middle of the nineteenth century.[90] Serbo-Croat language was declared the primary tongue of Serbians, Croatians, Slovenes, and Bosniaks (as well as Montenegrins and Herzegovians) and was given officially-recognized regional dialects, which were also standardized, following the Vienna Literary Agreement of 1850. However, the possession of a common language did not unify these groups ethnically. There were still communities, in the words of the Serbian geographer Jovan Cvijić [1865–1927], who were "nationally floating"[91] and did not conform to the fixed, standard categories of identity. They blended different languages and cultural traditions, and in some cases, they even drew on opposing conceptions of ethnicity.

As highlighted by the historian of fascism Roger Griffin, possessing a sense of belonging to a particular ethnic or national group can enhance the human experience by minimizing *anomie* and isolation and connecting the individual to a larger whole.[92] However, often, "ethnicity is politicized," as noted by the social anthropologist Ernest Gellner [1925–1995].[93] This can result in highly undesirable outcomes precisely because ethnic nationalists believe that "the boundaries of ethnicity should also be the boundaries of the political unit." Particularly at moments of crisis for the national community, "outsiders," "others," "foreigners," and immigrants can be seen as unwelcome intruders into the nation and be targeted as scapegoats. Based upon national myths of martyrdom and suffering, ethno-nationalism could easily turn into visceral hatreds, political animosities, ethnic rivalries, and religious conflicts. The great romantic project to create and consolidate nation-states did not always end in success.

The history of the twentieth century abounds in examples of the dangerous liaisons between nationalism, xenophobia, and racism. The case of South Africa demonstrates this point powerfully.[94] Most historians trace the origins of Apartheid back to 1948, when the Afrikaner Nationalist Party came to power under the Calvinist pastor turned politician, Daniel François Malan [1874–1959]. Equally important were the legislative reforms introduced by Hendrick F. Verwoerd [1901–1966], in his attempts to create "a white nation-state" during the early 1960s.[95] These reforms institutionalized a unique system of white supremacist rule: one in which a Western style of democracy for a minority of the population, who were whites of European origin, co-existed with a repressive, segregationist police state, which was imposed upon the majority of the population, who were native black Africans.[96]

The first landing of Europeans in the Cape occurred in 1652, when Dutch and German settlers arrived. The Dutch ruled the Cape until 1806, when the British took over the colony and ruled it until 1910. For over a century, Dutch and British white settlers struggled for mastery over South Africa and for control of the country's vast natural riches, especially diamonds and gold. The first great drama in this war between two competing white nationalisms was the mass migration of the Boers—descendants of the original Dutch settlers—after 1835, when they fled into the interior to escape British rule at the Cape. After conquering the African kingdoms in the north, the *Voortrekkers* (Afrikaans and Dutch for "pioneers"), as they were known, founded the independent Boer Republics. This Great Trek of 1835–1846 was a significant epoch in the epic myth-making which resulted in the formation of a distinct and strong Afrikaner identity and nationalism. Although High Dutch was the official language of the Boer Republics, Afrikaans, which was a spoken dialect, was the vernacular of the *Volk* and a rallying point for Afrikaner nationalists.

Scholars have identified a fundamentalist and salvationist interpretation of Calvinism as the core set of ideas informing the "Christian Nationalism" which became the cornerstone of Afrikanerdom.[97] In the nineteenth century, Afrikaner theologians and nationalists propounded a national mythology of the Boer people which was based upon their belief in pre-ordination and *"apartheid"* (Afrikaans for "separateness" or "apartness", denoting the need for separate racial development). According to this faith, God had created a great diversity of races, colours, nations, and cultures, and these all had an assigned role to play in history. The pre-destined vocation of the Afrikaner nation was to rule, Christianize, and civilize the others. The nation was, therefore, divinely ordained and had to be ruled according to God's design. According to Malan: "Our history is the greatest masterpiece of the centuries. We hold this nationhood as our due for it was given to us by the Architect of the Universe [. . .] Indeed, the history of the Afrikaner reveals a will and a determination which make one feel that Afrikanerdom is not the work of men, but the creation of God."[98]

Afrikaner nationalism made nation worship into a form of God-worship. Nations and races were defined as precious objects of divine grace, whose differences had to be preserved by all God-fearing people. In 1879, Afrikaner Christian nationalists joined together into an anti-British association, the *Bond (Union)*, which was under the command of a church minister, Reverend Stephanus J. du Toit [1847–1911]. The purpose of this organization was to fight for the nation's survival; the Afrikaner *Broederbond (Brotherhood Association)* followed in 1918; this organization, with a vast membership, functioned as a secret society and a Christian brotherhood, devoted to a single goal, as its manifesto declared: the "Afrikanerisation of South Africa's state on Christian-National lines."[99]

Similar to the westward expansion of the American people, which occurred contemporaneously, the Great Trek became the primary cultural myth and symbol of the Boer people. It is prototypical and "archetypical" too, for the story of the heroic flight from servitude tells the tale of the rebirth of the Boer nation, one which was consecrated in nationalistic accounts as a sacred deed of the ancestors and was, consequently, imprinted upon the living memory of the people. Afrikaner nationalists such as theologian Willem Postma [1874–1920] placed the trek on a par with the legend of "The Exodus" of the Israelites from slavery in Egypt, told in the Old Testament and Torah.[100] The epic narrative about how the Boers eventually vanquished their enemy, the British, was told and re-told, replayed and re-enacted continuously, in the decades which followed; it became the founding myth of the Apartheid regime. For example, the grandiose centenary celebrations of the event, marked by a re-enactment, began on 8 August 1938, with a procession of nine ox wagons, which symbolized the first flight to freedom. This recreation served as a major stimulus not just to Afrikaner nationalism, but also to South African Nazism. The philo-fascist, terrorist movement known as the *Ossewabrandwag* (*OB* or Ox-Wagon Sentinel; founded in 1939), which boasted its own paramilitary wing, the *Stormjaers* (*Stormtroopers*), took the Great Trek as their inspiration, which they defined as a "pilgrimage of martyrdom" of their persecuted people. This ultra-nationalist, racist, pro-Nazi, and anti-British organization fancied itself as the keeper of the "true" spirit of the Boer people; written in Afrikaans, its motto read "My God. My *Volk*. My Country, South Africa."[101] Dreams of a Boer People's State have never really disappeared.[102] As many nationalists in Europe during the nineteenth and early twentieth centuries, the Afrikaner nationalists assumed that their race would become a glorious, unified "People-Nation," waiting to be realized and reborn as a political entity.

National Races

In order for nations to be regenerated and reborn, however, nationalists must appeal to the hearts and minds of their peoples by means of national mythologies. As seen, myths of the ancestry, descent, and destiny of a chosen people are the cornerstone of racism, in a multitude of ways, over a long period of time, and in numerous and varied places around the world. One of the more fascinating examples of national races in the modern period is manifest in the precepts of State Shintöism, which provided legitimacy to the emperor-system that was revived and bolstered during the Meiji period [1868–1912] in Japan.[103]

In 1868, the Japanese government introduced a new method of chronological time, known as *nengö*, in which years would be labelled by reference to the reign of the Emperor. So in 1867, the death of Emperor Komei was followed by the accession to the throne of the Emperor who took the name "Meiji" (meaning "enlightened rule"). The Meiji era, also known as the time of Renovation, Restoration, Revolution, or Regeneration, inaugurated a state-sponsored drive towards industrialization and modernization, the rapidity and transformative quality of which was comparable to that of Imperial Germany, which was becoming, at the same time, the scientific powerhouse of Europe.[104] Fast-paced economic development under government control, which saw Japan emerge as the pre-eminent military, industrial, and expansionist power of the Far East, however, was coupled with a race revival based upon the state's conscious and managed use and manipulation of ancient mythology to implant national values within all social institutions and impose rigid conformity upon the Japanese people. The imperatives behind this experiment at social engineering and nationalization were the political goals of nation- and empire-building.[105]

Meiji Japan can be compared with Wilhemine Germany, which, in some respects, left much of its old imperial-autocratic-dynastic-and feudal structure intact during the process of industrialization and democratization that began after unification in 1871. In many ways, Japan was a traditional society still. The institutions and values which made Japan traditional were the Shintö religion, Buddhist ideals, Confucian philosophy and, of course, the emperor-system around which all these revolved. According to one of the foremost historians of modern Japan Richard Storry [1913–1982], there is no adequate English translation for the Japanese word for Emperor, *Tenno*. The literal "Heavenly Ruler" or "Son of Heaven," he wrote, sounds too ornate, whilst the term "Emperor" does not do justice to the sacerdotal nature of the Japanese imperial throne. The Japanese, he explained, never referred to foreign monarchs as *Tenno*; only the Japanese Emperor deserved the supreme respect and the total devotion of a *Tenno*.[106]

As a direct descendant of the Shintö Gods, the Emperor was the very focus of the Japanese perception of nationhood, as developed by the scholars who interpreted and disseminated the ancient wisdom of the national histories. This was made clear by the most important historian of the Meiji period Shiratori Kurakichi [1865–1942] who connected the imperial family to the unbroken continuity of the Japanese race.[107] During the Meiji period, nationalism in Japan became a religious faith based upon the tenets of the divinity of the Emperor and the sacred duty of racial devotion to the nation.[108] Many Japanese intellectuals, alongside military officers and the young who joined the many hyper-nationalist associations and insurrectionary secret societies in the period between the 1890s and the 1930s proclaimed their total allegiance to the ideas, embedded in the Meiji Constitution that: "The Empire of Japan shall be reigned over and governed by a line of emperors unbroken for ages eternal" and "The Emperor is sacred and inviolable."[109]

Similar to their counterparts in Europe, a new generation of Japanese authors such as Shiga Shigetaka [1863–1927], the editor of the nationalist magazine *Nihonjin* (*The Japanese*), propounded to define Japan's national essence (*kokusui*) and national character (*kokuminsei*).[110] As they sought to uncover and protect the essence of their people, Japanese nationalists, such as Shigetaka, took the message of Herder and Fichte very much to heart. Like many others of his generation, Shiga called for the preservation of Japan's cultural identity and rejected the government's indiscriminate programme of Westernization and modernization, which he argued were damaging to the social, spiritual, and racial unity and inseparableness of the Japanese. In his *Nihon Fūkeiron* (*Japanese Landscape*, 1894), which is widely considered his greatest work, and was a book read by every Japanese schoolchild and many of his compatriots, for decades, Shiga sought to revive national pride in the elegance (*shōsha*), beauty (*bi*), and power (*tettö*) of the geography and landscape of Japan, which he used to describe and symbolize the uniqueness and excellence of the Japanese. For Shiga, the interaction of the environmental factors of Japan, such as its climate, weather, soil, and the configuration of the land and water, together with the people's habits, customs, experiences, history, and development, over thousands of years, gave rise to a unique national essence and character in the Japanese race. Shiga saw himself as a pioneer and an advocate of a new type of nationalism which would bridge the divide between the past and the future, protect the continuity of the bloodline, and unleash the latent strength (*sensei ryoku)* of the Japanese upon the world.[111]

This ethnicized version of Japanese nationalism imagined the nation as a family, with all members connected to each other and to the supreme authority, the Emperor, by blood. We have already highlighted the importance of race in shaping definitions of national identity, and early twentieth-century Japan was no exception. As the sociologist Kosaku Yoshino has noted, in Japan, "race is a marker that strengthens ethnic identity," whilst the symbol of "Japanese-blood" augments the conviction that the Japanese "are members of the extended family that has perpetuated its lineage," but also that they "possess unique qualities."[112]

The belief in the divine mission and innate superiority of the Japanese people also markedly influenced their imperial expansion, in Hokkaido and elsewhere in the region.[113] According to some authors, the Japanese were a

Chosen People specially created by the gods to conquer the world. As one of them put it in 1924, "Japan has leapt from the ignoble position of an isolated island in the Far East, nay, a nation of pagans, to the status of a world empire blessed by God."[114] These elements—race, national character, nation—blended together to create a form of nationalism which functioned both as a civic religion under state sponsorship and as a sacred creed backed by the belief in Japan's historical destiny. A particularity of Japanism under Meiji was that it unified the religious and the secular and in acting in unison with the particular national variants of Buddhism and Confucianism it gave Japanese society a degree of conformity, cohesion, and homogeneity which was unknown in the West. It proved to be the perfect breeding ground for the especially virulent varieties of nationalism, militarism, and imperialism that arose in Japan, and, eventually found expression in the fascism of the 1930s.[115]

Scholars are now very familiar with the manifold means by which nationalists and governments "invent traditions" or national cultures in order to foster social cohesion, create a sense of ethnic belonging and unity within the nation, and legitimize political authority. The narratives which they seek to perpetuate and strengthen are often held to be "self-evident," "fundamental," or "eternal" truths about a people and nation and are felt to be worthy of being transmitted from generation to generation.

This was certainly the case in Meiji Japan and Imperial Germany, which both experienced state-directed rapid and unprecedented modernization at the same time. The concept of invented tradition pertains specifically to nationalism and accounts for the ways in which historical narratives can strengthen the legitimacy of a claim to a specific geographic region (such as in the case of Macedonia or Transylvania), self-autonomy or self-determination (such as in the successor states to and the micro-nationalisms of the Ottoman, Habsburg, and Russian empires, as well as the secessionism of the Basque, the Scottish, and others), or consolidating a sense of group identity (such as in an ethnically, religiously, and linguistically heterogeneous society, as in those in East-Central Europe and many parts of the Middle East); all these endeavours serve a nationalistic agenda with the nation-state as their focus.

The concept of an invented national tradition imposed from above by nationalist movements or governments, of course, does not take into account competing narratives that are not nationalistic or nation-centric. Indeed, other types and foci of identity, such as regional or local, can co-exist or compete with the forms of state identity which invented traditions seek to encourage and propagate.[116] As the cases of Italy, Greece, and Romania illustrate, cultural and racial mythologies have been an important part of the history of nationalism and the nation-state in the modern period. In the eighteenth century and the first half of the nineteenth, patriotic writers and scholars in Germany and elsewhere sought to revive national customs, languages, and cultures. As the case of South Africa exemplifies, these narratives could become essential constituents of the more vehement forms of racist, xenophobic, and chauvinistic nationalisms which emerged as the world became a far more competitive and hostile place. In the case of Japan, however, because it consisted of an existing literary and religious tradition substantiated by a written body of work, constituting sacred and ancient texts, Shintöism made it somewhat easier for Japanese nationalists to construct myths about the national character and the racial superiority of their people.

Ideas of national character enabled race's continuity through decades of historical change and ruptures with the past. Equally important, discussions of national character prompted the need for scientists to offer evidence and "proof" of the primordial nature of their peoples, nation, and race. During the nineteenth and twentieth centuries, as we shall see next, invocations of the past to create a sense of permanence and continuity received additional support from human sciences, above all from comparative linguistics and anthropology.

CHAPTER FOUR

Genealogy

[T]he builders of the Aryan civilization were of the type of "Uncle Sam" or, to use the terminology most suitable from the anthropological point of view, were of the race H[omo] Europaeus.[1]

As discussed in the previous chapters, before the nineteenth century, the term race referred primarily to a people or group unified by language, history, culture, or geography. However, a change in thinking and orientation occurred in the nineteenth century. No longer defined culturally only, race came to be associated with a group or people in possession of specific physical and psychological traits perpetuated for centuries, and ideally of a territory of their own with recognized physical borders. As the nation-state became the dominant and ideal form of political and social organization after 1789, modern ideas of race became increasingly intertwined with the nation, seen as a biological community in which a people became aware of their unique cultural heritage.

Depending upon the historical context, the ethno-cultural community (in such compelling evocations as "the Idea of Italy" or the Greek "Great Idea") for example, can predate the nation-state or the reverse can be the case, as in the argument that the French state created the French nation. Nonetheless, the importance of the association of the nation and race with the state cannot be stressed enough in modern history. The symbiotic bond between these concepts received its greatest underpinning under the influence of Rousseau, who defined the nation as inevitable and "natural" expressions of a people's will. The corollary of this transformation was the ascendancy of a cluster of ideas, which, penetrating deep within culture and science, reshaped political and nationalist movements at the end of the nineteenth century, and Fascism, Communism, and Nazism during the inter- and post-war periods. Embodying the unity of race and nation, the concept of a *völkische Staat* (ethnic state), for instance, which found its ultimate expression in Nazism, was predicated upon the reconfiguration of the national community as a living, racial entity whose purity had to be protected from the Jews, the Slavs, the Roma, and other "undesirables"—all those who were not considered to be a part of the national race.[2]

European nations were in need not only of protection but also of sound racial genealogies. The effort to invent these is discernible in the writings and thinking of those intellectuals, writers, and politicians who had taken part in the construction of a worldview based on race since the eighteenth century, if not earlier. One component of this racial philosophy of belonging deserves additional consideration: the Aryan myth. In many ways, the Aryan myth perfectly embodies the belief in the superiority of Europeans, demonstrating the intimate interplay between race, culture, and civilization,[3] whilst at the same time revealing the problematic objectivity claimed in the name of science.

Over the course of the nineteenth century, Aryanism went from being a linguistic movement to a pan-European idea to a key component in the historical process surrounding the foundation myths of the individual national races of Europe.[4] At the end of the nineteenth century, with the publication of James G. Frazer's *The Golden Bough* (1890), Aryan theories were embedded into the nativist revivalism of tradition and peasantry. By observing popular rituals and festivals, Frazer argued that peasants in Europe had preserved ancient Aryan myths. According to Frazer, the "primitive Aryan, in all that regards his mental fibre and texture, is not extinct. He is amongst us to this day."[5] Unaffected by centuries of written culture and civilization, the archaic peasant cultures of Europe provided the perfect testimony to the resilience of Aryan racial strength.

Although it was comparative linguistics and the study of religions that first brought the idea of the Aryan race to a broader audience, it was amongst racial authors, particularly during the first half of the twentieth century, and in countries such as Britain, Germany, Sweden, the USA, or Croatia, that the Aryan myth acquired a national and political role. As is well known, the Manichean interpretation of history as a conflict between races strengthened the widespread pessimism and the loss of faith in human reason following the First World War. The post-war generation not only carried on but, more importantly, amplified the racial radicalism of some of the nineteenth-century writers. Their revolt against modern civilization was not only spiritual and cultural but also biological, linked to a profound concern for the lost unity of individual human beings. Ideas of Aryan solidarity, transcending national boundaries, revitalized the slow decline of the intellectual persuasiveness of European culture and civilization. According to the historian Athena S. Leoussi, "Aryanism constructed a blood bond, between the Europeans and God, a bond which was stronger than had hitherto been claimed by the Jews as God's 'chosen people.'"[6]

Under the Nazi regime this "blood bond" and the Aryan racial utopia it fostered reached its genocidal personification. Racial hygiene and racial protectionism became embedded into the political ideology of a state determined to purify its nation of any contamination, both internal and external. To protect the Aryan race was to safeguard the future of Germany, and Nazi ideologues and politicians aspired to create a new German national community fortified against cultural decay and biological degeneration. This ideal of a healthy national community presupposed racial enrichment and physical regeneration; it also required the purging of "defectives" and "racially inferior" individuals. Sterilization and euthanasia were applied to protect the hereditarily healthy Germans and to strengthen the race as a whole. Furthermore, the Jew was declared the eternal enemy of the Aryan German and its elimination from the "national body" (*Volkskörper*) deemed essential, not only in Germany but also elsewhere in Eastern Europe, which the Nazi state reconfigured as the essential space needed for its racial expansion. The ensuing "final solution to the Jewish question" (*Endlösung der Judenfrage*) resulted in the murder of six million Jewish men, women, and children in concentration camps spread across Eastern and Central Europe.[7]

Yet, it was not only in Europe and in the USA that the Aryan myth contributed to the shaping of racism and nationalism. In India, too, this myth has influenced the emergence and dissemination of historical narratives about the national past and was often used by right-wing Hindu nationalists.[8] The myth of an Aryan race, alleged to be the common ancestors of all Indo-European peoples, functioned similarly to other historical narratives mentioned previously. Additionally, however, it reinforced the superior status of European civilization based on Hellenistic and Roman heritages, by trying to marginalize or even exclude completely the Hebrew one. In *The Birth of Tragedy*, the German philosopher Friedrich Nietzsche made the connection clear, describing the Greek god Prometheus "as the indigenous property of all Aryan peoples, and a testament to their talent for profundity and tragedy."[9]

When it emerged in the mid-nineteenth century, the main debate was between those who interpreted the Aryan race as a linguistic category and those who pushed the argument further, drawing connections between these ancient peoples and modern races in Europe and elsewhere.[10] For both academic traditions, however, the Aryans were a superior race whose past was rightly claimed by Europeans as theirs, and then quickly absorbed into mainstream European and American racism during the twentieth century. Tellingly, the Aryan myth appealed to many racial authors because it "entertained the flattering notion" of the West's "superior civilization" as a "birth-right," as the historian of anti-Semitism Léon Poliakov [1910–1997] observed decades ago.[11] Equally important, it fitted perfectly with the growing crisis of cultural confidence and its multiple reconfigurations exploited so vigorously by philosophers such as Arthur Schopenhauer [1788–1860] and Friedrich Nietzsche. In a world that was becoming increasingly fragmented, the Aryan myth attracted supporters in so many different countries, partly because of what appeared to be the strength of the scientific evidence favouring its credence; mostly because this mythological narrative about the racial origins of Europeans gave it both power and authority. As the British science writer Samuel Laing [1812–1897] argued in a popular lecture *On the Indo-European Languages and Races* (1862), the Aryan race was "eminently the intellectual race, the race of science, art, poetry, philosophy, conquest, colonization, and progress."[12]

Comparative Linguistics

In his study *The Aryans*, published in 1926, the Australian archaeologist V. Gordon Childe [1892–1957] argued that "by the time Aryan genius found its true expression in Greece and Rome, the pure Nordic strain had been for the most part absorbed in the Mediterranean substratum." Tellingly, he continued, "the lasting gift bequeathed by the Aryans to the conquered peoples was neither a higher material culture nor a superior physique, but [. . .] more excellent language and the mentality it generated."[13] Childe was not the first to place the discussion of the Aryans within the field of comparative linguistics rather than anthropology, literature, or politics. One of the greatest popularizers of the Aryan myth in nineteenth-century Europe, Friedrich Max Müller [1823–1900] first presented his ideas about the existence of a distinct Aryan language and civilization in Paris in 1849, in a study awarded the prestigious Prix Volney, given annually by the Institute of France to the best work in comparative philology.[14]

Müller remains to this day one of the most celebrated Indologists and Sanskritists, and is considered one of the founders of the study of comparative religion and linguistics in the nineteenth century. Such was his fame and acclaim that, in a novel written in 1870 by Benjamin Disraeli, who himself believed in the Aryan myth, he appears in the guise of a Mr. Phoebus, a painter who expressed his views on the genius of the Aryans to the young Lothair.[15] Like his fictional depiction, Müller settled in Oxford in 1848, as Professor of Comparative Philology and Vedic Studies, and remained there for the rest of his life.

During the 1850s, Müller was keen to take credit for being the first scholar to identify the existence of what he considered to be humanity's earliest civilization and Europe's ancestral race, the Aryans. Müller's assertion was, however, inaccurate. Other scholars such as the Swiss linguist Adolphe Pictet [1799–1875], argued along the same lines that the Aryans were linguistically, culturally, and racially the ancestors of the Indo-Europeans.[16] Academic philology had already "discovered" the Aryans as a linguistic and racial family in the late eighteenth century, when scholars realized that languages changed over time, and began to study the evolution of grammar and vocabulary.[17] In keeping with the spirit of Enlightenment scientism, they founded a new "science," philology, which sought to study the origins, history, and relationships of languages. As Stephen G. Alter noted, "The impetus for this new field came with the realization that Europe's classical languages bore close genetic ties to Sanskrit, the ancient language of the Hindus."[18]

However, it was not only linguists who were interested in the history and comparison of languages. European colonial administrators such as Sir William Jones [1746–1794], also attempted to decipher, classify, and compare the world's old languages in order to identify words, rules, and laws which were held in common. The Sanskrit language, for instance, was described by Jones to be "more perfect than the Greek, more copious than the Latin, and more exquisitely refined than either; yet bearing to both of them a stronger affinity."[19] Literary critics and philosophers such as Friedrich Schlegel [1772–1829], broadened the discussion by focusing not only on language but also on nature and culture. For instance, in his lectures on the world's history at the University of Cologne, which he published in 1808 under the title *Über die Sprache und Weisheit der Indier* (*On the Language and Wisdom of the Indians*), Schlegel suggested that this Sanskrit-speaking race, the Aryans, left the Himalayas and brought civilization to India, Egypt, and Europe.[20] A decade later, in 1819, he proposed that the term "Aryan" must denote a racial group who spoke the "Aryan language." He conflated language, myth, and culture with race, placing emphasis on the scientific credibility of linguistic criteria. Schlegel's appropriation of language for ethnic affiliation was embraced by succeeding generations of racial authors. As the literary scholar Bill Ashcroft aptly noted, "In his enthusiastic prospectus for a science of comparative philology Schlegel's lasting legacy was to galvanize German youth with the myth of an Aryan race."[21]

By the beginning of the nineteenth century, various terms were proposed to describe the outcome of this racial migration across continents, including Aryans, Indo-Europeans, and Indo-Germans. Comparative linguistics now supplemented anthropology and history with new evidence for the racial classification of mankind.[22] To some extent, comparative linguistics embraced a much wider mission, for its practitioners hoped to grasp the meaning of all knowledge and wisdom by studying that which, they believed, gave it expression—language. Linguists sought to identify and examine the oldest extant linguistic sources for clues as to the origin of language. Research into comparative linguistics relied heavily upon attempts to deconstruct and decode the sacred texts of the world's great religions, which were considered to be the oldest records of early languages and beliefs. Language and religion together, scholars maintained, would unlock the mysteries of human thought, endeavour, and culture.[23]

One of the first scholars to describe the derivation and descent of related languages in the form of a genealogical tree was the German linguist August Schleicher [1821–1868]. As a follower of Charles Darwin, Schleicher envisaged a "great tree" with many branches of sister-languages, together comprising a whole family of sometimes quite different sibling-idioms and all issuing forth from an ancient, proto-Indo-European mother tongue.[24]

Schleicher and other linguists, including Franz Bopp [1791–1867], Eugène Burnouf [1801–1852], and Friedrich Schelling [1775–1854], had a major impact outside their immediate field, since anthropologists keenly followed the latest trends in linguistic research. These authors also influenced Max Müller,[25] who devised and led one of the most extraordinary and painstaking editorial and intellectual enterprises of Victorian Britain, a project which was only completed after his death.

The Sacred Books of the East, as this project is known, consists of 50 volumes and was published by Oxford University Press between 1879 and 1910.[26] Müller personally edited and partially translated material from the Vedas, Uphanishads, and other fundamental Hindu scripture, as well as the Buddhist unabridged Dhammapada. He also edited the translations of his fellow Orientalists on Islam, Buddhism, Zoroastrianism, Confucianism, and other ancient religions.[27] But it was India that loomed large on Müller's agenda, which was, in Hegel's words, "the land of imaginative inspiration [. . .] a fairy region, an enchanted world."[28] India, or the Orient, more broadly, appealed to the European intellectuals, and not only to those with a Romantic bent such as Fichte and Herder,[29] but also to those such as Mircea Eliade for whom it embodied a primordial imaginative freedom and sexual creativity that were lacking in the West.[30] As home to one of the world's oldest books, the Rig Veda, India also represented the birth of civilization and the promise of culture. To Romantic idealists, it also represented, in a Hegelian sense, a transcendental spirit. Read as history, not legend, the Rig Veda, Müller believed, documented not only the invasion of the northern region of India (the Punjab and the Indus) by marauding Aryans, but also the birth of Western civilization. Europe's Aryan progenitors brought civilization and the sword from the highlands of Central Asia to the West.[31]

Müller was not the only scholar who believed in the Aryan Invasion myth. He was, in fact, following in the footsteps of the first great Orientalist, Abraham Hyacinthe Anquetil-Duperron [1731–1805], who travelled to India in 1754 and who was the first to translate Indian religious texts into European languages (French and Latin). Anquetil-Duperron used the term "Aryan" to mean an historic, warlike people who originally descended from Persia into the Indian subcontinent, before making their way into Europe.[32]

Müller presented the case for use of the term Aryan to describe a set of related Indian and European languages and a race of people. In a work published in 1855, he argued that those who first spoke the ancestral language Avestan, from which Sanskrit putatively derived, should be entitled to give "the name by which they called themselves" to the family of languages which they founded. This name was Aryan, according to Müller.[33] But did these ancient people really call themselves Aryan? On this crucial point, Müller was imprecise, but suggestive. They probably did, he contended, in some very remote past. He admitted, however, that the Sanskrit word for Aryan gradually disappeared from the language and culture over time. In the later Sanskrit literature, he claimed, "Arya," or "ārya", more precisely, meant no more than "of good family," "noble," "venerable," and "Lord." It referred, specifically, to the Brahmins, who were members of the highest or priestly caste in Hindu society. But Müller believed that it once had meaning as a national name, since, in his opinion, the Sanskrit "Arya-avarta" meant the holy land and abode of the Aryans. Moreover, he maintained, the term "Aryan" was preserved as a national name by the Medians and the Persians. Herodotus, he related, was told in his oriental travels that the Medians called themselves Aryans. Although the word "Aryan" fell into disuse amongst the Hindus, Müller argued, and was never used anywhere in the literature in association with an entire people or even a language, he felt it should still be retained as a nominative. The people whom it originally described, the top castes of Brahminic society, spoke Sanskrit, he explained, which was the "seed" which they planted widely and which flowered abundantly in both Europe and Asia. Members of a "whole Aryan family," with offshoots in both the East and the West, shared a common language and grammar.[34]

Müller was aware that the historical evidence for his vision of the Aryans as a heroic, conquering race who founded Europe's ancient civilizations was weak; however, he was swept away by the power of his own mythopoetic narrative. In the Vedic literature, the word "ārya," from which the English "Aryan" derived (and the name "Iran"), is, according to scholars today, nowhere defined in connection with a people, nation, "race," or language; rather, it refers to "gentleman," "good natured," "righteous person," "nobleman," and is often used like "Sir," before the name of a person (such as Aryaputra). Moreover, as the word "Aryan" apparently appears no more than four times in the whole of the Rig Veda, which is a collection of 1,028 hymns and 10,600 verses, in ten books, any argument based on the weight of the linguistic evidence alone was destined to be weak.[35] Nonetheless, Müller imbued the term Aryan with a racial meaning, describing the Aryans in 1895, as "the true ancestors of our race."[36] In so doing, he gave scholarly authority to the increasing tendency to believe that it was, in fact, true.

Müller wrote that the word Aryan fell into disuse amongst the Hindus, but was preserved by the Medians and the Persians in the *Zend-Avesta*, the canonical texts of Zoroastrianism, written in the otherwise unrecorded language of the ancient Persians, Avestan or Zend (with letters derived from old Pahlavi-Aramaic).[37] What Müller defined as a racial link between the ancient Indians and Iranians was based on the similarity between the Sanskrit "ārya" and the Avestan "ariya," also meaning noble. Müller, along with other Aryanists, noted that the ancient Persians seemed to have a highly developed sense of nationality. According to Müller, the earliest references to Aryans appeared in the Avestan literature as "ariya," meaning noble, and "airyanem vaego," meaning land of the Aryans. But the term seemed to have been adopted in remote antiquity by early Iranians to denote their national identity and even their racial affiliation. Müller remarked that it was significant that, in cuneiform inscriptions, Darius the Great [549–486 BCE] identified himself as "a Persian, son of a Persian, an Aryan of Aryan descent."

In later Pahlavi literature, Müller stated, the word Aryan was transmuted into Īrān, meaning the homeland of the Ariyas or Aryans, and the root of the modern word Iran.[38]

Because of their grounding in normative rules, scientific imaginings such as Müller's philological exegeses about language and meaning, appeared as "knowledge" and "fact." The Aryan myth, which he helped create and propagate, demonstrates just how far-fetched scientific imagination can be. He, his contemporaries, and his successors, who subscribed to this myth saw what they wished to see in the religious literature of India and then Persia. Müller provided clues as to the reason why he was so prepared to make up a story about a fictional race and create an entire narrative about its origin and descent. His personal archive, held at Oxford University, holds manuscript sources which reveal his thinking. They give a wonderful glimpse into the workings of racial myth-making: they reveal Müller's mental universe and capture the nature of his subjective understanding. The notes which he prepared for his first course of lectures in comparative philology at Oxford begin in 1851 and the very first notations show that he was concerned with demonstrating that "the nations of Europe are the best nations of the world." This greatness was evidenced in "modern society's innovations and revolutions"; these achievements, however, were traceable all the way back "to the first beginnings."

According to Müller, the present day was the result of "an aggregate experience" and the product of a genealogy that began with the "dawn of history." The entirety of European culture, comprising such splendours as the "sacred customs of the Teutonic race" and the "codes of the Roman emperors" had a common origin and a source, which was not in Europe, but in Asia.[39] The geologist, he continued, goes "back to periods previous to the beginnings of history." The philologist does the same, by examining the architectonics of language. "The history of a nation can only begin after its language has been formed."[40] Deep in a mysterious primeval epoch, an "ante-historical period," "one original people" populated the "valleys of Northern India" and this "primitive stock" was the seed of the "Indo-European nations." The earliest Brahmans who migrated towards the South and the Indus River shared the same god that the Teutons later did on the mountains of Scandinavia.[41] The primitive aboriginal races of Europe were eventually vanquished and often driven into mountainous and marshy tracts by the powerful prehistoric tribes of Aryan invaders. The Hungarians were the only example, Müller believed, of the surviving Finnic aborigines, who settled in the midst of Indo-European nations and successfully resisted the invasion.[42]

For Aryanists, the most important source of information about the Aryans came from the Rig Veda, which, as Müller explained in 1892, provided "something of our own intellectual growth, some recollections, as it were, of our own childhood, or at least the childhood of our race."[43] In his Oxford lectures, Müller argued that the book was probably "composed nearly 4,000 years ago" and formed an essential part of the oral tradition of the Brahminical priesthood, before being committed to written form about 1100–1200 BCE.[44] He also made a number of assumptions which formed the basis of the myths of an Aryan race and an Aryan invasion of India.

Müller believed that the Rig Veda was the product of the pantheistic religion of the highborn "Aryan" Brahmins, whom he called "our spiritual kith and kin."[45] The claim that the Brahmins were actually called Aryans by themselves or by other contemporaries was highly speculative, however. Western scholars, including Schlegel and Müller, derived the basis of this theory from what is now widely considered to be a highly flawed misreading of the Vedic literature.[46] Rather than see the Vedas as literary texts alone, Western scholars thought that they outlined an early history of India. The hymns of the Rig Veda seemed to contain fragmentary references to actual historical events, most notably to a war between the early Vedic peoples (the Aryans) and their enemies.

The Rig Veda also appeared to describe a Late Bronze Age material culture based on a presumed extensive use of metal tools and implements by alleged "Aryans." And even more fancifully, Müller and others believed that they found depictions of Aryans using horse-drawn chariots. The Vedas also used expressions, translated as "children of light" and "children of the sun," possibly, as some scholars now contend, to signify the struggle between the forces of good and evil.[47] Aryan theorists, including Müller, interpreted these poetic metaphors as references to the actual skin pigmentation of the putative Aryans. They began to construct an elaborate mythology concerning the ancient Aryan progenitors of Western civilization. An essential part of the creative process of myth-making was to see Aryans in their own image and to give them a European physiotype.

The imagined bearers of European civilization, Aryans were divided into two branches. One migrated north-westward and civilized the whole of Europe. The other branch which migrated south-eastward invaded and conquered India. Although the archaeological evidence of this was lacking in both respects, the idea that one branch of the nomadic Aryans settled in northern India and created Vedic culture and that the other, through subsequent migrations, which followed the course of the sun, founded European civilization itself was not questioned.[48] As argued by the historian of religion Dorothy Matilda Figueira: "The truth regarding the Aryans was less to be found in their literature than in what it was no longer able to express. Truth was not to be discovered in words, but rather in the lacunae, the message that had been lost through decay, inaccessibility, and the loss of ability to read correctly."[49]

Aryanism and its Enemies

Already in the 1850s, the above-mentioned Adolphe Pictet, who pioneered the method of "linguistic palaeontology" of the family, argued not only that primitive Aryans spoke an ancient dialect which gave birth to the family of Indo-European languages but also that the Aryan race was "destined by Providence some day to dominate the entire globe." Its superiority came both from "the beauty of its blood" and from the "richness, vigour, harmony, and perfection of form of its language."[50]

Aryanists bestowed upon the "noble" Aryans characteristics which they considered to be significant and desirable elements of their vision of European civilization. They put selected textual fragments together into a picture of early Aryans as a fair-skinned, heroic race of warriors who were devoted equally to the worship of nature and their deities and to the pursuit of war and territorial conquest. Though their natural religion was primitive and their social organization simple, early Aryans supposedly practised monogamy and lived together in clans. Thereby, they created the institutional rudiments of civilized society, which were marriage, family, and community. Their economic system was also quite sophisticated. A pastoral people, prehistoric Aryans mainly bred cattle for their livelihood, but they also subsisted by farming. These assumptions should not be discounted as symptoms of a collective delusion. As the philosopher of culture S. N. Balagangadhara observed, the false conjectures and misreadings which formed the basis of the Aryan myth possess an "internal logic" which derived from the realities of the Romantic scientific imagination and the cultural experience of nineteenth-century Europeans.[51]

The Aryan myth has possessed such persuasive power over Westerners for more than two centuries. In the first half of the nineteenth century, the tenets of Aryanism seemed to be established as incontrovertible historical facts, supported by a mass of linguistic and literary evidence, and endorsed by a host of scientists. Indeed, where the most disagreement prevailed concerned not the matter of the actual existence of the Aryans as such, but rather the question of whether Persia or India, or somewhere else entirely in Central Asia, could claim to be the true birthplace of this race of conquerors and civilizers. By the second half of the nineteenth century, however, the dynamics of the debate had changed, as some authors began to dispute the notion of the Asian provenance of the Aryans altogether. Dissenting voices such as the American historian and educator Joseph Pomeron Widney [1841–1938], argued that the primordial origins of the Aryans and the Western world were European rather than Asian. According to Widney, the cultural achievements of the Aryans were unrivalled in history, confirming the long-established assumption about Europe's dominant place in the world. "Every masterful race of the world's history has its epic," he noted and the Aryan racial story "was the tale of the race life, not told in words, but lived in deeds done."[52]

The "European hypothesis" was increasingly endorsed in the 1870s and 1880s by the work of racial authors such as Houston Stewart Chamberlain, who took a leading role in transforming Indic Aryan Man into a born-and-bred European with a robust Teutonic identity. As the dogmas and certainties of racial science claimed a foothold in the culture of Europe towards the end of the nineteenth century, the case for a European cradle of the Aryans increasingly gained supporters in France, particularly, and, then, in Germany and Scandinavia.[53] Works such as *Crania Britannica,* published in 1865 by Joseph B. Davis [1801–1881] and John Thurnam [1810–1873][54] or *Anthropologica Suecica* (Swedish Anthropology), published in 1902 by Gustaf Retzius [1842–1919] and Carl M. Fürst [1854–1935],[55] although concerned mainly with prehistoric crania did not hesitate to speak of "Teutonic nations" and "Teutonic blood," and put forward the theory that "racially pure" Germanic populations had survived in modern times. Initially, Retzius was hesitant to endorse the Aryan myth, but in his Huxley Lecture, given in London in 1909, he spoke positively of "that branch of the blond long-headed race in Europe which, from ancient times, has had its home in my native country of Sweden" and which also formed the "increasingly large element in the white population of North America and other continents."[56]

A new generation of Aryanists argued from a Eurocentric perspective and focused their attention on the great branches of the Aryan family in Europe: the Celtic, the Teutonic, the Italic, the Hellenic, the Slavonic, or the Getae.[57] Historians, archaeologists, and anthropologists in different countries maintained that their own ancestral national races were the actual progenitors of civilization. In some cases, additional support for Aryanism came from popularizers of science, many of them professional writers and journalists. In Norway, for instance, it was the ethnographer Andreas M. Hansen [1857–1932] who put forward a national narrative centred on the connection between the Aryans and the Germanic peoples and on the argument that ancient Aryans originated not from Central Asia but from Central Europe.[58]

Disagreement continued over who was the "purest" Aryan type and about whether the Aryan Prometheus of Europe originated in France, south of the Baltic, or in some Nordic-Scandinavian birthplace. But the idea that the Aryans were now European—"Homo Europaeus" according to the French anthroposociologist Georges Vacher de Lapouge [1854–1936]— became a new dogma for believers in this racial nationalist mythology. The European hypothesis found its supreme *raison d'être* in the fact that it unashamedly asserted the superiority of the "blond races of Europe" over all others.[59] As Alfred Ploetz argued in his 1895 *Grundlinien einer Rassen-Hygiene (The Foundations of Racial Hygiene)* the Aryan race was "the cultural race *par excellence.* To advance it is tantamount to the advancement of all humanity."[60]

As the century progressed, different varieties of Aryan racial theory arose and some of these grew increasingly focused on uncovering evidence of the superiority of one Aryan national type over another and the inferiority of all non-Aryan races to the superior Aryan. No education and cultural progress, Karl Pearson assumed, could, at least not in the foreseeable future, challenge the dominance of the Aryan Europeans.[61] Aryanism could be and often was extreme chauvinism disguised as the truths of scientific rationality. Aryan ideology fed fears about the "Decline of the West" and gave encouragement to new political forms of anti-Jewish sentiment, as well as race hatred. Georges Vacher de Lapouge's *L'Aryen, son role social (The Aryan: His Social Role)*, published in 1899, is an important example in this tradition, as it enunciated fears about the degeneration of Europe through Aryan racial dilution.[62]

Yet, the most important contribution to the development of Aryan race theory was that of German writers, who devised the concept of a "Nordic race" to showcase their belief that Northern Europeans were superior to "Latin," "Slavic," and other lesser Aryan peoples of Europe, as well as to the Jews.[63] For these theorists, the "Nordic race" comprised peoples of Germanic culture and speech who resided in Europe and North America.[64] The Nordic branch of the Aryan racial family represented an ideal to them. They believed that the Nordic race, whom they depicted as being tall, blond, blue-eyed, slim-faced, narrow-nosed, and long-headed, represented the very best of the Aryan physical and mental type. As the German racial popularizer Hans F. K. Günther [1891–1968] put it: "If an illustrator, painter, or sculptor wants to represent the image of a bold, goal-determined, resolute person, or of a noble, superior, and heroic human being, man or woman, he will in most cases create an image which more or less approximates the image of the Nordic race."[65]

Houston Stewart Chamberlain described history as a constant struggle between Aryans (Teutons) and Jews. Chamberlain's *The Foundations of the Nineteenth-Century* was bleak in its appraisal of the prospects for advancement and even survival of non-Nordic peoples. He considered Aryans to be the creators of Western culture and civilization.[66] Of all Aryans, the "Indo-Germans," who were physical embodiments of the very best of the Teutonic spirit and character, should be considered the chosen peoples of Europe. Because of their genius, morality, industry, and strength, they laid the foundations of nineteenth-century modernity and were destined to have mastery over the new century that was beckoning. Yet, the Germanic races should not take their final victory for granted since a "racial struggle" was unfolding, one which threatened to imperil the Aryan race and its civilization, and throw European culture into chaos, by means of the malicious spread of the Jewish race.

Chamberlain's anti-Semitism combined biological and cultural racism. The former pointed to the somatic characteristics of the Jews, to their physical particularity. "This one race," he noted admiratively, "has established as its guiding principle the purity of the blood; it alone possesses, therefore, physiognomy and character."[67] According to the latter the Jews possessed a "negative mentality," expressed in their cultural and moral inferiority, and their lack of religious sensibility. The aim was to expose what Chamberlain (and many after him) claimed to be the Jews' "absolute mental poverty," confirming the popular assumption of their racial degeneration. In this context, Chamberlain presented Christianity as a "moral revolt against decadence and degeneration," with modern Germans as the heralds of the new world order—the saviours of Europe and the creators of the modern mind, on account of luminaries, such as the theologian Martin Luther [1483–1546] and the philosopher Immanuel Kant.

Other European racists similarly elaborated on the Aryans and the Jewish "menace." In Romania, the prolific author on this topic was the political economist Alexandru C. Cuza [1857–1944]. He endorsed a biological vision of the race as a dynamic component of nationalism and assumed that anti-Semitism was synonymous with the defence of the nation. In 1908, Cuza published *Naţionalitatea în artă* (*Nationalism in Art*), in which he outlined his theories on "Jewish racial inferiority" and "the danger of racial mixing." The Jews, Cuza suggested, were the main threat to the development of a modern Romanian culture. Equally worrying, he noted, the "vigorous Romanian race" was constantly weakened by alcoholism and the spread of venereal diseases, both believed to be controlled by the Jews. Cuza's description of the Jews as "strangers, belonging to another race, having different laws and other cultural principles, incapable of assimilation" synthesized the main arguments put forward by anti-Semites everywhere, then as now.[68] Threatened and undermined by the "alien" Jews the Romanian race could barely protect itself from degeneration. "Jewish preponderance in any society and any profession," he maintained, was "a *cause of illness*—in any case *the symptom* of national weakness and degeneration."[69] Only when Romanians would "depart from the Semitic spirit, and energetically affirm their specific Aryan characteristics"[70] would they be moving towards fulfilling their historical destiny.

But there were many racial authors who did not embrace Aryanism. For instance, in his oft-quoted *The Races of Europe*, the American racial cartographer William Z. Ripley [1867–1941] rejected the grouping "of all peoples of Europe under a single title of the white, the Indo-Germanic, Caucasian or Aryan race. Europe," he argued, was not "a monotonous entity," but instead "a most variegated patchwork of physical types."[71] He rejected the application of the term Aryan to any modern physical types, in Europe and elsewhere. To some extent, Müller was also concerned about how his views were used by other scientists. "To me," he said, "an ethnologist who speaks of an Aryan race, Aryan blood, Aryan eyes and hair, is as great a sinner as a linguist who speaks of a dolichocephalic dictionary or a brachycephalic grammar."[72] In 1888, he further asked his "Scandinavian friends," as he called them, whether they could prove "or in any way make plausible, that the people who spoke an Aryan language near the northern course of the Indus, and at least 2000 BC, were emigrants from Scandinavia?" It would have been great, if they did, Müller continued. He too wanted to be "as proud as anybody to look upon Germany as the cradle of all Aryan life, and upon Teutonic speech as the fountain of all Aryan thought."[73] There was, of course, no proof to substantiate this theory, but that mattered little, particularly to Nazi ideologues and indeed to a number of white supremacists, reactivating the Aryan myth after the Second World War.

This glorification of European origins and genealogy represents a certain form of racism as secular religion which is founded upon ritualized ancestor-worship and an obsessive veneration for past achievements. In Europe and the USA, this reading of history is based on always looking backward; the nation and the race become a museum full of historical relics from long ago or a mausoleum for the living dead, which is no place for forward thinking or planning in an ever-changing world bringing new challenges and opportunities. The myth of one people-one nation-one race which has prevailed in many countries throughout the nineteenth and twentieth centuries remains, however, a powerful narrative, although it has always been contested.

Aryanism was a set of ideas at the core of European culture and had a fundamental impact upon political developments in individual countries, as well as pan-European geopolitics and relations. In the transition from the Romantic nationalism of the first half of the nineteenth century to the hyper-nationalism of the age of New Imperialism and the Fascist Epoch, from the 1870s to the 1940s, it helped shape European and national identities. If in the nineteenth century Aryanism legitimated British colonialism and the missionary crusade to Christianize the subcontinent, during the twentieth century it provided self-proclaimed "defenders of Western civilization" in Europe and the United States with a powerful common agenda.[74] Moreover, in the Asian East, the Aryan myth has outlived most of its European manifestations, as present-day Hindu nationalists are still eager to propagate a vision of India as the fountain of all culture and knowledge.

Aryan supremacist ideas have not entirely disappeared from the political culture of the West; they still linger on in the depths of politics in Europe and the United States, in the extreme underbelly where militant right-wing racism and neo-Nazism reside. Like so many other white supremacists today, the Norwegian mass-murderer, Anders Behring Breivik [b. 1979], revelled in grandiose fantasies that he himself was a fine specimen of Aryan manhood. On 22 July 2011, he killed eight bystanders by detonating a van bomb in central Oslo. Then, posing as a policeman, in some witness accounts, or merely dressed in some kind of Nazi-type uniform, in others, he shot dead 69 people, mostly teenagers, and attempted to murder 33 more. These victims were attending a Workers' Youth League summer camp on a quiet and beautiful resort island northwest of Oslo. Judged to be sane by court-appointed medical experts, Breivik was found not to be suffering from any psychotic delusions during his killing spree. When his guilty sentence was pronounced, the judge explained that Breivik was a terrorist, who acted out his murderous fantasies of being an Aryan avenging angel. In his manifesto, which he distributed electronically on the day of the attacks, Breivik explained that he was a "fascist," a "National Socialist," an "Aryanist" and an "ethno-nationalist," whose mission was to protect Europe from committing "cultural suicide" by appeasing Islam, Marxism, and Feminism.[75]

The disillusioned world of Breivik may seem far apart from that of Max Müller, Houston Stewart Chamberlain, and of nineteenth-century German, American and French "anthroposociologists," such as Otto Ammon [1842–1916], Carlos C. Closson and, most notably, Georges Vacher de Lapouge. The latter, as many in Nazi Germany during the 1930s, entertained romantic dreams about tall, blond, long-skulled, charioteered Aryan warriors conquering the world, following the path of the Sun-God to the West. It was these authors who elevated the European Aryan race and its "dolichocephalic blond" type to its superior status. The reality, however, is that potent racial myths such as the Aryan one, retained currency within culture and science and continue to be highly susceptible to the most imaginative and, often, dangerous interpretations. The ideological version of the Aryan myth continues to attract supporters to this day, as Breivik's disturbing beliefs and actions all too painfully demonstrate.

CHAPTER FIVE

Science

The Poet Who Lost His Head.[1]

In late 2003, the University of Padua proudly announced that it would be exhuming the body of Francesco Petrarch [1304–1374] from his pink marble sarcophagus in the Church of Santa Maria Assunta in Arquà, a nearby town.[2] Indeed, on 18 November, Vito T. W. Marin, a professor of anatomo-pathology in the Faculty of Medicine and Anthropology at Padua University, together with a group of oral surgeons, orthopaedists, and geneticists, assembled from various European countries, opened the casket of the great Renaissance poet, essayist, scholar, and humanist. The exhumation took place right in the main square of Arquà and was accompanied by a ceremony attended by local dignitaries, townspeople, and the media.

Professor Marin and his colleagues hoped to verify nineteenth-century reports that Petrarch stood at 1.83 metres (about 6 feet tall), an uncommonly tall height for his day. The team also planned to examine Petrarch's skull in order to construct a computerized image of his face and features. With the help of an Italian sculptor and German scientists, they aimed to create a three-dimensional portrait of Petrarch. This would be revealed during the many festivities which authorities were arranging to mark Petrarch's 700th birthday on 20 July 2004. When they opened the tomb, Marin and the others discovered that the skull was in hundreds of tiny splinters. However, the fragments allowed for the retrieval of sufficient mitochondrial DNA (mtDNA) for genetic analysis. The researchers extracted DNA from a rib and a tooth and sent the samples off to various laboratories in North America, England, and Italy, where mtDNA sequences were produced. They were surprised to discover that the DNA profiles from the tooth and rib were not identical, indicating that they belonged to different individuals. The researchers were fairly certain of the authenticity of Petrarch's skeleton, due to the fact that it bore evidence of injuries mentioned by the poet in his writings, including a kick from a donkey to his right leg when he was 42.

Molecular gender determination, however, revealed conclusively that the skeletal remains belonged to a male, whilst the skull belonged to a female.[3] Widely reported in the international press, the incident of the "Poet Who Lost His Head" is something of a mystery. The fact that the DNA test showed that the skull was that of an unknown woman, rather than that of the venerated poet is only part of the intrigue surrounding the matter, however.

Every country has a national pantheon of their revered dead, which includes those figures considered worthy of gratitude and remembrance. On Italy's list of famous people literary giants such as Petrarch figure prominently. The discovery that the skull did not belong to Petrarch was a tremendous blow to all concerned. In Arquà, where Petrarch died in his library at his daughter's home at the age of 70, he is considered a local hero, despite the fact that he was born in Arezzo, Tuscany. All of Italy, in fact, lays claim to Petrarch. He is widely celebrated as the "father of the Renaissance," and is warmly embraced as a great national writer whose verse established Italian as a literary language for the first time. Even in his own lifetime, Petrarch was a living legend, becoming a cult figure in Italy and the rest of Europe. Over the centuries, he never went out of fashion.[4]

November 2003 was, in fact, not the first time that admirers and scientists raided Petrarch's tomb. Nor was the question of the whereabouts of the poet's missing head the only mystery surrounding the remains of the venerable Petrarch. In 1843, Count Carlo Leoni [1812–1872], the celebrated nineteenth-century theatre historian and literary critic, paid for the restoration of Petrarch's tomb, where the body had been placed six years after the poet's death. On the occasion of the restoration, Leoni opened the tomb and, according to a letter which he wrote to Giovanni Canestrini in 1873, he saw that the entire arm was gone. But the head was not missing. Professor Antonio Meneghelli, Leoni recounted, was also present at the opening and could confirm the details of the discovery. Leoni stressed to Canestrini that "his science and his conscience" forbade him from lying about what exactly he found in the casket.[5]

But Leoni's science and conscience did not prevent him from stealing one of Petrarch's right ribs and a piece of his tunic on that day. Somehow, these eventually ended up in the hands of Austrian government officials, who ordered that they be returned to their rightful place. So, on 10 July 1855, the heavy lid on Petrarch's tomb was lifted once more. According to the surgeon and anatomist Ferdinando Moroni [1815–1885], who was present at the time and undertook an anthropometric examination of the skeleton, all was well with the "cerebral organism with the vast intelligence of a poet and politician like Petrarch." Apart from a few missing teeth, the cranial bones were complete.[6]

In attempting to explain the mystery of Petrarch's missing skull, Marin recalled the third official opening of the tomb, which occurred in 1873 under the supervision of Canestrini [1835–1900]. Canestrini is best remembered today for his translation, along with Leonardo Salimbeni [1830–1889], of the first complete and authorized Italian edition of Darwin's 1859 *The Origin of Species*.[7] A keen biologist, naturalist, and Darwinist, Canestrini also had an interest in anatomy and craniology, which explained his selection as the leader of the scientific team entrusted with the important task of taking measurements of the great poet's skull and bones.

In his testimony, Canestrini recounted his immense nervous anticipation of the event. He came prepared with various metric instruments to make the calculations, as well as a whole entourage of assistants to help hold and measure the bits and pieces of the remains. But his hopes were in vain, as he described. The skull "which for five centuries had resisted the destructive action of time, had, sometime between 1855 in 1873, weakened to such an extent" that when exposed to air it spontaneously disintegrated. Canestrini could just catch a glimpse of Petrarch's skull before it "was reduced to a multitude of fragments which offered no means to make a proper anthropological examination."[8] With only a few intact shards of the parietal (which forms part of the sides and top of the skull), frontal, and upper jaw bones, Canestrini had no choice, as he explained, but to abandon his dream of completing a full anthropometric analysis of the remains and constructing a model of the poet's head. The only explanation which he could offer for the extraordinary, spontaneous and rapid decomposition which he claims to have witnessed was that the remains rested upon a base of larch-wood and may have become saturated with damp, which rendered them vulnerable to disintegration on contact with air.[9]

The whole tale told by Canestrini in his account may well have been a cover-up to hide the simple truth that, in his irrepressible excitement, to which he readily admitted, he may have dropped the poet's cranium on the ground and then replaced it with another out of embarrassment at his clumsiness. Perhaps he could only find a damaged substitute cranium, so exchanged this with the original. Canestrini may have taken the real skull of the illustrious poet for himself, but, if so, he succeeded in being very secretive about it, because no such thing was ever reported to be amongst his possessions before or after his death. He may also have stolen it for someone else. Canestrini the thief does not sit well with contemporary appraisals of him as a virtuous and upstanding individual. In any event, the poet's head has never been found and probably never will be.

Whatever the truth may ultimately be, this story demonstrates one thing clearly: that nineteenth-century tomb raiders, despite their claims to the contrary, were not strictly ruled by the noble dictates of conscience and science. The quest for knowledge clouded their judgement and made them prone to fantasy, delusion, and deception. So confident was Canestrini of his own authority and that of the scientific method which he practised that he felt able to conclude his investigation with a discussion of the disputed authenticity of Petrarch's skull. He related that he had heard a certain rumour over the years that the putative head of Petrarch was a fake.

Canestrini wrote, however, that there was absolutely no reason whatsoever to believe that the skull which he saw on 6 December 1873 did not belong to Petrarch. It looked exactly like all the other remains in the tomb and was in exactly the same state of conservation. Although the skull partly disintegrated and the skeleton did not, he stated, they belonged to one and the same person.

Backed by data furnished by Italy's foremost craniologist, Giustiniano Nicolucci [1819–1904], Canestrini's analysis of the cranial bones confirmed that they represented an "ancient Etruscan type," as he assumed Petrarch's would have been.[10] Although the notion of "type" was notoriously contested, Canestrini suggested that "rigorous" phrenological examinations that he carried out "confirm[ed] beyond any doubt that it belong[ed] to a person of extremely elevated mental faculties [...] therefore, it had to belong to Petrarch."[11] This "proof" of Petrarch's genius is what Canestrini was looking to find in the fragments, after all. To have found it, as he, of course, did was confirmation not just of the intellectual superiority of a great poet, but also that of the people from whence he came. Therein lies the stimulus behind the fascination with the skulls and bones of distinguished dead people.[12]

Canestrini's claims about the power of science to reveal significant truths about human beings capture the deep faith which formed a backbone to anthropology during the nineteenth century. Canestrini and others of his generation across Europe and the USA invested in their science's objectivity, efficacy, and exactness, a commitment which may seem very naïve today. Their obsession with the measurement and classification of human diversity encapsulated many of the anxieties and aspirations of the age. Canestrini, for instance, expressed his slight disappointment that the volume and form of the skull which he studied showed few truly outstanding characteristics, measured in terms of cephalic index, facial angles, and cranial capacity, using the latest methods and tools. More cheering was the fact that the best comparative data at his disposal demonstrated Petrarch's unquestionably "superior intelligence and creativity." Canestrini was delighted to inform his readers that Petrarch's skull, though smaller than that of Georges Cuvier, was reassuringly greater in size than those of other eminent Europeans, including Immanuel Kant.[13]

The urge to collect and compare data about crania was a major driving force for nineteenth-century anthropology.[14] Already in the 1820s the Austrian Franz Joseph Gall [1758–1828] began studying the development of brain contours in order to provide empirical evidence for how the brain functioned and how it influenced human faculties and emotions. His theory of cranial bumps, or phrenology (from the Greek words for "mind" and "knowledge"), reduced psychological categories to physiological attributes, and endorsed the view, propounded by many other scientists, including the Italian criminologist Cesare Lombroso [1835–1909], that certain regions of the brain were correlated with certain physical aptitudes and moral behaviour. According to Gall, violent propensities, like combativeness and destructiveness, for instance, were located at the back of the brain; intellectual aptitudes, like memory and language, were situated at the front; whilst human affections, like veneration and benevolence, were found towards the top of the head. Gall and his followers in Europe and the USA, such as Johann Gaspar Spurzheim [1776–1832] and George Combe [1788–1858], believed that, by examining the physiognomy of the skull and the brain, the psychological character of the individual could be revealed and evaluated, thus enabling scientists to demonstrate and, ultimately, control human difference.[15] In the USA, in particular, phrenology was hugely popular, and not only amongst white scientists. Black phrenologists and abolitionists also embraced the methods of "reading" and "examining" heads, albeit for reasons to do less with race and more with abolitionism and social reform. As the literary historian Britt Rusert suggested, phrenology was mobilized "as a fugitive science that destabilized the racist science of craniology from within its own methodology [. . .] mobilizing it instead for a set of experiments oriented toward black elevation and emancipation."[16] It needs emphasis, therefore, that the craniologists and the phrenologists were a diverse group of varying political persuasions and religious affiliations. They did, however, concur that the fusion between science and politics should serve the harmonious development of the body politic of the nation. In the USA, for instance, it was Christian values that most supporters of phrenology advocated.[17] Harmonizing these ideals with the new political and social environment resulting from the Civil War [1861–1865] was an essential test for such esteemed educators and social reformers as Horace Mann [1796–1859] and Samuel Gridley Howe [1801–1876].[18]

To some extent, many of these theories about the presumed direct and determining correlations between body, brain, and behaviour drew inspiration from the work of Johann Friedrich Blumenbach, whose celebrated *Of the Varieties of the Human Species* (1795), a lengthy treatise in Latin, was influential everywhere in Europe.[19] Blumenbach was considered by many of his contemporaries and successors as being the first scientist to codify and systematize the "skulls of different nations, giving each a provenance."[20] He identified five primary races: the "Caucasian," the "Mongolian," the "Aethiopian," the "American," and, finally, the "Malayan." He endowed each of them with a "racial face"; the "Mongolian," for instance, had a wide and flat face, whilst the "Aethiopian" one was narrow with prominent lips. Although he did not endorse the idea of inferior and superior races, he elaborated his ideas of racial difference within the intellectual tradition discussed in chapters 1 and 2 that placed the Europeans above all others, in terms of intellect, beauty, culture, and civilization.

This idealized representation of the European "race" was in transition from the mid-nineteenth century onwards. There were a number of causes for this change, not least the decline of phrenology and the emergence of comparative ethnology and linguistics. The publication of Charles Darwin's

The Descent of Man, and Selection in Relation to Sex and E. B. Taylor's *Primitive Culture*, both in 1871, also "helped to further strengthen the significance of new forms of developmental theories within the recently amalgamated discipline of anthropology."[21] Blumenbach's racial typology was no longer considered to be sophisticated enough to explain the complexity of human diversity. The vocabulary used to describe cranial shapes had also changed. Fashions in science came and went, and the Bristol doctor turned anthropologist James C. Prichard [1786–1848] was gradually becoming the most respected authority in the field.[22] His ideas acted "as a bridge between social and biological theories of difference: culture and climate initiate change, but also legitimize the distinction and description of various congenital 'races.'"[23] Importantly, Prichard retained Blumenbach's simple schema of cranial conformation, and argued that all other types were variations or combinations of these "fundamental racial forms." But unlike Blumenbach, Prichard endowed cranial differences with cultural value, arguing that the formation of the skull reflected the level of civilization reached by the race to which it belonged. Not surprisingly, then, the Greek cranium he examined from Blumenbach's collection was deemed the most perfect, in terms of its size and its beauty.[24]

Blumenbach had bequeathed an initial tool of analysis, the cranial index (the ratio of the width of the skull to its length, usually represented as a percentage), but methods and measurements were becoming ever more complicated and numerous. The Swedish anatomist Anders Retzius [1796–1860] identified jaw shapes as being either prognathic (jutting forward) or orthognathic (sloping back); and, in 1842, he invented the influential cephalic index (the ratio of the maximum breath of the skull, divided by the maximum length, multiplied by 100), which provided to a generation of anthropologists in many different countries a seemingly more sophisticated and accurate numerical means to calculate even the smallest differences in crania.[25]

Followers used Retzius's index as a signifier of race and based a whole ranking system upon it; his index differentiated people with round heads (those with high ratios of skull width to length; brachycephalic; associated with Africans) from those with long heads (those with low ratios of skull width to length; dolichocephalic; associated with Europeans). Ever more complex quantitative measures, sometimes numbering in the thousands, were being made of human skulls and skeletons. Often politicians responded to these developments in anthropometry with excited agendas whose purpose was to perpetuate the alleged differences between Europe's colonial populations, but the desire to measure and quantify cranial differences between the races had also become somewhat of a fixation of anthropologists across Europe.[26] In Hungary, for instance, anthropologists József Lenhossék [1818–1888] and Aurél Török [1842–1912] were particularly active in this field, nationally and internationally. In 1875, Lenhossék published his acclaimed study of human craniology, and was the first Hungarian

SCIENCE

93

anthropologist to study cranial deformation, caused by accident or injury.[27] Another direction of research was to focus on cranial differences in order to classify them and describe groups of people who were presumed to share the same features. Already in 1882, Török offered one of the first detailed investigations of the ethno-cranial characteristics of Romanians in Transylvania.[28]

From the 1880s, a growing scepticism about the utility of cranial research for racial purposes led many leading anthropologists to question its scientific credentials in Hungary, Italy, Germany, and elsewhere. In Europe, it was Török who produced one of the simultaneously most comprehensive discussions and substantial critiques of craniology in 1890. His main scientific opus, *Grundzüge einer systematischen Kraniometrie (Principles of Systematic Craniometry)*, is arguably the most detailed craniological analysis of a single skull in the history of craniology, including an astounding 5,371 measurements. This meticulous exercise, however, did not improve Török's views on craniology. He argued that the cephalic index was ultimately entirely irrelevant to racial differentiation and that there was no scientific possibility of proving the existence of a "pure" dolichocephalic or brachycephalic race.[29] As the social historian of medicine Benoit Massin aptly argued, "craniometry, taken by itself, did not provide an adequate basis for racial classification."[30] However, such sceptical views about the usage of craniology did not deter other physical anthropologists concerned with racial cartography from further elaborating schemes of racial classification and specific racial physiognomies. This was, after all, the period in which racial sciences flourished.

Broadly, two primary strands of anthropology existed in Europe during the late nineteenth and early twentieth centuries, comprising those who studied the anatomy of the human races and those who focused upon the cultural specificities of "civilized," meaning white Europeans, and "uncivilized" peoples, encompassing blacks and other ethnic minorities peoples.[31] From roughly the 1860s to the 1910s, alongside professional consolidation and institutionalization, anthropology in its entirety was preoccupied with the category of race. The development of the field was heavily influenced by the theoretical and methodological approaches of the French school of Paul Broca [1824–1880], a remarkable anthropologist and neurologist.[32] Another prominent scientist was criminologist Alphonse Bertillon [1853–1914], who devised the so-called "metric anthropology," consisting of a system of physical measurements of body parts, especially the head and the face, and whose manual of anthropometry remained standard teaching material for both criminologists and anthropologists until late in the twentieth century.[33]

In the first half of the twentieth century, as colonialism assimilated the racism of anthropological thinking, the number of "races" described by investigators proliferated. Though the categories used to describe white Europeans as a group, such as Caucasian, and, increasingly, Aryan, remained in circulation, discussions of sub-groups within Europe also increased as the focus shifted to national races within individual countries. Attempts to work through this problem are detectable in the efforts to standardize racial taxonomy and cartography.[34] Old anthropological models such as that of Blumenbach competed with new ones, such as the one proposed by the French naturalist and anthropologist Joseph Deniker [1852–1918], who identified six primary races: Northern; Eastern; Ibero-Insular; Western or Cenevole; Littoral or Atlanto-Mediterranean; and Adriatic or Dinaric; along with four sub-races: sub-Northern; Vistulian; North-Western; and sub-Adriatic.[35] William Ripley outlined another competing model, suggesting that there were only three European races: Teutonic, Alpine (Celtic), and Mediterranean.

In turn, the German racial anthropologist Hans F. K. Günther [1891–1968] proposed that there were five European races: Nordic; Western; Dinaric; Eastern; and Baltic.[36] Importantly, all three authors considered the cephalic index to be a reliable instrument for classification, meaning that what fundamentally differentiated races was their cranial capacity: some were dolichocephalic (long-headed), mainly Northern and Ibero-Insular races; others were brachycephalic (short-headed), like Eastern, Western, and Dinaric races; and, finally, some races were mesocephalic (medium-headed). The more a race possessed dolichocephalic and brachycephalic characteristics, the prevailing opinion was, the more it could legitimately claim a superior position within the hierarchy of European races.[37]

During the age of empire and in the long nineteenth century, anthropology endorsed the idea of racial differences between nations, and many nationalists invoked the pernicious power of racialized categories to reassert ideas of historical superiority in moments of international and domestic crises and instability.[38] This inclination was not the sole preserve of any ideological movement, for racialized motifs and orderings of the world infiltrated mainstream European and North American politics and public discourse, and reverberated in the proliferation of social agendas for the protection of mothers, children, the birth rate, and the family from a number of perceived internal and external "threats" to the nation and race.

The interwar period was characterized by a crisis of liberal democracy, an assault on humanistic values, the rise of fascism and Nazism, a tendency towards economic protectionism, a new era of political nationalism and an isolationist retreat within the nation-state. By the 1930s, race had acquired a dominant, albeit contested role, not just within human sciences, but also in inter-governmental (in national parliaments) and extra-governmental (in the public domain and on the streets) politics and, more broadly, throughout the entirety of European and North American popular culture.[39]

Anti-Racism

The highly visible presence of race in science, society, and politics was not without its critics. In Britain, as early as the 1840s, the Aborigines' Protection

Society (established in 1837), "actively campaigned against the racial depredations of the age of empire"[40] and popularized the importance of indigenous rights in Africa. Committed individuals such as the Quaker activist Catherine Impey [1847–1923], who founded Britain's first anti-racist journal *Anti-Caste*, campaigned persistently for the unity of the human race.[41] She and others who shared her convictions condemned the carefully orchestrated but largely unconvincing ideas of racial difference that prevailed in the society at large and amongst most European educated elites at the time. José Martí [1853–1895], the Cuban poet and philosopher, similarly questioned these ideas, in his essay "Nuestra América" ("Our America") published in 1891. Martí explicitly rejected the existence of different human races and chastised "theorists and feeble thinkers" for turning "bookshelf races" into real entities, which "the well-disposed observer and the fair-minded traveller" would not find in Nature.[42]

By the beginning of the twentieth century, the growing condemnation of theories of racial hierarchy and of scientific racism became more intense. In the USA, it was anthropologist Franz Boas who provided one of the most serious and persistent criticisms of racism.[43] Boas did not challenge the overriding assumption of anthropology that races existed, but he did reject one of its guiding tenets, namely that racial differences were caused by physical traits. The existence of biological races, Boas felt, was a scientific hypothesis, which had erroneously been raised to the level of a natural law by its racist advocates. This belief emanated from his observation that variation within racial groups was often more pronounced than were differences between races.

Sampling a large population of immigrants to the United States and their offspring over time, he observed that cranial size changed cross-generationally due, in his opinion, to the beneficial effects of non-biological factors. He postulated that culture, rather than biology, determined races. In his study *Changes in Bodily Form of Descendants of Immigrants*, published in 1910, Boas strikingly concluded: "the head form, which has always been considered one of the most stable and permanent characteristics of human races, undergoes far-reaching changes coincident with the transfer of the people from European to American soil."[44] Boas used this research to expose notions of racial permanence in favour of his theory of human biological plasticity, suggesting that differing social, mental, moral, and even anatomical and physiological characteristics of human groups were the result of environmental, historical, and cultural circumstances which were both variable and changeable.[45]

Boas deflated the importance of race as an all-encompassing explanatory factor for understanding the origins and history of humanity. He, therefore, revolutionized the very nature of anthropology's domain of knowledge. His influence was social as well as political. He laid the theoretical foundations for what has become known as cultural relativism (and later multiculturalism) within science and, more broadly, society.[46] His arguments about the plasticity of the cranium became the scientific basis for a new understanding of race as well as the platform for a new politics of race. Demands for an end to racial discrimination against African-Americans found a compelling rationale in his theory that assimilation and integration would eliminate any inequalities in the intelligence and the cultural achievements of blacks and whites. For Boas and the generation of anthropologists which he influenced, race was no longer biological; it had become a cultural construct rooted in racism: a consequence, not a cause of racial inequality.[47]

Attempts to re-conceptualize, and even abandon the concept of race entirely, gained momentum in the late 1930s and early 1940s. In Britain, for example, biologist Julian Huxley [1887–1975] and anthropologist Alfred C. Haddon [1855–1940] published We Europeans. A Survey of "Racial" Problems in 1935, arguing that it was "very desirable that the term race as applied to human groups should be dropped from the vocabulary of science."[48] At the same time in Czechoslovakia, anatomist Karel Weigner [1874–1937] edited a collective volume On the Equality of European Races and Ways for Their Betterment, in which contributors across a number of academic disciplines voiced their criticism of ideas of German racial superiority,[49] whilst, in Romania, hygienist Iosif Glicsman [1871–1938] denounced racism as the greatest "swindle" in history.[50]

These and other scientists in Europe and elsewhere, such as the American anthropologist Ruth Benedict [1887–1948], who trained under Boas at Columbia University, challenged belief in the existence of separate and distinct racial groups which were made unequal either by God or by nature.[51] Ashley Montagu was another scientist to argue that the concept of race had no scientific validity and should be abandoned completely in scientific and social usage. His book on the fallacious nature of race, published in 1942, emphasized the ability of environment, education, and culture to shape human behaviour and nature.[52] A year earlier, Theodosius Dobzhansky [1900–1975], the Ukrainian-born professor of zoology at Columbia University, too attempted to shed some light on the "perennial discussion of the nature of races, particularly of those in man," admitting that his own academic discipline, biology, had so far not been successful in dismantling scientific racism. The problem, Dobzhansky remarked, was that the debate about the concept of race was less about science and more about everything else.[53]

After the Second World War, these scientists were joined by a new generation of biologists and anthropologists who embraced the strains of progressive thought and civil rights movements of the period.[54] These new critics of race started from the proposition that race should be understood as a socio-cultural reality that existed independently of the biophysical diversity found in human beings; and they asserted that the classification of human beings by cranial size or shape, or other anatomical characteristics, such as skin colour, hair colour, eye colour, or facial angle, had no taxonomical precision whatsoever and led to no greater understanding of biological diversity. Rethinking along these lines led to the assertion that genes or geography had more relevance to an appreciation of the meaning and nature of human variation than did race. Natural selection and migration patterns determined variability between human beings not innate racial characteristics. Human variation is distributed geographically, not racially.[55]

In a study published in 1972, Richard C. Lewontin [b. 1929], the celebrated American evolutionary biologist and population geneticist, attempt to resolve the debate about race once and for all. He analysed a large data-set involving blood samples from seven different population groups around the globe, demonstrating clearly that "race" does not reveal very much at all about human evolution and variability. Equally important, his research uncovered what he believed to be a truly remarkable degree of biological affinity between what are conventionally known as racial groups. For his definition of races, Lewontin adhered to the classic schema which divided the world into the principal groups—variously named, but broadly corresponding to "Whites," "Blacks," "Yellows," "Browns," and "Reds"— and their subdivisions. Variability rates differed from one local population to the next, so that a large and diverse one, such as that in the United States, affected as it was by a great deal of immigration from a broad range of different populations, would be very genetically variable, whilst a small and isolated island population would show a high degree of uniformity. Of the remaining 15 per cent of human variation, Lewontin's research revealed, between a quarter and a half was between local populations, representing national or linguistic "racial" subdivisions, such as the Italians and the French (sub-groups of whites, "Caucasians" or Europeans) or the Japanese and the Koreans (sub-groups of the Asiatic or "Yellow" Race). Only a relatively small amount of the total human variation possible, representing between 6 and 10 per cent, existed between the "races." He found that the human species as a whole exhibits a great deal of biological variation, but most of this occurs between individuals who are unrelated. Moreover, whilst each classically defined "race" shares many biological traits with other "races," the differences between people (measured by DNA sequences) are great, making it impossible to draw clear distinctions along racial lines.[56]

Professional scientists, Lewontin maintained, had led many members of the general public to believe, mistakenly, that race was an objective biological reality rather than an arbitrary social construct. The existing system of racial classification in operation since the nineteenth century was flawed, shifting, and imprecise, he argued. Racial classification should be abandoned, Lewontin claimed, because it perpetuates the unpalatable politics and culture of racism and because it has little taxonomical value from a scientific point of view. Furthermore, in evolutionary terms, the extraordinary differentiation which occurs within *Homo sapiens* is very gradually breaking down because of the high level of migration and inter-group mating that has taken place over thousands of years.[57]

Old Wine in New Bottles

Contrary to their valiant efforts, scientists did not succeed in definitively shifting physical anthropology and biology away from a taxonomical approach, which focuses on labelling and dividing human beings. This taxonomical approach to population diversity continued to be in use after the Second World War, and even thrived in the changed and challenging political circumstances which beset so many different countries during the Cold War. The concept of race remained a central element of a post-war transnational physical anthropology.[58] This relationship was also reaffirmed in *Rassengeschichte der Menschheit* (*The Racial History of Mankind*), edited by anthropologists Ilse Schwidetzky [1907–1997] and Karl Saller [1902–1969] and published in 14 volumes between 1968 and 1993. This impressive collection of studies provides the standard post-war narrative of the race as an integral biological unit surviving centuries of ethnic mixing and territorial displacement. Schwidetzky, a former assistant of the influential German racial scientist Egon Freiherr von Eickstedt [1892–1965], was a prolific writer of popular books on anthropology and genetics during the 1950s. She rephrased her racial theories under a new concept, "national biology" ("*Völkerbiologie*"), described as the most recent development in comparative human biology, and as part of the "new racial science" ("*die neue Rassenkunde*").[59]

Significantly, Schwidetzky also secured contributions from anthropologists from communist East-Central Europe, including the Romanian Olga Necrasov [1910–2000] and the Bulgarian Peter Boev [1920–2006].[60] The social, cultural, and political context was markedly different in those countries in Europe, which after the Second World War fell under Soviet influence. The idea of race and racism were denounced as "imperialist" and products of previous "bourgeois" regimes. Physical anthropology was the scientific discipline to suffer most from its association with the idea of race and racial thinking, and particularly so in the countries of East-Central Europe which fell under Soviet occupation. After a short period of revival immediately after the war, when new professional associations were formed, such as the Anthropological Division of the Museum of Natural History created in 1945 in Budapest and the Commission of Psychometrics and Anthropology established in 1946 by the Romanian Academy in Bucharest, the early 1950s brought such hopes to an end. In Romania, for instance, some physical anthropologists were imprisoned, university chairs and departments were dissolved, and the "bourgeois" racial anthropology was deemed "incompatible" with the new scientific ideologies imported from the Soviet Union.

With the establishment of the communist republics in East-Central Europe, physical anthropology in this region had entered a new period, one in which the concept of race became fully integrated into official re-definitions of the nation and ethnicity. What the historian Francine Hirsh aptly termed "state-sponsored evolutionism"—namely the "Soviet version of the civilizing mission that was grounded in the Marxist conception of development through historical stages and also drew on European anthropological theories about cultural evolutionism"[61]—also fittingly describes the conceptual reorientation of physical anthropologists in Hungary, Romania, and Bulgaria during the 1950s.

Interestingly, in a period when a concerted campaign was launched in Western Europe and the United States against the concept of race, the evolutionary framework and the idea of typological races professed by Soviet anthropology, in fact, provided the perfect conditions for interwar anthropological methodologies to survive the ideological orientation of the new political regimes.[62] As noted by anthropologist Katarzyna Kaszycka, "Eastern European countries were not burdened by past colonialism, and, moreover, the philosophy of 'brotherhood and unity' was officially imposed on citizens and implemented. Both the existence of races and their equality were therefore strongly affirmed in politics and science."[63] Not surprisingly, then, the Hungarian anthropologist János Nemeskéri [1914–1989] retained the use of race when distinguishing the main areas of research in Hungarian anthropology: "1) the problems of ethnic anthropology (Raciology); 2) the investigation of certain morphological and physiological traits; and 3) anthropogenesis (paleoanthropology)."[64]

Importantly, physical anthropology remained connected to the investigation of ethnic identities, and thus contributed significantly to the re-canonization of national identity in communist countries in Eastern Europe after the 1960s. Furthermore, whilst in Western Europe and the United States anthropology became increasingly defined as "cultural" and "social," in East-Central Europe it continued to be referred to as "physical anthropology."[65] As the Czech anthropologist Milan Dokládal [1928–2004] and psychologist Josef Brožek [1913–2004] explained: "As taught and studied in Czechoslovakia, anthropology [. . .] refers to the Science of Man in the narrower sense. It may be defined as the science of human physique, man's phylogenetic evolution and ontogenetic development, and the varieties ('races') of man."[66]

Whilst the political engagement of physical anthropology was much more overt in Eastern Europe during the Cold War, the discipline continued to remain important in Western Europe and the USA as well. One particular aspect of this continuous history deserves highlighting. The study of crania as signifiers of race has, in recent decades, re-emerged as a widely perceived legitimate method of analysis. The computer age has given the quantitative approach to the study of crania a new life, as university-based researchers across the globe seek to compile huge comparative databases on world population groups. They place these data at the disposal of governments, international bodies, and police organizations. There is now a large body of literature documenting the use, since the 1970s, of craniometrics in determining differences in skull size and shape between prehistoric populations and in documenting human evolutionary trends and migratory patterns. Now divested of its overt racism, craniology, re-fashioned as craniometrics, stands aloof from its past and presents itself as a neutral tool of contemporary forensic archaeology and anthropology. An imagined neutrality, of course, was one of the original claims of the old craniology of the nineteenth century.

The continuing appeal of craniometrics is based on the fact that, unlike non-metric methods, "measuring man" from within appears to go beneath the surface of superficialities, like skin, eye, and hair colour, whose significance can more easily be contested, to uncover the seeming "hard" and supposed eternal, physical verities of racial difference, which, according to this line of reasoning, are embedded in the very core of human beings—the skull and the skeleton. The idea that essential, and, in many scientific scenarios, permanent, biological differences are imprinted on bones and bodies may, in and of itself, not be such a controversial notion. As seen, this methodology has been used by anthropologists as the conceptual framework for a divisive way of seeing human beings as being separated into distinct races and ethnic sub-groups. The corollary of this has been the tendency to equate a presumed, but by no means proven biological dissimilarity with racial inequality. And what strikes the historian, if not the scientist, is that for much of its history, modern anthropology has been determined to demonstrate the existence of a division of *Homo sapiens* into distinct groups and to go beyond a strict scientific remit by attributing social meaning to this species diversity and, in some cases, prescribing political solutions, such as slavery or segregation, to the socio-biological problems which they perceived were the consequence of racial diversity.

The Harvard-based American anthropologist, William W. Howells [1908–2005], always firmly maintained that craniometry would eventually lead to important discoveries about human evolution and variation. For decades, he ignored the mounting scientific and ethical objections to the methods which he and his colleagues used. After he joined Harvard University in 1954, as Professor of Anthropology, Howells spent the next 20 years building the largest and most comprehensive collection of statistical analyses of crania in the world. On their many travels, he and his wife, Muriel Gurdon Seabury [1910–2002], took and recorded a total of 68 measurements of about 3,000 human crania from sites in Europe, Africa, Asia, and the Pacific.[67] The Howells' painstaking documentation of craniometric variation became the basis for the forensic anthropology computer programme known as CRANID, developed by anthropologist Richard Wright, at the University of Sydney, and FORDISC, developed by Stephen Ousley and Richard Jantz at Mercyhurst Archaeological Institute in Pennsylvania, and which are in wide use today. Howells' data-set had large gaps, however, which subsequent researchers have sought avidly to fill.

The anthropologist Michael Pietrusewsky endeavoured to cover crania from East Asian and Pacific populations with a higher level of thoroughness and detail than did William Howells.[68] As part of the Australian National University at Canberra's ongoing and long-term "Project Craniometry," Raghavan Pathmanathan and his colleagues are currently accessing and measuring collections of human skulls across India, with a view to compiling the largest existing database of measurements for this population group. Recently, Pathmanathan made an invaluable addition to his research when he began measuring the skulls and skeletons of human specimens found in the world's largest three-tier prehistoric cemetery in India.[69] The bio-anthropology of today shares with the physical anthropology of old its need to unearth and use bones and bodies from sacred, secular, ancestral, and burial sites, both ancient and modern. Pathmanathan's findings on the Punjab crania have made their way into CRANID, which aims to be the cutting-edge research resource of its kind and the definitive directory of comparative data on human variability in so-called modern craniometrics.[70]

But just how much better are modern craniometric techniques than were earlier, nineteenth-century craniological ones? The latest edition of CRANID states that it allows the researcher to do a "linear discriminant analysis and a nearest neighbour discriminant analysis, with 29 measurements on an individual cranium." The cranium under investigation "is classified after comparison with 70 samples that include 3,163 crania from around the world."[71] The bulk of the data bank represented within CRANID, and indeed within the various editions of FORDISC (which allows for up to 21 cranial measurements), is the Howells' measurements taken from recovered remains found in existing, and, therefore, older museum collections from around the world (but mainly in Europe and the United States). Using instruments that have varied little from the ones which the French anthropologist Paul Broca first devised in the nineteenth century, the researcher takes measurements, which are then subjected to computer-assisted multivariate statistical procedures originally developed by Karl Pearson.[72]

Old and new anthropological ideas coalesce in the methods of modern craniometrics. CRANID and FORDISC work by coming up with the best fit with the existing samples of their databases, but the method is not without flaws. The quality of the identification of a cranium by these programmes, as defined by their own criteria of accuracy and usefulness, is determined by the representativeness of the samples within their databases. But the databases of both programmes are exceedingly limited, despite the drive to expand them. FORDISC, for example, relies entirely upon the Forensic Data Bank, which was developed largely from North American forensic cases, so it has no wide applicability whatsoever. With its varied base-line samples, taken from dispersed populations groups across the world, CRANID contains a much broader pool of cranial comparators, making an accurate match between an unidentified skull and one within the database more likely. Finding an unknown cranium's "nearest neighbour" within the database is not always possible. Researchers from the Smithsonian Institution recently disclosed the major errors which FORDISC made when attempting to determine the sex and ancestry of 95 crania found in a sixteenth- to seventeenth-century church ossuary in north-western Spain. The skulls are known to have belonged to members of the church. FORDISC classified some of the crania into groups, such as Chinese, Japanese, American Indian, and Vietnamese, with no geographic, historic, or ancestral connections at all with the samples, which it identified as typically Spanish. The probability of these ethnic groups actually being represented within the Spanish skeletal collection was very low. FORDISC could not identify the sex or ethnic group affiliation of a significant portion of the crania.

Researchers entered the measurements into both the Howells and the Forensic Data Bank collections and were surprised to see the wildly differing results from each of the two sets of references. According to the Howells collection, half of the Spanish sample contained crania from non-European and North African sources. The findings of the Forensic Data Bank were that fewer than half of the skulls belonged to members of the "White race."[73] Other scientists have used FORDISC with similar disappointingly poor results. Though it claims to have "standardized the attribution of population affinity for forensic analysis" and to have provided a "user-friendly method for ascribing 'social race' to unknowns," FORDISC has now been repeatedly tested and has been repeatedly found to produce erroneous and, in some instances, bizarre classifications.[74] The CRANID system is by no means foolproof either. By the admission of its inventor, CRANID has only a 68.2 per cent "classificatory success rate."[75]

Presented as scientifically neutral and politically correct by advocates of FORDISC, these new techniques employ the term "social race" in order to differentiate their biases from the old category of biological race; but this new terminology is ambiguous and, like the old thinking behind it, still clings to the notion that outward physical differences are significant, determining, and measurable with scientific precision. It is, in fact, misleading in that it is used solely to designate probable biological affiliation, based on the measurement of craniofacial morphology alone. The new forensic anthropology defines races as multivariate clusters of "standard" metric traits. It assumes that the racial attributes which are supposed to be measurable on the human skull are constant over time and space and are not subject to environmental or evolutionary influences.

These assumptions represent a recapitulation of old arguments about the immutability of race. The heterogeneity of cranial formation, both in terms of size and shape, from individual to individual within groups and between sexes is not a consideration for analysts employing the craniometric method of racial determination. In addition, the terminology used by these programmes to identify a cranium is folkloristic, stereotypical, vague, and inconsistent. Biology alone is presented as the criterion of racial assignment, but the categories proffered by these programmes have non-biological origins and character. The names for the "races" identified by FORDISC and CRANID vary from the socio-historical (such as black or white) to the national, such as Chinese or Japanese, to the linguistic (Hispanic). To this effect, indeterminate labels such as Caucasian and Mongoloid are also used to define the biological group to which unknown crania supposedly belong.[76]

Whether there is actually a correlation between cranial form and ancestry, geography, or race remains a highly contested issue within anthropology. The utility of the term race to describe human beings has also been questioned. But some practitioners refuse to reject this concept or the thinking behind it in favour of an alternative way of looking at humanity. Giustiniano Nicolucci would, perhaps, be amused to know that some of his skulls continue to have relevance to scientists working within the parameters of the new bio-anthropology. Data from the osteological collection which he originally sold to the Royal College of Surgeons in 1870, with the assistance of the English physician and craniologist Joseph Barnard Davis [1801–1881], have made their way into the CRANID series as the only sample within it of a so-called "Southern European population group."[77] The crania from the Nicolucci collection represent a significant find for the makers and supporters of CRANID.

As CRANID, like FORDISC, identifies an unknown cranium by naming the closest morphological neighbours to it within its original database of 2,900 crania, the addition of statistics from an entirely new population is seen by craniometricians as a major development. Hitherto, the European samples within CRANID were rather limited, as they contained only skulls from Poundbury, Dorset (dating from around 150 CE), the Oslo Museum (reputedly Viking), and from Zalavár, Hungary.[78] With the contribution of the Nicolucci collection of 163 crania, together with some other recent inclusions (from Australia, Denmark, and the Punjab), the current CRANID database has increased to 3,163 in total. Within CRANID, the Nicolucci skulls are presented as being representative of a "Southern European" or "Mediterranean" type of cranium.[79]

Nicolucci and his successors, such as the anthropologist Giuseppe Sergi [1841–1936], who developed a theory of the "Mediterranean race" in the 1890s that was very influential in Fascist Italy, would, no doubt, approve of this nomenclature.[80] However, the assumptions behind this classification of the Nicolucci skulls raise a number of important issues. By CRANID's own criteria of racial demarcation, according to geography (and then, by implication, ancestry), the skulls in the Nicolucci collection do not represent a natural or discrete population subset, but are used as if they did so. The term "Mediterranean" has little classificatory meaning, as it cannot be used to describe a human geographical variation.

To what extent do crania actually have distinctive features, the measurement of which possesses statistical coherence? The crania from the Nicolucci collection were subjected to the same 29 measurements as were others in the database. As many as 520 different measurements are today taken on a human skull (including quite a few of the teeth, which are considered quite crucial for identification in forensic cases), whilst over

2,000 routinely used to be taken by nineteenth-century craniologists. But which measures exactly of the 29 or more are considered particularly distinctive for the crania for the purposes of classification? Nicolucci himself believed that crania found within Italy showed marked morphological differences by region. In selecting crania for his collection, he may very well have pre-selected certain ones, because in his mind they conformed to his image of what, for example, a "perfect" Tuscan variety should be. So just how representative the skulls actually are as a whole remains just as problematic for today's forensic researchers as it was for Nicolucci and his contemporaries. The provenance of skulls within museum and university collections remains a decidedly nagging problem too.

The Hunterian Museum at the Royal College of Surgeons in London acquired the Nicolucci collection of 166 ancient and modern skulls in 1870 through the English collector and craniologist Joseph Barnard Davis [1801–1881], who acted on Nicolucci's behalf in respect of the sale. In addition, the College received the Barnard Davis osteological collection in 1880. Held by the Royal College of Surgeons, the letters regarding the acquisition of the Nicolucci skulls reveal that the purchase received the full support of George Rolleston [1829–1881], Thomas H. Huxley [1825–1895], and Edwin Saunders [1814–1901], Queen Victoria's personal dentist, who travelled to Italy to view the skulls prior to the sale, before William H. Flower [1831–1899], the conservator at the Hunterian Museum, agreed to fund the project. According to Nicolucci's own hand-written catalogue of the collection and Barnard Davis's manuscript copy and English translation of it, which were prepared in advance of the sale, certain skulls had special significance for Nicolucci. Amongst these were crania 12–14 from his "ancient Italian skulls" series in the collection; according to Nicolucci, these originated from Fasano (which he called ancient Gnathia) in Bari, Rugge (ancient Rudine) in the province of Oltrano and Ceglie (ancient Colium). Nicolucci considered these skulls to be unique representatives of the root-source of modern Italians, a kind of progenitor race. Of what worth are these skulls to modern forensic anthropology? The skull from Rugge, to which Nicolucci assigned such significance, was then and is now in over 20 fragments, which make any kind of topographical analysis and careful measurements of cranial conformations and parameters, on which the accuracy of CRANID depends, difficult at best. The skull from Ceglie was and is currently in better condition, although its mandible broke into six parts at some stage.[81]

Most scientists today who advocate a craniometric approach admit that ancient skulls reveal little about the origins and identity of prehistoric people because these crania exhibit none of the specific traits of regionality that modern skulls do. The regional variations in skull topography which today's craniometricians claim to observe are a relatively recent phenomenon and are attributable to the evolutionary effects on physiognomy of environmental influences. But another issue must be considered when evaluating the efficacy of the new computer-based craniometry in identifying skulls. Nicolucci never questioned the provenance of the skulls which he acquired. In his catalogue, he listed all his skulls by their number in the collection, their number in the series, their sex, and their place of origin. The "whence derived" list gives only the place-names where skulls were found, with no elaboration as to their provenance.

How Nicolucci came to possess "modern" skulls is never explained; whether he bought or stole them is not clear.[82] As to the "ancient" specimens, Nicolucci provided some details about how they came to be included in the collection. Many of the "ancient" skulls were collected from a necropolis at Aquinum; Nicolucci dated them from between 2 BCE to 2 CE. He could not be more precise. The others are from "pre-Christian and later" tombs, though he did not identify these in any more detail. Number 50 is a "cast of a skull from a tomb anterior to the Christian era, probably the skull of an ancient Celt found in a very ancient tomb near Turin." Not only is this specimen not the original, but the information about its origins is very vague. It is worth considering the import of these entries when evaluating the scientific worth of these crania for modern-day scientists. Their contribution to the CRANID 6 programme is the matter at hand. Surely, Davis exaggerated wildly when, in a letter to William Henry Flower, whose purpose was to convince the latter to purchase the entire collection for a mere £120, Davis described it as the "finest in existence."[83] The vagueness about the origins of the skulls, and the questions which arise as to their authenticity, have significance because the new forensic anthropologists present their science as an exact one and their methods as flawless. In the nineteenth century, scientists did not have any reliable means to authenticate or date the skulls, which they found in the field or acquired on the market, at their disposal.

When skulls are entered into the CRANID samples, they are not subject to any testing to verify origin or age, but even if they were, radiocarbon dates are not precise enough. Age matters only in so far as modern-day craniometricians believe that ancient skulls have insufficient topographical markers to be of any use. The term "Caucasoid," for example, is in common usage to lump all prehistoric crania of a "White" or European type together. Provenance unquestioned, the measurements are taken and these are introduced into the programme. This raises a number of questions. Did data from the presumed "Celtic" skull, for example, make its way into CRANID 6 as a representative of a Southern European or Mediterranean geographic variety? If so, does a "Celtic" skull share enough commonalities with a so-called "Southern European" or "Mediterranean" one for its measurements not to affect detrimentally the statistical coherence of the Nicolucci samples within the database?

These and other questions about new craniometry remain largely unanswered.[84] When faced with the possibility that their science may have shortcomings, and its methods faults, craniometricians close ranks and become obdurate. Richard Wright, for example, refuses to contemplate that he might be wrong, so unassailable are his views that human racial—or "ancestral"—classification, as he prefers to call it, exists in nature and is verifiable statistically and that it has a cranial basis, which resides in skull morphology alone, rather than genes, for example.[85] Naturally, given its lineage in a shady past of phrenologists, racists, Nazis, and their bedfellows, the new craniometry has understandably gone on the defensive. But the burden of proof does still remain with those who support the theory that it is possible to trace neat lines on the world map, separating one group of people from another, and that these clear racial demarcations are determined by the shape of the skull. Some authors have even posited that technological advances, bringing new forensic applications to anthropology, have actually halted progress by encouraging the discipline to "retreat back to a neoracial approach and with it a resurgent interest in the methods of description."[86] It is difficult, it seems, to escape the legacy of what the French anthropologist Claude Lévi-Strauss [1908–2009] called anthropology's "original sin" of discriminating between various human communities.[87]

Conclusions

Race life is broader, deeper, richer than the life of any man, or of any men[1]

In his inauguration speech delivered on Capitol Hill in Washington, DC on 20 January 2017 Donald J. Trump promised to make "America great again!" and to restore its "national pride."[2] Used throughout his presidential campaign this slogan, as many critics point out, is not only a historical fantasy, but is also a dangerous one, as it evokes a past in which the United States was ruled by a political and economic elite that was white, Christian, heterosexual, and masculine. As part of his campaign against the political establishment, Trump's pronouncements on American national character were often generalized distillation of his perceptions of the desires of working-class men and women who, he thinks, are disadvantaged by globalization and immigration, and in need of a new sense of community.

Trump's brand of nativist populism has many adherents both within and outside the United States. Making one's country great again has become the political dream of many populist politicians across the world, from Hungary and Greece, to China and Russia.[3] Those who identify themselves with the New Right (in Europe) and the Alt-Right (in the USA and Britain) argue against social integration and assimilation not only of foreigners and immigrants, but also of those with disabilities, alongside a reaffirmation of an organic sense of ethnic belonging above and beyond the civic loyalty to the state. The current political climate promotes and encourages the re-writing of the ethnic canon and with it radical definitions of the national community. Once again, biological aspects of ethnicity, rather than cultural ones, are portrayed as the ideal form of identity. According to one such view, "a people or folk *(Volk)*" is "an organic cultural entity, possessing its own unique spirit and historical background, and existing in the world with its own, particular form of being."[4] This re-articulation of ethnicity also prompts a new emphasis on race and common racial origins. Europeans, for instance, are described as one racial community, "due to their close biological relatedness." They all share a "common racial type," which, importantly, "allows them to better relate to each other (in ways that they cannot relate to non-White peoples)."[5] Not surprisingly, then, authors of this orientation condemn ethnic and racial mixing, insisting on the protection of the same racial type.[6] They are not just longing for an idealized past; they are engaged in cultural and political wars on multiple fronts and what is at stake is the future of policies and politics which shape peoples' lives in many different countries around the world. This new form of racialized populism, like its earlier variants in the past, possesses broad mass appeal and seeks to undermine established liberal-democratic systems and values.

Only a day after Trump's inauguration, on 21 January 2017, European right-wing leaders met in Koblenz, Germany. Marine Le Pen, the leader of the French Front National, announced a new dawn of patriotism and national spirit. "2016," she claimed, "was the year the Anglo-Saxon world woke up. I am certain 2017 will be the year when the people of continental Europe wake up."[7] This claim is hardly surprising, but the racial undertones of her statement, such as the use of the term Anglo-Saxon for the British and the North Americans, are nonetheless disturbing. Her support of the "Anglo-Saxons" who in Britain voted for Brexit and in the United States voted for Donald Trump acquired a greater political importance during the presidential elections in France in April-May 2017. Certainly, Le Pen's views reflected the Eurosceptic radicalism of many in France and elsewhere in Europe.

If Le Pen spoke of the "Anglo-Saxons" regaining political power, the Dutch politician and leader of the Party for Freedom, Geert Wilders, drew attention to the other main tenets of populist ideology: the mourning for the loss of ethnic homogeneity and of a strong national state with clear borders and shared values. "Blonde Europeans," Wilders remarked, are now in danger of becoming "strangers in their own countries" because of "Islamization."[8] Racial tropes such as these have returned to our political language and are normalized in ways which would have been unthinkable only a few years ago. They are used to articulate the possibility of a future at a historical moment when the conception of the national state is undergoing a significant revival, and with it the rejection of multiculturalism and cosmopolitanism. Important political gains notwithstanding, none of these right-wing parties succeeded in winning the general or presidential elections in 2017.[9]

It is not only "new" immigrants but also "old" ethnic minorities that remain a constant focus of racial harassment in the United States and elsewhere.[10] Outside of science, the politics of race today is dominated by conflicting ideas about the appropriateness and use of racial constructs to determine policies by governments and their agencies relating to law and order, health, housing, education, and national security. The "Black Lives Matter" movement which was founded by Patrisse Cullors, Opal Tometi, and Alicia Garza in the United States in 2013 after the murder of 17-year-old Trayvon Martin by George Zimmerman, a police officer who was later acquitted of the crime, is a response to what it perceives as the "dehumanization of Black people" in the USA.[11] Although its remit extends far beyond exposing the "extra-judicial killing of Black people by police and vigilantes," its activities and aims have brought the issue of so-called "racial profiling" into the spotlight.[12]

According to the definition employed by the American Civil Liberties Union, the practice by law enforcement officials of targeting individuals for suspicion of crime based on the individual's race, ethnicity, religion, or national origin is widespread and commonplace within American society. Racial profiling, however, is not the exclusive preserve of the police; nor does it relate solely to crime. Other authorities acting in a policing capacity for public and private purposes, such as security guards and airport officials, employ the methods of racial profiling. Since the 11 September 2001 attacks on the World Trade Towers and the Pentagon, the detention of Arabs, Muslims, and South Asians, who are found to be in the country illegally, has become routine and occurs in the absence of any connection between issues of national security and minor violations of immigration law.[13]

The 9/11 attacks were carried out by Muslims from Arab countries; in response to these attacks the US federal government has engaged in a sweeping and far-reaching counterterrorism campaign focused on Arabs and Muslims. In some cases, Arabs and Muslims have been victims of the extremes of the new paranoia gripping Fortress America and draconian Homeland Security measures; in other cases, however, the employment of the crude techniques of racial profiling has resulted in the stopping, searching, and detention of persons who were perceived to be, but were not, in fact, Arabs and Muslims, such as Sikhs and other South Asians. Racial profiling, though deemed unconstitutional by the Supreme Court, on the grounds that it violates the right to equal protection of the law, is known to operate at an institutional and systemic level in American society and to be extremely pervasive.

Longing for protection and security has also brought forward a yearning for racial solidarity, which was allegedly lost in the decades after the Second World War. The idea of race has always permeated the omnipresent historical narratives about the country or the nation's past glory, aspiring to restore its former greatness. In the twenty-first century, the assumption is that race, as a meaningful social and biological category of analysis, has been de-ritualized and de-politicized, but the truth is that race continues to lend itself to theories of social, cultural, and political inequality. Combined with an aggressive rhetoric of national protectionism and ethnicity, race issues— meaning political programmes and platforms framed around issues of race, ethnicity, and immigration—are now part of the mainstream politics in countries with very different histories of race, such as Ireland, the United States, South Africa, Britain, Hungary, and Greece.[14] In others, such as France and the Netherlands, openly racist and right-wing politicians, with hard-line anti-immigrant agendas, are rapidly transforming the political landscape and have a real chance of attaining power and leading their countries in the near future.

Traditions of civic nationhood, which are premised upon the idea that citizenship is open to anyone who assents to the liberal-democratic principles of the nation-state and the society to which she/he belongs or wishes to belong, have been under attack in recent decades. But there are also authors who offer an interesting counterpoint to those focusing on race, ethnicity, and history as the cornerstones of identity. The Canadian writer Michael Ignatieff, for instance, has been a prominent advocate of a new kind of civic nationalism, which he has defined as a way forward for the West into an increasingly uncertain and frightening future. For him, the civic nation, as epitomized in countries such as the United States, France, and Canada, which all celebrate a universal conception of liberty, is "a community of equal, rights-bearing citizens, united in patriotic attachment to a shared set of political practices and values."[15] In order to refashion it, disassociate it from the Right, and make it into an engine of social progress, Ignatieff attempted to turn nationalistic sentiment from an irrational drive into a rational choice; like many liberal nationalists, he saw no clash between nationalism and liberalism. However, the concept of civic nationalism, though high-minded, inclusive, egalitarian, multicultural, and liberal-democratic—at least in intent—has come under much criticism since its inception in the late eighteenth century.

In a post-Brexit Britain and in Trump's America, Ignatieff's endeavour to celebrate the universality of neo-liberal ideals and proclaim, confidently, that the "postmodern" nation-state can be a cosy haven of all-inclusiveness seems like an especially anachronistic and naïve throwback to the 1990s, a decade which was characterized by the global rise of multiculturalism as a concept and as a conscious policy for social inclusion adopted throughout the West. The utopian aspirations of the era were captured fully by the United Nations, when it declared 1995 the official Year for Tolerance. At the time, multiculturalism was an aspiration which sought to bridge the divide between cultural diversity and universal values. It aimed at creating a *rapprochement* of the various cultures within historically evolved, increasingly diverse modern societies in the West by reinforcing a commitment to the idea of the toleration of cultural and ethnic diversity and the creation of inter-religious and inter-cultural dialogue for the purposes of peace and harmony within and between nations.[16] Gone now is much of the idealism of that decade. It largely disappeared, as polarization and divisiveness— often defined along lines relating to "identity," religious, cultural, ethnic, sexual, gendered, racial, or otherwise—are increasingly voiced in a sustained upsurge in discrimination, racism, intolerance, xenophobia, radicalization, and violence throughout the world.

The truth is that the great European project to create and consolidate nation-states did not always end in success. Peoples could be conjoined linguistically, but divided along ethnic, cultural, or religious lines. One needs only to remember the case of the former Yugoslavia, which confounds the simple idea of nationhood imbedded in Romantic nationalism. The Yugoslav kingdom which was first established between 1918 and 1922 (and re-named and re-founded in 1929, 1946, and 1963) never enjoyed more than a strained and artificial unity. The forces and fault-lines which eventually tore the nation asunder had been there from the start; it was officially dissolved in 1992, after bloody wars were precipitated by rising internecine strife and ethnic nationalism from the late 1980s.[17]

Yugoslavia had been an illusory nation-state, divided along illusory ethnic and sharp religious lines, with ethno-nationalists (and fascists before and during the Second World War) always willing to exploit the differences in faith between Muslim Bosniaks, Eastern Orthodox Serbs, and Catholic Croats. Between 1992 and 1995, a campaign of mass expulsions, ethnic cleansing, and genocide, which included the systematic use of unlawful confinement, child murder, gang rape, and torture as weapons of war, was carried out in areas controlled by Bosnian Serbs, and was organized under the command of General Ratko Mladić. These atrocities, which resulted in the death of an estimated 100,000 people killed in Bosnia and Herzegovina, targeted Muslim Bosniaks and Bosnian Croats "for extinction," as the United Nations' International Criminal Tribunal for the Former Yugoslavia (ICTY) made very clear in its official ruling of 2001. The ICTY declared the 1995 Srebrenica massacre of 8,327 Bosnian Muslims a "crime against humanity" by Bosnian Serb forces, who "stripped all the male Muslim prisoners, military and civilian, elderly and young, of their personal belongings and identification, and deliberately and methodically killed them solely on the basis of their identity."[18] This example helps illustrate one of the central arguments put forward at the beginning of this book, namely that the ideology of race and ethnic discrimination have gone through many incarnations from their Enlightenment origins to the right-wing populism and nationalism of our day.

As we have seen in this book, a long tradition dating back to the sixteenth and seventeenth centuries links the concept of race to theories of culture and civilization and, during the nineteenth and twentieth centuries, also to ideas of nation and ethnicity. Regarding the latter, many nationalist writers believed that the people were united in a single, holy bond which promised to elevate them above others. In this context, the national idea was both a subjective reality—existing as an abstract ideal in the hearts and minds of the people—and an objective construct—embodied in the political institutions and territory of the nation-state. The urge for national union and ethnic communion has not disappeared. Imaginings about what constitutes a race and nation are remarkably persistent in contemporary societies. Indeed, since the nineteenth century, there has been a great deal of continuity in the perceptions, stereotypes, and myths concerning the question of what makes one a member of a given race and a particular nation.[19]

The concept of race survived into the twenty-first century, and in some cases even thrives in contemporary societies, notwithstanding the genocide, oppression, and marginalization carried out in its name in the previous centuries. To reject only traditional or conventional descriptions of race based on skin colour is insufficient. There is need now for a new hermeneutics of the idea of race, one that engages with and reflects critically on the "*new* anomalies, *new* ambiguities, and a *new* ambivalence in contemporary life."[20] These new interpretations and other alterations of existing historiographic canons can prove unsettling, but they certainly are necessary. According to the forensic anthropologist Amade M'Charek, "the challenge in studying race is to denaturalize without dematerializing it, and to simultaneously attend to [its] materiality without fixing [it]" in different scientific practices and legal arrangements.[21]

The failure of the multicultural experiment to create cohesive societies and, since 2014, specifically, the surge in non-European immigration by economic migrants and asylum seekers from North Africa and the Middle East, have led to what EU officials call a "migration crisis" and what some observers see as a complete *déracinement* of Europeans. In this context, the Brexit campaign before the referendum of 23 June 2016 re-asserted the principle of national sovereignty as one of its central claims. A restoration of the power of the nation-state, Nigel Farage and his UK Independence Party, as well as other Brexiters within the British political establishment, such as Boris Johnson, repeatedly argued, was a legitimate response to the threat that an overbearing, supra-national, super-state in Brussels posed to the national interests. They portrayed the European Union as the main hindrance to the preservation of the British "way of life." Brexiter populism succeeded in deflecting anger about the real causes of the people's misery caused by years of government-imposed austerity which brought cuts to state spending, the erosion of the welfare state, and the collapse of the National Health Service, as well as a protracted economic crisis adversely affecting growth, employment, and incomes. It was not successive Labour, Tory, and coalition governments which were blamed for these misfortunes, but the European Union. Appeals to stop immigrants and the EU from impinging upon national sovereignty were matched by calls to "make Britain great again." The Brexit campaign purposefully sought to stir a sense of loss for a Glorious Past, when Crown, Country, Empire, and People were One, and Britain was Greater. The Brexit vote has, as some commentators put it, reopened "on the British body politic" many painful and "deep wounds of race, citizenship and belonging."[22]

Other European countries experience similar anxieties concerning national identity. In the summer of 2016 France was embroiled in a controversy called "Burkinigate" which encapsulated many of these issues. When 30 out of some 36,000-odd French municipalities sought to impose a ban on the burkini at seaside resorts, like Nice, the divisions within French society came to the fore. The republican concept of secularism defines the burkini as a "political provocation" by radical Islam, as Manuel Valls, the French Prime Minister, member of the Socialist Party, and defender of the ban, explained.[23] One of the West's most vocal enemies of Islamism, even before the *Charlie Hebdo* terrorist attacks took place on 7 January 2015, Valls has consistently claimed that the charge of "Islamophobia" to describe policies aimed at protecting people, defending women's rights, and fighting terrorism is a weapon by Islamists to silence their critics. However, opponents of the interdiction, which include other prominent socialists, such as Najat Vallaud-Belkacem, the first French woman to be appointed Minister of Education, Higher Education, and Research, claim that the burkini ban contravenes two cornerstones of the French Republic: freedom of religion and individual rights. Even its proponents must realize that the results of the measure have been disappointing. By appearing as an unfair, discriminatory act targeting Muslims, it has hardly endeared the nation's disaffected minority communities to the Republic and its secularist agenda. Instead of promoting a unifying, secular mind-set, the ban has also become a tool of radical Islamists, who portray it as an act of war against Islam and the Caliphate, a symbol of their martyrdom, and proof of their victimization by a compulsory Westernization.[24]

As can be seen from these examples, on both sides of the Atlantic, the nationalist and ethnic appeals of right-wing populism continue to exploit familiar notions about the past, which have been ingrained in the culture and consciousness by over three centuries of race and racism. During one of the most brutal electoral campaign in the history of the United States, Donald Trump eschewed entirely the traditional conservatism of the Republic Party and ran on an openly racist and misogynistic ticket which has repeatedly been endorsed by members of the self-styled Alt-Right such as Alex Jones, a notorious and inflammatory right-wing blogger, and white supremacists such as David Duke, the former leader of the Ku Klux Klan.[25] Post-Brexit Britain and Trump's America may be lost causes, at least temporarily, but the challenge facing the European Union and all Americans and Europeans today is to restore and preserve their increasingly diluted and weakened collective identities without pandering to rising xenophobia and chauvinism within individual nations. This is a difficult challenge whose outcome is by no means certain.

More than 1.32 million migrants crossed the Mediterranean Sea to Europe in 2015. More than 66,000 refugees, mainly from Africa, arrived in Italy in the first six months of 2016 alone. More than 150,000, mainly Syrians, Afghans, and Iraqis, entered Greece in the first half of 2016 and, according to a joint investigation by Europol and Interpol, more than 400,000 in Libya alone sought passage to Europe in the autumn of 2016.[26] Countries such as Britain and the United States seek to build a fortress against threats to "national sovereignty," which the hordes of nameless and faceless "immigrants" represent to the popular psyche. During the electoral campaign Trump had called for a complete ban on Muslims entering the USA. Then, on 27 January, Holocaust Memorial Day, he signed an executive order banning individuals from seven Muslim countries including Syria,

Iran, Iraq, and Somalia from entering the United States for 90 days.[27] Not since the 1930s has the appeal of economic protectionism, populism, and geopolitical isolationism had so much appeal amongst politicians in the West.

This book has, therefore, argued that, in order to understand the current challenges posed by the revival of ethnic nationalism, populism, and nativism, one needs to concentrate not only on economic and social factors but also on historical traditions of race, alongside scientific, cultural, and political versions of race postulated across time and geographical borders. It is worth recalling here what the historian Michelle Brattain has said about the evolution of race after the Second World War: "What race *was* is not what race *is*, but understanding how it has been constructed in the past is essential to understanding and contributing to debate about its current construction."[28] It is this approach that guided our efforts in the preceding chapters. Whilst a great deal of work has been devoted to debunking the science of race, much less attention has been devoted to understanding race as one of the foundational elements of modern culture and modern societies, and explaining its persistence as a historical reality; for example, in constructions of national identity in countries such as China, Japan, and Brazil.[29]

As discussed in this book, race has been a central concept of the modern representation of society; its history has been fraught with complexities and contradictions. To understand its historical traditions, we examined race from a distinctive perspective, its historicity. More specifically, the argument put forward here is that race continues to have a significant role across culture, science, and politics. It has furthermore been part of the argument of this book that race was and is perceived as historically contingent because of developments not only in the humanities and social sciences but also in politics and in the public's perception of human difference. Such challenging issues touch upon the question of incongruity between the denouncement of racism by scientists and the subtle or not-so-subtle re-employment of it by politicians. This is the paradox of the current use of race, particularly in the United States. According to the sociologist Michael Banton, a possible "conflict between scientific knowledge" of race and its "public practice has arisen because scientists and legislators have different objectives and use different vocabularies in order to attain them."[30] Indeed, how to deal with race remains problematic, at both scientific and political levels.

The race-based worldview that took hold in modern cultures and societies after the eighteenth century has proved to be remarkably persistent, despite the fact that the concept of race has been discredited within science and by society at large from the 1960s onwards.[31] Race as an analytical category still exists within science.[32] As observed in this book, the methodological foundation of this new craniometrics is the same as the old craniology. Rooted in eighteenth-century biology, the impulse to measure and classify human beings has been held to account as one of the primary means used to divide and separate humanity. And there are other sources of concern. There is growing unease at the idea of using human specimens, located in natural history and ethnological collections, for scientific research. Increased sensitivity to public displays of human crania, bones, and skeletons in museums has led in many instances to the withdrawal of osteological material from general access and its placement in restricted access sites, such as at the Royal College of Surgeons in London, which houses one of the largest collections of comparative anatomy in the world. Indigenous peoples, including First Nation/Native Americans and Native Hawaiians in the United States, as well as Aboriginals in Australia and New Zealand, have also, in recent decades, mounted highly publicized campaigns for the repatriation of the "stolen" physical remains, as well as the cultural artefacts, of their ancestors.[33] Recent official estimates are that about 164,000 human aboriginal remains are to be found in British museums and another 200,000 are in American collections; many thousands more are located in continental European countries.[34] Though some of these specimens were acquired legally and consensually, a significant portion of them were obtained unethically. None other than Franz Boas wrote in 1888 that grave-robbing was "repulsive work," but "someone had to do it."[35] Within physical anthropology, archaeological and osteological collections became the mainstay of the discipline's global research enterprise at an early date; colonization facilitated the acquisition of human bodies, crania, and bones.[36] Museums became not only agents of cultural change and sources of collective knowledge but also, problematically, public sites defined by the interconnections between colonialism, racism, and human exploitation.[37]

Perhaps, it is not the purview of the historian to be didactic or judgemental about the past. Some scientists have no such qualms or restraints.[38] To give just one notable example: in 2007, James Watson [b. 1928], the eminent biologist who shared the 1962 Nobel Prize for describing the double-helix structure of DNA and who headed the American government's part in the international Human Genome Project, was forced to resign his position as Chancellor of the Cold Spring Harbor Laboratory on Long Island after publicly questioning the intelligence of people of African descent and asserting that people of European descent possessed a genetic advantage and superior intelligence.[39] It is surely right, from any perspective, to acknowledge that the foundations of natural, social, and biological sciences and the grounds of much modern thinking about race were based upon unethical practices, as well as easily controvertible evidence. Also, now more than ever, the examination of those cultural, philosophical, scientific, and political foundations upon which racial ideas are based requires that we engage critically with the "deeply anchored racialization" which is situated "in the somatic field of the human."[40] In this context, the emphasis on the human body in all its complexity is bound to be invested with historical significance. As argued in this book, we need to see this historical significance fully in accord with the unsettling reconfiguration of the concept of race within current political discourse and social practices.

Most books on the history of race conclude with a warning and a call for more active engagement of scholars and academics on all levels of public and political life. Our motivation here was not simply to bring a number of instances in the complex history of race to light but to illuminate their relevance to our society today. Perhaps this way we may come to terms with our own problematic history, whilst at the same time attempting to improve educational quality in our societies with respect to racial equality and social justice. It is, therefore, fitting that at the end we return to one of main sources of inspiration for this book, the eminent biologist Stephen Jay Gould [1941–2002]. He wrote *The Mismeasure of Man* in the early 1980s, a time which he described as one "of political retrenchment," and one which favoured the rise of biological determinism in society and politics. His warnings against the rise of racial prejudice, biological labelling, and chauvinistic descriptions of ethnic, social, and sexual minorities were as effective then as they are now: "We pass through this world but once. Few tragedies can be more extensive than the stunting of life, few injustices deeper than the denial of an opportunity to strive or even to hope, by a limit imposed from without, but falsely identified as lying within."[41]

This book pursued this aim differently from Gould's, of course, but we share with him the same respect for human differences and the unrelenting concern with the perpetuation of arguments about social and cultural worth derived from biological factors. Ultimately, our analysis and choice of topics are influenced by the political issues of our own time but we nevertheless hope that the book invites the reader to go beyond our conceptual and historiographic examples and find those important universal values in which genuine feelings of solidarity, compassion, care, and ultimate hope reside.

NOTES

Introduction

1 Jean-Baptiste Alphonse Karr, *Les guêpes (sixième série)* (Paris: Michel Lévy, 1862), 305 [originally published in *Les guêpes*, January 1849, vi].

2 Karim Murji and John Solomos, eds., *Theories of Race and Ethnicity: Contemporary Debates and Perspectives* (Cambridge: Cambridge University Press, 2015), 8.

3 See the recent collection by Amos Morris-Reich, Dirk Rupnow, eds., *Ideas of 'Race' in the History of the Humanities* (Basingstoke: Palgrave, 2017).

4 See Sadiah Qureshi, "Displaying Sarah Baartman: The 'Venus Hottentot,'" *History of Science* 42, 136 (2004): 233–57. Qureshi focuses on Cuvier's anatomical studies, carried out in 1815–1816, of the corpse of Sarah Baartman, a black South Africa immigrant, who came to Europe and was displayed as an oddity in travelling circuses. These studies of her remains formed the basis of Cuvier's racial thinking about the fixity of types. Seeing her as the lowest of the lowly races, Cuvier expressed a fascination, none the less, for her "ape-like" physiognomy, with its prominent genitalia and high rear-end. He thought that she might be an evolutionary throwback or "missing-link".

5 See Bruce S. Hall, *A History of Race in Muslim West Africa, 1600–1960* (New York: Cambridge University Press, 2014).

6 Tanya Golash-Boza, "A Critical and Comprehensive Sociological Theory of Race and Racism," *Sociology of Race and Racism* 2, 2 (2016): 129.

7 Social scientists working on 'multi-ethnic' societies emphasize the role played by the multiple (origins) and the shifting locations of race within current processes of identification amongst second and third generations of immigrants. See, for example, Tamsin Barber, *Oriental Identities in Super-Diverse Britain: Young Vietnamese in London* (Basingstoke: Palgrave, 2015). See also Panikos Panayi, *Immigration, Ethnicity and Racism in Britain, 1815–1914* (Manchester: Manchester University Press, 1994).

8 Laura Tabili, "Race is a Relationship not a Thing," *Journal of Social History* 37, 1 (2003): 125–30.

9 This is a methodology put forward by the Italian idealist philosopher and historian Benedetto Croce. For him, "ogni vera storia è storia contemporanea" ("every true history is contemporary history"). See Benedetto Croce, *Teoria e storia della storiografia*, 2nd revised edn (Bari: G. Laterza, 1920), 4.

10 As Channel 4 programme, entitled "Things We Won't Say about Race are True," shown on 15 March 2015, clearly revealed. Available at http://www. channel4.com/programmes/things-we-wont-say-about-race-that-are-true [accessed 22 December 2016].

11 Eduardo Bonilla-Silva, *Racism without Racists: Color-Blind Racism and the Persistence of Racial Inequality in America*, 4th edn. (Lanham, MD: Rowman & Littlefield, 2014).

12 For instance, many commentators described some of the speeches made by Donald J. Trump during the presidential election as racist.

13 Hayden White, *Tropics of Discourse: Essays in Cultural Criticism* (Baltimore: The Johns Hopkins University Press, 1978), 1.

14 The Italian "CasaPound," for instance, claims inspiration from Benito Mussolini's brand of fascism, whilst the Golden Dawn promotes the 4th of August regime of Ioannis Metaxas, in power between 1936 and 1941, as the ideal form of government for Greece. See Sophia Vasilopoulou and Daphne Halikiopoulou, *The Golden Dawn's 'Nationalist Solution': Explaining the Rise of the Far Right in Greece* (New York: Palgrave Macmillan, 2015).

15 See Nadine Ehlers, *Racial Imperatives: Disciplines, Performativity, and Struggles against Subjection* (Bloomington, IN: Indiana University Press, 2012) and Ramy M. K. Aly, *Becoming Arab in London: Performativity and the Undoing of Identity* (London: Pluto Press, 2015).

16 Judith Butler, *Bodies that Matter: On the Discursive Limits of "Sex"* (London: Routledge, 1993).

17 François Hartog, *Regimes of Historicity: Presentism and Experiences of Time*, trans. by Saskia Brown (New York: Columbia University Press, 2015) [first published in French in 2003].

18 See Luigi Luca Cavalli-Sforza, *Genes, Peoples and Languages*, trans. by Mark Seielstad (London: Penguin Books, 2001), 9. In his *Mankind Evolving: The Evolution of the Human Species*, published in 1962, geneticist Theodosius Dobzhansky similarly tried to retain the use of race to explain human diversity, proposing a genetic (that is scientific) definition of race.

19 Michael Kent and Peter Wade, "Genetics against Race: Science, Politics and Affirmative Action in Brazil," *Social Studies of Science* 45, 6 (2015): 818.

20 Paul Gilroy, *Between Camps: Nations, Cultures and the Allure of Race* (London: Penguin Books, 2000), 29.

21 *The Future of Multi-Ethnic Britain. Report of the Commission of Multi-Ethnic Britain* (London: Profile Books, 2000), 24.

22 Michael Skey, *National Belonging and Everyday Life: The Significance of Nationhood in an Uncertain World* (Basingstoke: Palgrave, 2011), 5.

23 See René Girard, "The Scapegoat as Historical Referent," *The Girard Reader*, ed. James G. Williams (New York: The Crossroad Publishing, 2003), 97–106.

24 Ian Traynor, "Migration crisis: Hungary PM says Europe in Grip of Madness," *The Guardian*, 3 September 2015. Available at https://www.theguardian.com/world/2015/sep/03/migration-crisis-hungary-pm-victor-orban-europe-response-madness[accessed 22 January 2016]. The same rhetoric was used

prior to the "quota referendum" ("kvótareferendum") held in Hungary on 2 October 2016 in response to the European Union's migrant resettlement plans.

25 As Paul A. Hanebrink has shown, the idea of a Christian Hungary, defender of European civilization, has been a cornerstone of modern Hungarian nationalism. See his *In Defense of Christian Hungary: Religion, Nationalism, and Antisemitism, 1890–1944* (Ithaca, NY: Cornell University Press, 2006).

26 See Craig S. Smith, "Poor and Muslim? Jewish? Soup Kitchen is not for you," *The New York Times*, 28 February 2006. Available at http://www.nytimes.com/2006/02/28/world/europe/poor-and-muslim-jewish-soup-kitchen-is-not-for-you.html [accessed 24 January 2016].

27 "President Obama's Farewell Address," Chicago, 10 January 2017. Available at https://www.nytimes.com/2017/01/10/us/politics/obama-farewell-address-speech.html?_r=0 [accessed 11 January 2017].

28 Rita Chin, Heide Fehrenbach, Geoff Eley, and Atina Grossmann, *After the Nazi Racial State: Difference and Democracy in Germany and Europe* (Ann Arbor: The University of Michigan Press, 2009) and Zoë Burkholder, *Color in the Classroom: How American Schools Taught Race, 1900–1954* (Oxford: Oxford University Press, 2011); and Ann Morning, *The Nature of Race: How Scientists Think and Teach about Human Difference* (Berkeley: University of California Press, 2011)

29 Fatima El-Tayeb, *European Others: Queering Ethnicity in Postnational Europe* (Minneapolis: University of Minnesota Press, 2011), xv.

30 See Neil MacMaster, *Racism in Europe: 1870–2000* (Basingstoke: Palgrave, 2001).

31 See Richard Graham, ed., *The Idea of Race in Latin America, 1870–1940* (Austin, TX: University of Texas Press, 1990).

32 Frank Dikötter, "The Racialization of the Globe: Historical Perspective," in Manfred Berg and Simon Wendt, eds., *Racism in the Modern World: Historical Perspectives on Cultural Transfer and Adaptation* (New York: Berghahn, 2011), 20–40.

33 Linda Martín Alcoff warns, however, not to essentialize "whiteness as necessarily, fundamentally, and centrally about white supremacy." Alcoff, *The Future of Whiteness* (Cambridge: Polity, 2015), 20.

34 See the excellent discussion of the relationship between border management in Europe and race in Amade M'Charek et al., "Topologies of Race: Doing Territory, Population and Identity in Europe," *Science, Technology & Human Values* 39, 4 (2014): 468–87.

35 Arun Kundnani, *Muslims are Coming! Islamophobia, Extremism, and the Domestic War on Terror* (London: Verso, 2014), 10–11. The independent review into opportunity and integration in Britain published by Dame Louise Casey in December 2016 confirmed this assumption. According to the Casey Review "65% [of the British population] agreed that Islamophobia is common in Britain today." Available at https://www.gov.uk/government/publications/the-casey-review-a-review-into-opportunity-and-integration [accessed 5 December 2016].

36 Norwegian Social anthropologist Fredrik Barth [1928–2016] suggested the same interpretation already in the late 1960s. Human groups, he believed, tend

to define themselves not by reference to their own characteristics but by exclusion, that is, by comparison to the 'Other.' See his *Ethnic Groups and Boundaries: the Social Organization of Culture Difference* (Boston: Little, Brown, 1969),

37 See, for example, Douglas Murray, *The Strange Death of Europe: Immigration, Identity and Islam* (London: Bloomsbury, 2017).

38 See Arthur Herman, *The Idea of Decline in Western History* (New York: The Free Press, 1997).

39 David Theo Goldberg, *Racist Culture: Philosophy and the Politics of Meaning* (Malden, MA: Blackwell, 1993), 6.

40 Martin Bernal, *Black Athena. The Afroasiatic Roots of Classical Civilization*, vol. 1 *The Fabrication of Ancient Greece, 1785–1985* (London: Vintage, 1991), 73 [first published in 1987].

41 Frantz Fanon, *Black Skins, White Masks*, trans. by Richard Philcox (New York: Grove Press, 2008), 1 [first published in French in 1952].

42 Josiah Royce, *Race Questions: Provincialism and Other American Problems* (New York: The Macmillan Company, 1908), 5.

43 See Albert Atkin, *The Philosophy of Race* (Abingdon: Routledge, 2014) and the collection of chapters published in Naomi Zack, ed., *The Oxford Handbook of Philosophy and Race* (Oxford: Oxford University Press, 2017).

44 *Kant's Critique of Judgement*, trans. with introd. and notes by J. H Bernard, 2nd edn revised (London: Macmillan, 1914), 63–4.

45 To some extent, this reference to race's function in society echoes Michel Foucault's interpretation of racism as a form of biopolitics. For a discussion of this view see Kim Su Rasmussen, "Foucault's Genealogy of Racism," *Theory, Culture & Society* 28, 5 (2011): 34–51.

46 One author whose approach to race is similar to the one adopted here is Linda Martín Alcoff. See, especially, her *Visible Identities: Race, Gender, and the Self* (New York: Oxford University Press, 2005).

47 Amade M'Charek, "Beyond Fact or Fiction: On the Materiality of Race in Practice," *Cultural Anthropology* 28, 3 (2013): 421–3.

48 Robert Bernasconi, "On Needing Not to Know and Forgetting What One Never Knew: The Epistemology of Ignorance in Fanon's Critique of Sartre," in Shannon Sullivan and Nancy Tuana, eds., *Race and Epistemologies of Ignorance* (Albany, NY: State University of New York Press, 2007), 236.

49 Thomas C. Holt, "Marking: Race, Race-Making, and the Writing of History," *The American Historical Review* 100, 1 (1995): 1–20.

50 Charles W. Mills, *Blackness Visible* (Ithaca, NY: Cornell University Press, 1998), xiv.

51 Already in 1996, Walter Laqueur noted that the "defense of Europe" has become one of the mantras of the European neo-fascists. See Walter Laqueur, *Fascism: Past, Present, Future* (Oxford: Oxford University Press, 1996), 93.

52 See Lisa McGirr, *Suburban Warriors: The Origins of the American New Right*, with a new preface (Princeton: Princeton University Press, 2015) [first published 2001]; Mark Bassin, "Lev Gumilev and the European New Right,"

Nationalities Papers 43, 6 (2015): 840–65; Tamir Bar-On, *Rethinking the French New Right: Alternatives to Modernity* (Abingdon: Routledge, 2013); and Cass Mudde, ed., *The Populist Radical Right: A Reader* (London: Routledge, 2017).

53 As clearly illustrated by the electoral success of such parties as The People's Party Our Slovakia and Alternative for Germany at the national elections in Slovakia (6 March 2016) and regional elections in Germany (13 March 2016), respectively.

54 Susan Sontag, *Styles of Radical Will* (London: Penguin Books, 2009), 75 [first published in 1966].

55 Larry Siedentop, *Inventing the Individual: The Origins of Western Liberalism* (London, 2014), 1.

1 History

1 W. E. B. du Bois, "The Conservation of Races" (1897), in W. E. B du Bois, *On Sociology and the Black Community*, eds. Dan S. Green and Edwin D. Driver (Chicago: University of Chicago Press, 1978), 238.

2 In trying to understand how race functions in society, in terms of both ideas and practice, we are indebted to the methodology proposed by Peter L. Berger and Thomas Luckmann in their study on *The Social Construction of Reality* (New York: Doubleday, 1966).

3 Mircea Eliade, *Myths, Dreams and Mysteries* (London: Collins, 1968), 24 [emphasis in the original].

4 See Elijah Anderson, *The Cosmopolitan Canopy: Race and Civility in Everyday Life* (New York: W. W. Norton, 2011).

5 Pierre L. van den Berghe, "Does Race Matter?" *Nations and Nationalism* 1, 3 (1995): 357–68.

6 Karl Pearson, *The Academic Aspect of the Science of National Eugenics* (London: Dulau, 1911), 5.

7 Karl Pearson, *The Academic Aspect of the Science of National Eugenics*, 6.

8 Alexander Etkind, *Internal Colonization: Russia's Imperial Experience* (Cambridge: Polity Press, 2011), 93.

9 Amos Morris-Reich, *Race and Photography: Racial Photography as Scientific Evidence, 1876–1980* (Chicago: The University of Chicago Press, 2016), 21–7.

10 Quoted in George W. Stocking, Jr., "Bones, Bodies, Behavior," in George W. Stocking, Jr., ed. *Bones, Bodies, Behavior: Essays on Biological Anthropology* (Madison: University of Wisconsin Press, 1988), 4. See also Pliny the Elder, "Natural Histories," in Rebecca F. Kennedy et al., eds., *Race and Ethnicity in the Classical World: An Anthology of Primary Sources in Translation* (Indianapolis, IN: Hackett Publishing, 2013), 48–9.

11 Quoted in Ania Loomba and Jonathan Burton, eds., *Race in Early Modern England: A Documentary Companion* (New York: Palgrave, 2007), 60.

12 Christopher L. Miller, *Black Darkness: Africanist Discourse in French* (Chicago: University of Chicago Press, 1985).

13 Surekha Davies, *Renaissance Ethnography and the Invention of the Human: New Worlds, Maps and Monsters* (Cambridge: Cambridge University Press, 2016).

14 See Margo Hendricks, "Race: A Renaissance Category?" in Michael Hattaway, ed., *A Companion to English Renaissance Literature and Culture* (Oxford: Blackwell, 2003), 691.

15 See Patrícia Ferraz de Matos, *The Colours of the Empire: Racialized Representations during Portuguese Colonialism*, translated by Mark Ayton (New York: Berghahn, 2013).

16 Quoted in Loomba and Burton, eds., *Race in Early Modern England*, 272.

17 Charles White, *An Account of the Regular Gradation in Man, and in Different Animals and Vegetables; and from the Former to the Latter* (London: C. Dilly, 1799).

18 White, *An Account of the Regular Gradation in Man*, 98.

19 White, 134–5.

20 Victor Courtet (de l'Isle), *Tableau ethnographique du genre humain* (Paris: Arthus Bertrand, 1849), 2. Courtet is often considered one of the first theorists of racial inequality. See Jean Boissel, *Victor Courtet (1813–1867), premier théoricien de la hiérarchie des races. Contribution à l'histoire de la philosophie politique du romantisme* (Paris: Presses Universitaires de France, 1972).

21 Peter H. Boulle, "François Bernier and the Origins of the Modern Concept of Race," in Sue Peabody and Tyler Stovall, eds., *The Color of Liberty: Histories of Race in France* (Durham, NC: Duke University Press, 2003), 11–27.

22 See H. Samy Alim, John R. Rickford and Arnetha F. Ball, eds., *Raciolinguistics: How Language Shapes our Ideas about Race* (New York: Oxford University Press, 2016).

23 See Helge Jordheim, "The Nature of Civilization: The Semantics of Civilization and Civility in Scandinavia," in Helge Jordheim and Margrit Pernau, eds., *Civilizing Emotions. Concepts in Nineteenth-Century Asia and Europe* (Oxford: Oxford University Press, 2015), 25–44.

24 See Thomas McCarthy, *Race, Empire and the Idea of Human Development* (Cambridge: Cambridge University Press, 2009) and Benedikt Stuchtey, ed., *Science across the European Empires* (Oxford: Oxford University Press, 2005).

25 Herodotus, *The Histories*, trans. and intro. by Aubrey de Selincourt (Harmondsworth: Penguin Classics, 1954), 7–10.

26 See Benjamin Issac, *The Invention of Racism in Classical Antiquity* (Princeton: Princeton University Press, 2004).

27 Wayne Ambler, "Aristotle on Nature and Politics: The Case of Slavery," *Political Theory* 15, 3 (1987): 390–410.

28 *The Politics of Aristotle*, trans. by E. Barker, with intro. and notes by R. F. Stalley (Oxford: Oxford University Press, 1995), vii-xxxviii; and Malcolm Heath, "Aristotle on Natural Slavery," *Phronesis: A Journal for Ancient Philosophy* 53, 3 (2008): 245.

29 See Miriam Eliav-Feldon, Benjamin Isaac, and Joseph Ziegler, eds., *The Origins of Racism in the West* (Cambridge: Cambridge University Press, 2009).

30 Francisco Bethencourt, *Racisms: From the Crusades to the Twentieth Century* (Princeton: Princeton University Press, 2013), 1–8.

31 Peter Wade, *Race: An Introduction* (Cambridge: Cambridge University Press, 2015), 3.

32 David Nirenberg, "Race and the Middle Ages: The Case of Spain and Its Jews," in Margaret R. Greer et al., eds, *Rereading The Black Legend: The Discourses of Religious and Racial Difference in the Renaissance Empires* (Chicago: The University of Chicago Press, 2007), 87.

33 George Yancy, *Black Bodies, White Gazes: The Continuous Significance of Race* (Lanham, MD: Rowman & Littlefield, 2008), 34.

34 One must be aware of what Rogers Brubaker called the unintentional "*doubling* or *reinforcing* the reification of ethnic groups in ethnopolitical practice with a reification of such groups in social analysis." See Rogers Brubaker, *Ethnicity without Groups* (Cambridge, MA: Harvard University Press, 2004), 10.

35 Hermann W. Siemens, *Race Hygiene and Heredity* (New York: D. Appleton, 1924), 175.

36 See *Dictionary of Races or Peoples*. Reports of the Immigration Commission (Washington: Government Printing Office, 1911), 5.

37 *Dictionary of Races or Peoples*, 8.

38 See Robert F. Zeidel, *Immigrants, Progressives, and the Exclusion Politics: The Dillingham Commission, 1900–1927* (DeKalb, IL: Northern Illinois University Press, 2004) and Desmond King, *Making Americans: Immigration, Race, and the Origins of the Diverse Democracy* (Cambridge, MA: Harvard University Press, 2000).

39 G. Spiller, ed., *Papers on Inter-Racial Problems* (London: P. S. King & Son, 1911), v.

40 Marcos Chor Maio and Richardo Ventura Santos, "Antiracism and the Uses of Science in the Post-World War II: An Analysis of UNESCO's First Statements on Race (1950–1951)," *Vibrant: Virtual Brazilian Anthropology* 12, 2 (2015): 1–26. See also Jenny Bangham, "*What is Race?* UNESCO, Mass Communication and Human Genetics in the early 1950s," *History of the Human Sciences* 25, 5 (2015): 80–107.

41 The first two UNESCO statements on race (in 1950 and 1951, respectively) were followed by the Proposals on the Biological Aspects of Race (1964), the Statement on Race and Racial Prejudice (1967). See *Four Statements on the Race Question* (Paris: UNESCO, 1969). For a discussion of these statements see Michael Yudell, *Race Unmasked: Biology and Race in the Twentieth Century* (New York: Columbia University Press, 2014), 148–52 and Michelle Brattain, "Race, Racism, and Anti-Racism: UNESCO and the Politics of Presenting Science to the Postwar Public," *The American Historical Review* 112, 5 (2007): 1386–94.

42 See Elazar Barkan, *The Retreat of Scientific Racism: Changing Concepts of Race in Britain and the United States between the World Wars* (New York:

Cambridge University Press, 1992), 341 and Gavin Schaffer, *Racial Science and British Society, 1930–1962* (Basingstoke: Palgrave, 2008), 122.

43 See William H. Tucker, *The Science and Politics of Racial Research* (Urbana, IL: University of Illinois Press, 1994), 170–9.

44 Erik Bleich, *Race Politics in Britain and France: Ideas and Policymaking since the 1960s* (New York: Cambridge University Press, 2003).

45 See Wendy D. Roth, "The Multiple Dimensions of Race," *Ethnic and Racial Studies* 39, 8 (2016): 1310–38.

46 Peter Wade, "'Race', Nature and Culture," *Man (new series)*, 28, 1 (1993): 17.

47 The debate about the "whiteness" of European philosophy has now reached the general public as shown on BBC2's Newsnight programme with Emily Maitlis on 9 January 2017, when she discussed the issue with the sociologist Kehinde Andrews and the historian Sir Anthony Seldon. Available on http://www.bbc.co.uk/iplayer/episode/b088k00m/newsnight–09012017 [accessed 10 January 2017].

48 Tsenay Serequeberhan, "The Critique of Eurocentrism and the Practice of African Philosophy," in Emmanuel C. Eze, ed., *Post-Colonial African Philosophy: A Critical Reader* (Oxford: Blackwell, 1997), 146.

49 See Kim F. Hall, *Things of Darkness: Economies of Race and Gender in Early Modern England* (Ithaca, NY: Cornell University Press, 1995); Marey Floyd-Wilson, *English Ethnicity and Race in Early Modern Drama* (Cambridge: Cambridge University Press, 2003).

50 Saree Makdisi, *Making England Western: Occidentalism, Race and Imperial Culture* (Chicago: Chicago University Press, 2014), xiii.

51 Makdisi, *Making England Western,* ix.

52 See John Darwin, *The Empire Project: The Rise and Fall of the British World System, 1830–1970* (Cambridge: Cambridge University Press, 2009).

53 Edward Said, *Orientalism: Western Conceptions of the Orient* (London: Penguin Books, 1995), 3 [first edition 1978].

54 Karl Pearson, "On the Coefficient of Racial Likeness," *Biometrika* 18, 1–2 (1926): 105–17 and idem, "The Application of the Coefficient of Racial Likeness to Test the Character of Samples," *Biometrika* 20B, 3–4 (1928): 294–300. And Carl C. Seltzer, "A Critique of the Coefficient of Racial Likeness," *American Journal of Physical Anthropology* 23, 1 (1937): 101–9.

55 Percy Amaury Talbot and H. Mulhall, *The Physical Anthropology of Southern Nigeria: A Biometric Study in Statistical Method* (New York: Cambridge University Press, 1962).

56 See Colin Kidd, *The Forging of Races: Race and Scripture in the Protestant Atlantic World, 1600–2000* (Cambridge: Cambridge University Press, 2000).

57 Not to be mistaken for "racial constructivism," a position adopted by Charles W. Mills to investigate the "view of race as both real and unreal, not 'realist' but still objectivist." See Mills, *Blackness Visible*, 47.

58 Catherine Bliss, *Race Decoded: The Genomic Fight for Social Justice* (Stanford, CA: Stanford University Press, 2012), 5. Further in the book, the "genomic racial expert" is described as the "biosocial scientist par excellence,

a scientist who reflexively considers the ethical implications of biological research from the first moment of inquiry." *Race Decoded*, 13.

59 Rogers Brubaker, *Grounds for Difference* (Cambridge, MA: Harvard University Press, 2015), 54.

60 Brubaker, *Grounds for Difference*, 54.

61 See Kenan Malik, *The Meaning of Race: Race, History, and Culture in Western Society* (New York: New York University Press, 1996).

62 Amongst the disciplines of the humanities, philosophy has of late received due attention from historians of race. See Robert Bernasconi, *Race and Racism in Continental Philosophy* (Bloomington, IN: Indiana University Press, 2003) and Peter K. J. Park, *Africa, Asia, and the History of Philosophy: Racism in the Formation of the Philosophical Canon, 1780–1830* (New York: SUNY Press, 2013).

63 Leopold von Ranke, *History of the Latin and Teutonic Nations, from 1494 to 1514*, trans. by Philip A. Ashworth (London: George Bell and Sons, 1887), 1.

64 Wolfgang J. Mommsen, ed., *Leopold von Ranke und die moderne Geschichtswissenschaft* (Stuttgart: Klett-Cotta, 1988).

65 Georg G. Iggers, *The German Conception of History: The National Tradition of Historical Thought from Herder to the Present*, revised ed. (Middletown, CN: Wesleyan University Press, 1983) [first published 1968].

66 See, for example, Heinrich von Treitschke, *Das deutsche Ordensland Preußen* (Leipzig: Insel Verlag, 1862).

67 Ettore Rota, *Il Giansenismo in Lombardia e le origini del Risorgimento italiano* (Pavia: Fusi, 1907).

68 Antonino de Francesco, *Mito e storiografia della 'Grande rivoluzione'. La Rivoluzione francese nella cultura politica italiana del '900* (Naples: Alfredo Guida, 2006).

69 Stuart J. Woolf, *The Italian Risorgimento: Problems and Perspectives in History* (London: Longmans, 1969), 94–5.

70 Stefan Berger and Chris Lorenz, "Introduction," in idem, eds., *Nationalizing the Past: Historians as Nation Builders* (Basingstoke: Palgrave, 2015), 1–25.

71 Edward A. Freeman, "Race and Language," in idem, *Historical Essays* (London: Macmillan, 1879), 181.

72 Freeman, "Race and Language," 188.

73 Freeman, "Race and Language," 191–2.

74 Freeman, "Race and Language," 194.

75 Freeman, "Race and Language," 198–9.

76 Freeman, "Race and Language," 199–200.

77 Freeman, "Race and Language," 200.

78 Alexandros Ypsilantis, "Fight for Faith and Motherland!", trans. by Mary Kitroeff, in Balázs Trencsényi and Michal Kopeček, eds., *Discourses of Collective Identity in Central and Southeast Europe*, vol. 2 National Romanticism (Budapest: CEU Press, 2007), 401–2.

79   J. P. Fallmerayer, *Welchen Einfluss hatte die Besetzung Griechelands durch die Slaven auf das Schicksal der Stadt Athen und der Landschaft Attika?* (Stuttgart: J. G. Cotta'sche Buchhandlung, 1835).

80   See David Bindman, *Ape to Apollo: Aesthetics and the Idea of Race in the 18th Century* (London: Reaktion Books, 2002), 81–92.

81   Suzanne L. Marchand, *Down From Olympus: Archaeology and Philhellenism in Germany, 1750–1970* (Princeton: Princeton University Press, 1996), 4.

82   See, for example, Comte de Gobineau, *Deux études sur la Grèce moderne: Capodistrias. Le Royaume des Hellènes* (Paris: Librairie Plon, 1905), 111.

83   Stathis Gourgouris, *Dream Nation: Enlightenment, Colonization and the Institution of Modern Greece* (Stanford: Stanford University Press, 1996), 145, n. 16.

84   See Andrew D. Evans, *Anthropology at War: World War I and the Science of Race in Germany* (Chicago: University of Chicago Press, 2010).

85   Jovan Cvijić, *La Péninsule Balkanique. Géographie humaine* (Paris: Armand Colin, 1918), 278–9.

86   Paul Vidal de la Blache, *Principes de géographie humaine* (Paris: Librairie Armand Colin, 1922).

87   See Katrin Steffen, "Ludwik Hirszfeld, the Great War, and Seroanthropology: Expectations and Unfulfilled Promises," *Ab Imperio* 2 (2016): 125–52 and Marius Turda, "Entangled Traditions of Race: Physical Anthropology in Hungary and Romania, 1900–1940," *Focaal* 58 (2010): 32–46.

88   See Rachel E. Boaz, *In Search of 'Aryan Blood': Serology in Interwar and National Socialist Germany* (Budapest: Central European University Press, 2012).

89   Lajos Méhely, "Blut und Rasse," *Zeitschrift für Morphologie und Anthropologie*, Festband Eugen Fischer, 34 (1934): 244–57.

90   P. P. Panaitescu, "Noi suntem de aici," *Cuvântul* 17, 38 (20 November 1940): 1.

91   For the relationship between the theme of rebirth and fascism, see Roger Griffin, *Fascism* (Cambridge: Polity Press, 2018).

92   See, for example, the work by the British-American anthropologist John Lawrence Angel [1915–1986]: "A Racial Analysis of the Ancient Greeks," *American Journal of Physical Anthropology* 2, 4 (1944): 329–76 and idem, "Social Biology of Greek Culture Growth," *American Anthropologist* 48, 4 (1946): 493–533.

93   For the Pelasgian origins of the Romanians see Nicolae Densușianu, *Dacia preistorică* (Bucharest: Inst. de Arte Grafice 'Carol Göbl, 1913). Pelasgians, near-mythical peoples, were considered to be the ancestors of all the Indo-Europeans.

94   According to Simon Mehedinți in his *Vechimea poporului român și legătura cu elementele alogene* (Bucharest: Cartea Românească, 1925).

95   John Koumaris, "On the Morphological Variety of Modern Greeks," *Man* 48 (1948): 126.

96 Koumaris, "On the Morphological Variety of Modern Greeks," 127.

97 Mark Bassin, "Nurture *is* Nature: Lev Gumilev and the Ecology of Ethnicity," *Slavic Review* 68, 4 (2009): 872–97. See also his *The Gumilev Mystique: Biopolitics, Eurasianism, and the Construction of Community in Modern Russia* (Ithaca, NY: Cornell University Press, 2016).

98 Katherine Verdery, *National Ideology under Socialism: Identity and Cultural Politics in Ceausescu's Romania* (Berkeley: University of California Press, 1995).

99 See Peter Boev, "Anthropological Data on the Ethnogenesis of the Ancient Thracians," *Mankind Quarterly* 16 (1975): 68–73.

100 Pál Lipták, *Avars and Ancient Hungarians* (Budapest: Akadémiai Kiadó, 1983).

101 Peter Boev, *Die Rassentypen der Balkanhalbinsel und der Ostägäischen Inselvelt und deren Bedeutung für die Herkunft ihrer Bevölkerung* (Sofia: Verlag der Bulgarischen Akademie der Wissenschaften, 1972).

102 Ion F. Buricescu, "Rasa și sufletul românesc," *Revista de Filosofie* 26, 1–2 (1941): 56–84.

2 Culture

1 Jules Harmand, *Domination et colonisation* (Paris: Ernest Flammarion, 1910), 69 [the original is in Latin: *Tu regere imperio gentes, "Europa" memento*].

2 Quoted in John E. Flint, *Cecil Rhodes* (London: Hutchinson, 1976), 248.

3 According to Reginald Horsman, Anglo-Saxonism in Britain can be traced back to the sixteenth century, coinciding with the break with Rome and the creation of the Church of England. He sees its origins as non-racial, as emphasis was placed on institutions, common law, and ideas of freedom. See Reginald Horsman "Origins of Racial Anglo-Saxonism in Great Britain before 1850," *Journal of the History of Ideas* 37, 3 (1976): 387–410.

4 Tellingly, this is a term which resonates today, when so-called Brexiters framed their arguments for leaving the European Union around the need to make Britain "Great" again.

5 Charles Wentworth Dilke, *Greater Britain: A Record of Travel in English-speaking Countries during 1866–7* (London: Macmillan, 1869), 347.

6 J. S. Mill, *Principles of Political Economy. Collected Works*, vol. 2 (Toronto: Toronto University Press, 1965), 319.

7 See Paul P. Rich, *Race and Empire in British Politics*, 2nd edn (Cambridge: Cambridge University Press, 1990), 12–26 and Douglas Lorimer, *Science, Race Relations and Resistance. Britain, 1870–1914* (Manchester: Manchester University Press, 2013), 27–36.

8 Civilization is here understood, in the words of Raymond Williams, as both a "historical process" and "an achieved condition of refinement and order," opposed to barbarity and savagery. See Raymond Williams, *Keywords: A Vocabulary of Culture and Society* (London: HarperCollins, 2014), 57 [first

published in 1976]. See also Brent Bowden, *The Empire of Civilization: The Evolution of An Imperial Idea* (Chicago: University of Chicago Press, 2009).

9   Sir J. R. Seeley, *The Expansion of England* (London: Macmillan, 1914), 10.

10   See Deborah Wormell, *Sir John Seeley and the Uses of History* (Cambridge: Cambridge University Press, 1980), 154–9 and Duncan Bell, *Reordering the World: Essays on Liberalism and Empire* (Princeton: Princeton University Press, 2016), 265–96.

11   Bernard Porter, *The Absent-Minded Imperialists: Empire, Society and Culture in Britain* (Oxford: Oxford University Press, 2004).

12   William Marsden, "Rooting Racism into the Educational Experience of Childhood and Youth in the Nineteenth- and Twentieth-Centuries," *History of Education* 19, 4 (1990): 333–53.

13   Two classic studies are: Jacques Barzun, *The French Race* (New York: Columbia University Press, 1932) and Eric Voegelin, "The Growth of the Race Idea," *The Review of Politics* 2, 3 (1940): 283–317.

14   Giovanni Bovio, *Il diritto pubblico e le razze umane* (Naples: A. Morano, 1887), 10.

15   Jules Harmand, *Domination et colonisation* (Paris: Ernest Flammarion, 1910), 156.

16   Alice L. Conklin, *A Mission to Civilize: The Republican Idea of Empire in France and West Africa, 1895–1930* (Stanford: Stanford University Press, 1997), 1–2.

17   De Matos, *The Colours of the Empire*, 226.

18   David L. Howell, "Civilization and Enlightenment: Markers of Identity in Nineteenth-Century Japan," in Joshua A. Fogel, ed., *The Teleology of the Modern Nation-State* (Philadelphia: University of Pennsylvania Press, 2005), 117–37.

19   Quoted in Komori Yōichi, "Rule in the Name of 'Protection': The Vocabulary of Colonialism," in Michele M. Mason and Helen J. S. Lee, eds., *Reading Colonial Japan: Text, Context, and Critique* (Stanford: Stanford University Press, 2012), 72.

20   Quoted in Robert Thomas Tierney, *Tropics of Savagery: The Culture of Japanese Empire in Comparative Frame* (Berkeley: University of California Press, 2010), 82.

21   Quoted in Herman, *The Idea of Decline in Western History*, 37–8.

22   J. M. Blaut, *The Colonizer's Model of the World: Geographical Diffusionism and Eurocentric History* (New York: The Guilford Press, 1993), 1.

23   Edward W. Said, *Culture and Imperialism* (New York: Vintage Books, 1994), 53.

24   For an excellent discussion of these authors and their ideas, see Klaus-Peter Koepping, *Adolf Bastian and the Psychic Unity of Mankind: Foundations of Anthropology in Nineteenth Century Germany* (St. Lucia, Qld.: University of Queensland Press, 1983); Woodruff D. Smith, *Politics and the Science of Culture in Germany, 1840–1920* (New York: Oxford University Press, 1991); Andrew Zimmerman, *Anthropology and Antihumanism in Imperial Germany* (Chicago: Chicago University Press, 2001); and Chris Manias, "The Growth of Race and

Culture in Nineteenth-Century Germany: Gustav Klemm and the Universal History of Humanity," *Modern Intellectual History* 9, 1 (2012): 1–31.

25 Edward B. Taylor, *Primitive Culture: Researches into the Development of Mythology, Philosophy, Religion, Art, and Custom*, 2. vols. (London: John Murray, 1871).

26 See the articles collected under the title *Race, Language and Culture* (New York: The Macmillan Company, 1940).

27 For early works see Frank H. Hankins, *The Racial Basis of Civilization. A Critique of the Nordic Doctrine* (New York: Alfred A. Knopf, 1926) and Ignaz Zollschan, *The Significance of the Racial Factor as a Basis in Cultural Development* (London: Le Play House Press, 1934).

28 See, for instance, the works on the history of anthropology published by the American scholar George W. Stocking Jr. [1928–2013].

29 Lorimer, *Science, Race Relations and Resistance*, 3.

30 Quoted in F. M. Barnard, *Herder's Social and Political Thought: From Enlightenment to Nationalism* (Oxford: Clarendon Press, 1965), 100.

31 For the Dutch case, see Gloria Wekker, *White Innocence: Paradoxes of Colonialism and Race* (Durham, NC: Duke University Press, 2016).

32 Said, *Culture and Imperialism*, 222.

33 Olindo de Napoli, "Race and Empire: The Legitimation of Italian Colonialism in Juridical Thought," *The Journal of Modern History* 85, 4 (2013): 820 [italics in the original].

34 For a discussion of this aspect, see Harry D. Harootunian, *Things Seen and Unseen: Discourse and Ideology in Tokugawa Nativism* (Chicago: University of Chicago Press, 1988).

35 See Justin E. H. Smith, *Nature, Human Nature, & Human Difference: Race in Early Modern Philosophy* (Princeton: Princeton University Press, 2015).

36 Denise F. da Silva, *Toward a Global History of Race* (Minneapolis: University of Minnesota Press, 2007), xiii.

37 See the chapters in Larry Wolff and Marco Cipolloni, eds., *The Anthropology of the Enlightenment* (Stanford: Stanford University Press, 2007).

38 Bernal, *Black Athena*, 32.

39 "Preface," to Wolff and Cipolloni, eds., *The Anthropology of the Enlightenment*, xii.

40 As recently demonstrated by Mostafa Minawi, the Ottoman Empire too had colonial ambitions in Africa in an attempt to reinvent itself as a global power. See his *The Ottoman Scramble for Africa: Empire and Diplomacy in the Sahara and the Hijaz* (Stanford: Stanford University Press, 2016).

41 J. A. Hobson, *Imperialism: A Study* (London: James Nisbet, 1902), 237.

42 See Helen Tilley, *Africa as a Living Laboratory: Empire, Development, and the Problem of Scientific Knowledge, 1870–1950* (Chicago: The University of Chicago Press, 2011).

43 See John Thornton, *Africa and Africans in the Making of the Atlantic World, 1400–1800*, 2nd edn (Cambridge: Cambridge University Press, 1998);

Nehemia Levtzion and Randall L. Pouwels, eds., *The History of Islam in Africa* (Athens, OH: Ohio University Press, 2000); Bruce S. Hall, *A History of Race in Muslim West Africa, 1600–1960* (Cambridge: Cambridge University Press, 2014).

44   See Gustave Le Bon, *Lois psychologiques de l'évolution des peuples* (Paris: Félix Alcan, 1895).

45   Léo Frobenius, *Histoire de la civlisation africaine* (Paris: Gallimard, 1936), 15.

46   See, for instance, the descriptions provided by Hegel in his five series of lectures on the philosophy of history delivered at the University of Berlin between 1822 and 1831.

47   George M. Fredrickson, *Racism: A Short History* (Princeton: Princeton University Press, 2012).

48   B. Disraeli, *Tancred: or, The New Crusade*, vol. 1 (New York: Walter Dunne, 1904), 191. See also Simone Beate Borgstede, *'All is Race': Benjamin Disraeli on Race, Nation and Empire* (Münster: LIT Verlag, 2011).

49   For the nineteenth century see Christine Bolt, *Victorian Attitudes to Race* (London: Routledge and Kegan Paul, 1971); Douglas Lorimer, *Colour, Class, and the Victorians: English Attitudes to the Negro in the Mid-Nineteenth Century* (Leicester: Leicester University Press, 1978); and Nancy Stepan, *The Idea of Race in Science: Great Britain, 1800–1960* (London: Macmillan, 1982).

50   Quoted in Horsman "Origins of Racial Anglo-Saxonism," 402.

51   Quoted in *Race and the Enlightenment: A Reader*, ed. by Emmanuel C. Eze (Oxford: Blackwell, 1997), 104.

52   Robert Knox, *The Races of Men: A Fragment* (Philadelphia: Lea & Blanchard, 1850), 7.

53   See Stephen Jay Gould, *The Mismeasure of Man*, rev. and exp. edn, with a new intro. (New York: W. W. Norton, 1996) [first published 1981] and Marvin Harris, *The Rise of Anthropological Theory: A History of Theories of Culture*, updated edition (Lanham, MD: AltaMira Press, 2001) [first published 1968]. See also Maria Sophia Quine, "The Destiny of Races 'Not Yet Called to Civilization': Giustiniano Nicolucci's Critique of American Polygenism and Defense of Liberal Racism," in Richard McMahon, ed. *National Races: Transnational Power Struggles in Science and Politics, 1840s–1940s* (Lincoln, NE: University of Nebraska Press, in press).

54   George W. Stocking, Jr., *Victorian Anthropology* (New York: The Free Press, 1987), chap. 1.

55   See the excellent discussion in Evelleen Richards, "The 'Moral Anatomy' of Robert Knox: The Interplay between Biological and Social Thought in Victorian Scientific Naturalism," *Journal of the History of Biology* 22, 3 (1989): 373–436. See also Alan Bates, *The Anatomy of Robert Knox: Murder, Mad Science and Medical Regulation in Nineteenth-Century Edinburgh* (Brighton: Sussex Academic Press, 2010).

56   Adrian Desmond and James Moore, *Darwin's Sacred Cause: How a Hatred of Slavery shaped Darwin's Views on Human Evolution* (New York: Houghton Mifflin Harcourt, 2009).

57 Knox, *The Races of Men*, 9–10.

58 Knox, *The Races of Men*, 46.

59 Knox, *The Races of Men*, 60 and 100.

60 These are theories that posit the extinction of the so-called "primitive" races following the contact with white races and their civilization. For this aspect, see Patrick Brantlinger, *Dark Vanishings: Discourse on the Extension of Primitive Races, 1800–1930* (Ithaca, NY: Cornell University Press, 2003).

61 See Lee D. Baker, *From Savage to Negro: Anthropology and the Construction of Race, 1896–1954* (Berkeley: University of California Press, 1998). Although traditionally Social Darwinism was used to justify the superiority of the "White race" over other races, there was also another tradition, which, in the USA in particular, used Social Darwinism to highlight the endemic erosion of the "White race's vital qualities" due to overexpansion, ruthless competition for resources, and not least moral depravity. See Malinda Alaine Lindquist, *Race, Social Science and the Crisis of Manhood, 1890–1970: We are the Supermen* (New York: Routledge, 2012), esp. ch. 1.

62 This topic has, as expected, generated a variegated scholarship. See, for example, Ann L. Stoler, *Carnal Knowledge and Imperial Power: Race and the Intimate in Colonial Rule* (Berkeley: University of California Press, 2002) and Miguel Vale de Almeida, *An Earth-Colored Sea 'Race', Culture and the Politics of Identity in the Post-Colonial Portuguese-Speaking World* (New York: Berghahn, 2004).

63 Henry Neele, "Survey of the Greek, the Roman, and the Modern Historians," *The Edinburg Review* 47, 94 (1828): 129.

64 Neele, "Survey of the Greek, the Roman, and the Modern Historians," 129.

65 Horsman "Origins of Racial Anglo-Saxonism," 410.

66 Reginald Horsman, *Race and Manifest Destiny: The Origins of American Racial Anglo-Saxonism* (Cambridge, MA: Harvard University Press, 1981), 5.

67 Arthur de Gobineau, *The Inequality of Human Races* (New York: Howard Fertig, 1999), 1.

68 Gobineau, *The Inequality of Human Races*, 1.

69 See John Nale, "Arthur De Gobineau on Blood and Race," *Critical Philosophy of Race* 2, 1 (2014): 106–24.

70 Tzvetan Todorov, *On Human Diversity: Nationalism, Racism, and Exoticism in French Thought* (Cambridge, MA: Harvard University Press, 1993), 131–6.

71 Michael D. Biddiss, *Father of Racist Ideology: The Social and Political Thought of Count Gobineau* (London: Weidenfeld, 1970) and idem, "Prophecy and Pragmatism: Gobineau's Confrontation with Tocqueville," *The Historical Journal* 13, 4 (1970): 611–33.

72 See Stuart C. Gilman, "Degeneracy and Race in the Nineteenth Century," *Journal of Ethnic Studies* 10, 4 (1983): 27–50 and Daniel Pick, *Faces of Degeneration: A European Disorder, c. 1848-c. 1918* (Cambridge: Cambridge University Press, 1989).

73 See Janine Buenzod, *La formation de la pensée de Gobineau et 'L'Essai sur l'inégalité des races humaines'* (Paris: A. G. Nizet, 1967).

74 Gobineau, *The Moral and Intellectual Diversity of Races, with Particular Reference to their Respective Influence in the Civil and Political History of Mankind* (Philadelphia: J. B. Lippincott, 1856). The foremost American polygenist Josiah C. Nott provided an appendix, "containing a summary of the latest scientific facts bearing upon the question of unity or plurality of species."

75 See Jerry Dávila, *Diploma of Whiteness, Race and Social Policy in Brazil, 1917–1945* (Durham, NC: Duke University Press, 2003).

76 Alejandro de la Fuente, *A Nation for All: Race, Inequality, and Politics in Twentieth-Century Cuba* (Chapel Hill: The University of North Carolina Press, 2001), 45. For Chile, see Karin Alejandra Rosemblatt, "Sexuality and biopower in Chile and Latin America," *Political Power and Social Theory* 15 (2002): 229–62.

77 See Paul A. Fortier, "Gobineau and German Racism," *Comparative Literature* 19, 4 (1967): 341–50.

78 See, for example, K. L. Schemann, *Gobineau und die deutsche Kultur* (Leipzig: Eckardt, 1910).

79 For the discussion of de Lagarde's and Fritsch's racial anti-Semitism see Ulrich Sieg, *Germany's Prophet: Paul de Lagarde and the Origins of Modern Antisemitism* (Waltham, MD: Brandeis University Press, 2013). For the impact of ideas of race on the production of scientific knowledge, see Suzanne L. Marchand, *German Orientalism in the Age of Empire: Religion, Race, and Scholarship* (New York: Cambridge University Press, 2009).

80 See, for example, Martin A. Ruehl, *The Italian Renaissance in the German Historical Imagination, 1860–1930* (Cambridge: Cambridge University Press, 2015).

81 The differences between "Kultur" and "Zivilisation" had generated much debate and a large scholarship. A very good discussion is provided in Lucien Febvre, "Zur Entwiklung des Wortes und der Vorstellung von 'Civilisation,'" (1930) in Lucien Febvre, *Das Gewissen des Historikers*, ed. Ulrich Raulff (Berlin: Wagenbach, 1988), 39–79 and Jörg Fisch, "Zivilisation, Kultur," in Otto Brunner, Werner Conze and Reinhart Koselleck, eds., *Geschichtliche Grundbegriffe: Historisches Lexikon zur politisch-sozialen Sprache in Deutschland* vol. 7 (Stuttgart: Klett-Cotta, 1992), 679–774.

82 For an early discussion of Kant's anthropology and his writings on race see Theodor Elsenhans, *Kants Rassentheorie und ihre bleibende Bedeutung* (Leipzig: Verlag von Wilhelm Engelmann, 1904). In the 1950s, Earl W. Count highlighted Kant's contribution to European racial thought, but his edited volume, *This is Race: An Anthology from the International Literature on the Races of Man* (New York: Henry Schuman, 1950), remains little known to this day. During the 1990s, Emmanuel C. Eze edited *Race and the Enlightenment: A Reader* (Oxford: Blackwell, 1997), which reignited interest in Kant's discussion of race. See also Jon. M. Mikkelsen, ed., *Kant and the Concept of Race. Late Eighteenth-Century Writings* (New York: State University of New York Press, 2013).

83 Immanuel Kant, "Of the Different Human Races," trans. by Jon Mark Mikkelsen, in Robert Bernasconi and Tommy L. Lott, eds., *The Idea of Race* (Indianapolis, IN: Hackett, 2000), 9.

84   Robert Bernasconi, "Kant as an Unfamiliar Source of Racism," in Julie K. Ward and Tommy L. Lott, eds., *Philosophers on Race: Critical Essays* (Oxford: Blackwell, 2002), 145–66.

85   Bernard Boxill, "Kantian Racism and Kantian Theology," in Zack, ed., *The Oxford Handbook of Philosophy and Race*, 44–53.

86   H. S. Chamberlain, *The Wagnerian Drama: An Attempt to Inspire a Better Appreciation of Wagner as a Dramatic Poet* (London: John Lane, 1923), trans. by John Lees [first published in German in 1892].

87   Lord Redesdale, "Introduction," to H. S. Chamberlain, *Foundations of the Nineteenth Century*, vol. I, trans. by John Lees (London: John Lane, 1910), l.

88   Chamberlain, *Foundations*, I, 495.

89   Chamberlain, *Foundations*, I, lxviii.

90   Chamberlain, *Foundations*, I, lxviii.

91   Chamberlain, *Foundations*, I, 269.

92   Chamberlain, *Foundations*, I, lxvi.

93   See Alfred Rosenberg, *Houston Stewart Chamberlain als Verkünder und Begründer einder Deutscher Zukunft* (Munich: H. Bruckmann, 1927). For the standard work in English see Geoffrey G. Field, *Evangelist of Race: The Germanic Vision of Houston Stewart Chamberlain* (New York: Columbia University Press, 1981).

94   Chamberlain, *Foundations*, I, 25.

95   Chamberlain, *Foundations*, I, lxvii.

96   Chamberlain, *Foundations*, I, xci. In making this point, as so often in this book, Chamberlain returns to Kant, and his "conception of the Imagination" ("Vorstellung der Einbildungskraft"), outlined in *Critique of Pure Reason* (1781).

97   Michael Biddiss, "History as Destiny: Gobineau, H. S. Chamberlain and Spengler," *Transactions of the Royal Historical Society* 7 (1997): 81.

98   C. Rădulescu-Motru, "Filosofia lui Houston Stewart Chamberlain asupra raselor," *Noua Revistă Română pentru politică, literatură, știință și artă* 2, 17 (1900): 168.

99   Charles Darwin, *The Descent of Man and Selection in Relation to Sex*, 2 vols. (London: John Murray, 1871).

100 Chamberlain, *Foundations*, I, 288.

101 For H. S. Chamberlain's impact on Romanian intellectuals see Marius Turda, "Conservative Palingenesis and Cultural Modernism in Early Twentieth-Century Romania," *Totalitarian Movements and Political Religions* 9, 4 (2008): 437–53.

102 See Martin Woodroffe, "Racial Theories of History and Politics: The Example of Houston Stewart Chamberlain," in Paul Kennedy and Anthony Nicholls, eds., *Nationalist and Racialist Movements in Britain and Germany before 1914* (London: Macmillan, 1981), 143–53 and Roderick Stackelberg, *Idealism Debased: From Völkisch Ideology to National Socialism* (Kent, OH: Kent State University Press, 1981).

103 See Hugo Meyer, *Houston Stewart Chamberlain als Völkischer Denker* (Munich: H. Bruckmann, 1939).

104 Marr first introduced the term "anti-Semite" into politics and, in 1879, founded the notorious League of Anti-Semites (*Antisemitenliga*), which represented the first popular political movement focused exclusively on anti-Jewish beliefs. In pamphlets such as *Der Weg zum Siege des Germanenthums über das Judenthum* (*The Way to the Victory of Germandom over Judaism*) Marr was amongst the first to define the Jews in racial, rather than religious or cultural, terms. See Mosche Zimmermann, *Wilhelm Marr: The Patriarch of Anti-Semitism* (New York: Oxford University Press, 1986).

105 Chamberlain, *Foundations*, I, 293–6.

106 Stjepan Radić, *Živo hrvatsko pravo na Bosnu i Hercegovinu* (Zagreb: Hrvatski dnevnik, 1907), 27–37.

107 Kerubin Šegvić, *Die gotische Abstammung der Kroaten* (Berlin: Verlag Klinkhardt & Biermann, 1936) and idem, *Die Kroaten und ihre Mission während dreizehn Jahrhunderte der Geschichte* (Zagreb: Kugli, 1942).

108 Nevenko Bartulin, *The Racial Idea in the Independent State of Croatia: Origins and Theory* (Leiden: Brill, 2014), 20–32.

109 For Croatia see Rory Yeomans, *Visions of Annihilation: The Ustasha Regime and the Cultural Politics of Fascism, 1941–1945* (Pittsburgh: Pittsburgh University Press, 2013); for Romania see Vladimir Solonari, *Purifying the Nation: Population Exchange and Ethnic Cleansing in Nazi-Allied Romania* (Baltimore: Johns Hopkins University Press, 2010).

110 Nichifor Crainic, "Rasă și religiune," *Gândirea* 14, 2 (1933): 57–66.

111 Liviu Stan, *Rasă și religiune* (Sibiu: Tiparul Tipografiei Arhidiecezane, 1942).

112 Nayden Sheytanov, "Bulgarian Worldview," trans. by Zornitsa Dimova-Hristova, in Diana Mishkova et al., eds., *Anti-Modernism: Radical Revisions of Collective Identity*, vol. 4 (Budapest: Central European University Press, 2014), 230.

113 See the chapters included in Francis Barker et al., eds., *Europe and its Others: Proceedings of the Essex Conference on the Sociology of Literature, July 1984*, 2. vols. (Colchester: University of Essex, 1985); and Paul Gifford and Tessa Hauswedell, eds., *Europe and Its Others: Essays on Interpretation and Identity* (Bern: Peter Lang, 2010).

114 Alex Drace-Francis, *The Traditions of Invention: Romanian Ethnic and Social Stereotypes in Historical Context* (Leiden: Brill Publishers, 2013).

115 Count Hermann Keyserling, *Europe*, trans. by Maurice Samuel (London: Jonathan Cape, 1928), 329.

3 Nation

1 Jean-Jacques Rousseau, "Plan for a Constitution for Corsica" (1765), in idem, *The Plan for Perpetual Peace, On the Government of Poland, and*

Other Writings on History and Politics, trans. by Christopher Kelly and Judith Bush (Hanover, NH: University of New England, 2005), 133.

2   Mircea Eliade, *Myth and Reality*, trans. Willard R. Trask (New York: Harper Torchbooks, 1963).

3   See the discussion in Benedict Anderson, *Imagined Communities: Reflections on the Origin and Spread of Nationalism*, revised ed. (London: Verso, 2006) [first published 1983].

4   Gérard Bouchard, "National Myths: An Overview," in idem, ed., *National Myths: Constructed Pasts, Contested Presents* (Abingdon: Routledge, 2013), 277.

5   Richard Slotkin, *Regeneration through Violence: The Mythology of the American Frontier, 1600–1860* (Norman, OK: University of Oklahoma Press, 1973), 6 and 8–9.

6   For the Romanian case, see Lucian Boia, *History and Myth in Romanian Consciousness*, trans. James Christian Brown (Budapest: CEU Press, 2001); for the USA see Martin Heusser and Gudrun Grabher, eds., *American Foundational Myths* (Tübingen: Narr, 2002); for Turkey see Hale Yilmaz, *Becoming Turkish: Nationalist Reforms and Cultural Negotiations in Early Republican Turkey, 1923–1945* (Syracuse, NY: Syracuse University Press, 2013).

7   David Prodan, *Supplex Libellus Valachorum or the Political Struggle of the Romanians in Transylvania during the 18th Century* (Bucharest: Publishing House of the Academy, 1971).

8   M. Obédénare, "Presentation de quelques cranes roumains," *Bulletins de la Société d'Anthropologie de Paris* 9 (1874): 725–6.

9   For the German case, see Woodruff D. Smith, *Politics and the Sciences of Culture in Germany, 1840–1920* (New York: Oxford University Press, 1991); for the Portuguese case see Patrícia Ferraz de Matos, "Anthropology in Portugal: The Case of the Portuguese Society of Anthropology and Ethnology (SPACE), 1918," in Regna Darnell and Frederic W. Gleach, eds., *Local Knowledge, Global Stage* (Lincoln: University of Nebraska Press, 2016), 53–97; for the Argentinian case, see Ashley Kerr, "From Savagery to Sovereignty: Identity, Politics, and International Expositions of Argentine Anthropology (1878–1892)," *Isis* 108, 1 (2017): 62–81.

10 Kemal H. Karpat, *The Politicization of Islam: Reconstructing Identity, State, Faith, and Community in the Late Ottoman State* (New York: Oxford University Press, 2001), 349–50.

11 Karpat, *The Politicization of Islam*, 388–96. See also Bora Isyar, "The Origins of Turkish Republican Citizenship: The Birth of Race," *Nations and Nationalism* 11, 3 (2005): 348–9.

12 See, for example, the case of Turkish anthropology, discussed in Nazan Maksudyan, "The *Turkish Review of Anthropology* and the Racist Face of Turkish Nationalism," *Cultural Dynamics* 17, 3 (2005): 305.

13 See Finn Pollard, *The Literary Quest for an American National Character* (New York: Routledge, 2009).

14 William R. Taylor, *Cavalier and Yankee: The Old South and American National Character* (New York: Oxford University Press, 1993), 21 [first published 1961].

15 Lung-Kee Sun, *The Chinese National Character: From Nationhood to Individuality* (New York: M. E. Sharpe, 2002), 11.

16 See Emilio Gentile, *La Grande Italia: The Myth of the Nation in the Twentieth Century*, trans. by Suzanne Dingee and Jennifer Pudney (Madison: The University of Wisconsin Press, 2009) [first published in Italian in 1997].

17 George L. Mosse, *The Crisis of German Ideology: Intellectual Origins of the Third Reich* (New York: Grosset and Dunlap Publishers, 1965) and idem, *The Nationalization of the Masses: Political Symbolism and Mass Movements in Germany from the Napoleonic Wars through the Third Reich* (New York: Howard Fertig, 1974).

18 Slotkin, *Regeneration through Violence*, 17.

19 Carlton J. H. Hayes, "Nationalism as a Religion," in idem, *Essays on Nationalism* (New York: Macmillan, 1926), 101.

20 Hayes, "Nationalism as a Religion," 102–3.

21 See Jonathan Israel, *Revolutionary Ideas: An Intellectual History of the French Revolution from the Rights of Man to Robespierre* (Oxford and Princeton: Princeton University Press, 2014).

22 Silvana Patriarca and Lucy Riall, eds., *The Risorgimento Revisited: Nationalism and Culture in Nineteenth-Century Italy* (Basingstoke: Palgrave Macmillan, 2012); Ahmet Ersoy et al., eds., 4 vols., *Discourses of Collective Identity in Central and Southeast Europe 1770–1945: Texts and Commentaries* (Budapest: CEU Press, 2006–2014).

23 Roger Chartier, *Cultural History: Between Practices and Representations* (Oxford: Polity Press, 1993) [first published in 1988], chs. 1–2.

24 See, for example, Bálint Varga, *The Monumental Nation: Magyar Nationalism and Symbolic Politics in Fin-de-siècle Hungary* (New York: Berghahn, 2016).

25 J. Michelet, *Le Peuple* (Paris: Hachette, 1846), xlii.

26 Originally the text was published in *Polemic* (January 1946). The present quote is from George Orwell, *In Defence of English Cooking* (London: Penguin Books, 2005), 10.

27 As formulated by Eugen Weber in his *Peasants into Frenchmen: The Modernization of Rural France, 1870–1914* (Stanford: Stanford University Press, 1976).

28 Hayes, "Nationalism as a Religion," 109.

29 Steven K. Green, *Inventing a Christian America: The Myth of the Religious Funding* (New York: Oxford University Press, 2015).

30 R. B. Bernstein, *Thomas Jefferson: The Revolution of Ideas* (Oxford: Oxford University Press, 2004), 78.

31 Quoted in Bernstein, *Thomas Jefferson*, 80. See also Ibram X. Kendi, *Stamped from the Beginning: The Definite History of Racist Ideas in America* (New York: Nation Books, 2016), 104–19.

32 David Hume, "Of National Characters," in idem, *Selected Essays* (Oxford: Oxford University Press, 1996), 360.

33 John P. Diggins, "Slavery, Race and Equality: Jefferson and the Pathos of the Enlightenment," *American Quarterly* 28, 2 (1976): 206–28. For a recent discussion see Gregory Laski, *Untimely Democracy: The Politics of Progress after Slavery* (New York: Oxford University Press, 2017).

34 Peter S. Onuf, *Jefferson's Empire: The Language of American Nationhood* (Charlottesville: University Press of Virginia, 2000).

35 Kendi, *Stamped from the Beginning*, 111.

36 Hayes, "Nationalism as a Religion," 125.

37 Anthony W. Marx, *Faith in Nation: Exclusionary Origins of Nationalism* (Oxford: Oxford University Press, 2003).

38 See the discussion in Roberto Romani, *National Character and Public Spirit in Britain and France, 1750–1914* (Cambridge: Cambridge University Press, 2002).

39 Robert Shannan Peckham, *National Histories, Natural States: Nationalism and the Politics of Place in Greece* (London: I. B. Tauris, 2001), 87. For a regional discussion of these developments see Diana Mishkova, Marius Turda, Balázs Trencsényi, eds., *Anti-Modernism: Radical Revisions of Collective Identity* (Budapest: CEU Press, 2014).

40 *The Essential Writings of Rousseau,* ed. by L. Damrosch and trans. by P. Constantine (New York: Random House, 2013) and *Herder on Social and Political Culture*, selected, translated and edited by F. M Barnard (Cambridge: Cambridge University Press, 1969).

41 Zeev Sternhell, *The Anti-Enlightenment Tradition*, trans. David Maisel (New Haven: Yale University Press, 2010) 21 [originally published 2006].

42 Isaiah Berlin, *Vico and Herder: Two Studies in the History of Ideas* (London: Hogarth Press, 1976), 145–216. See also Vicki A. Spencer, *Herder's Political Thought: A Study of Language, Culture, and Community* (Toronto: Toronto University Press, 2012).

43 Carl Ritter, "Attempt at a General Comparative Geography," trans. by Daniel Theisen, in *German Essays on Science in the 19th Century*, ed. by Wolfgang Schirmacher (New York: Continuum, 1996), 32.

44 Zsolt Beöthy, *A magyar irodalom kis-tükre* (Budapest: Athenaeum, 1896), 21.

45 See the discussion in Hippolyte A. Taine, *Histoire de la littérature anglaise*, 5 vols. (Paris: L. Hachette, 1866–1878).

46 See G. Michaut, *Le génie latine: la race, le milieu, le moment* (Paris: A. Fontemoing, 1900).

47 Mark Bassin, "Imperialism and the Nation-State in Friedrich Ratzel's Political Geography," *Progress in Human Geography* 11 (1987): 473–95.

48 See, for example, Andreas Wimmer, *Ethnic Boundary Making: Institutions, Power, Networks* (New York: Oxford University Press, 2013), 16–17.

49 J. G. Herder, "Government as Inherited Regimes (1785)", in J. G. Herder, *Another Philosophy of History and Selected Political Writings*, trans., with introd. and notes by Ioannis D. Evrigenis and Daniel Pellerin (Indianapolis, IN: Hackett Publishing, 2004), 128.

50 Sternhell, *The Anti-Enlightenment Tradition*, 200.

51 Stefan Collini, "The Idea of 'Character' in Victorian Political Thought," *Transactions of the Royal Historical Society* 35 (1985): 33.

52 *Mill on Bentham and Coleridge* (London: Chatto & Windus, 1950), 132.

53 Peter Mandler, *The English National Character: The History of an Idea from Edmund Burke to Tony Blair* (New Haven: Yale University Press, 2006).

54 Gyula Kozáry, "Az Eugenics kérdése," *Athenaeum* 16, 1 (1907): 68.

55 See for Russia, Marina Mogilner, "Beyond, Against, and with Ethnography: Physical Anthropology as Science of Russian Modernity," in Roland Cvetkovksi and Alexis Hofmeister, eds., *An Empire of Others: Creating Ethnographic Knowledge in Imperial Russia and the USSR* (Budapest: CEU Press, 2014), 81–120; for Japan, see Mariko Asano Tamanoi, "Knowledge, Power, and Racial Classification: The 'Japanese' in 'Manchuria,'" *The Journal of Asian Studies* 59, 2 (2000): 248–76.

56 See Ivo Banac and Katherine Verdery, eds., *National Character and National Ideology in Interwar Eastern Europe* (New Haven: Yale Center for International Studies, 1995).

57 Murat Ergin, *"Is the Turk a White Man?": Race and Modernity in the Making of Turkish Identity* (Leiden: Brill, 2016), 99.

58 See the overviews provided in Diana Mishkova, ed., *We, The People: Politics of National Peculiarity in Southeastern Europe* (Budapest: CEU Press, 2009).

59 Katherine Verdery, "The Production and Defense of 'the Romanian Nation', 1900 to World War II", in Richard D. Fox, ed., *National Ideologies and the Production of National Culture* (Washington, DC: American Anthropological Association, 1990), 85.

60 See Mandler, *The English National Character* and Balázs Trencsényi, *The Politics of 'National Character': A Study in Interwar East European Thought* (Abingdon: Routledge, 2012).

61 For an application of this argument to the Romanian case, see Marius Turda, "The Nation as Object: Race, Blood, and Biopolitics in Interwar Romania," *Slavic Review* 66 (2007): 413–41.

62 D. L. Williams, *Rousseau's 'The Social Contract': An Introduction* (New York: Cambridge University Press, 2014), 163–70.

63 Hans Kohn, *Nationalism: Its Meaning and History* (Princeton, NJ: D. van Nostrand, 1955), 21.

64 See Pauline Kra, "Rousseau et la politique du caractère national," in Robert Thiéry, ed., *Jean-Jacques Rousseau, politique et nation* (Paris: Champion, 2001), 813–22.

65 Jean-Jacques Rousseau, *The Government of Poland*, trans. by Willmoore Kendall (Indianapolis, IN: Hackett Publishing, 1985).

66 Jeffrey A. Smith, "Nationalism, Virtue, and the Spirit of Liberty in Rousseau's 'Government of Poland'," *The Review of Politics* 65, 3 (2003): 409–37.

67 See Balázs Trencsényi, Maciej Janowski, Monika Baar, Maria Falina, and Michal Kopecek, *A History of Modern Political Thought in East Central*

Europe. Volume I: Negotiating Modernity in the 'Long Nineteenth Century' (Oxford: Oxford University Press, 2016) and Partha Chatterjee, *The Nation and Its Fragments: Colonial and Postcolonial Histories* (Princeton, Princeton University Press, 1993).

68 Lord Acton, *Essays on Freedom and Power* (Boston: The Beacon Press, 1949), 188.

69 He put forward these arguments in Ion Dragoumis, Ελληνικός πολιτισμός (Alexandria: Grammata, 1914) and Ο Ελληνσμός μου και οι Έλληνες (Athens: Estia, 1927).

70 Maximos Kaliakatsos, "Ion Dragoumis and 'Machiavelli': Armed Struggle, Propaganda, and Hellenization in Macedonia and Thrace, 1903–1908," *Journal of Modern Greek Studies* 31, 1 (2013): 53–84.

71 See the discussion in Rogers Brubaker, *Citizenship and Nationhood in France and Germany* (Cambridge, MA: Harvard University Press, 1992).

72 G. Mazzini, "Europe: its Condition and Prospects," in *Essays: Selected from the Writings, Literary, Political and Religious of Joseph Mazzini*, ed. William Clark (London: Walter Scott, 1880), 261–98.

73 For a discussion of liberal notions of equality and unity see Maurizio Viroli, *For Love of Country. An Essay on Patriotism and Nationalism* (Oxford: Clarendon Press, 1995).

74 Augustin Thierry, *Dix ans d'études historiques*, 5th edn (Paris: Furne, 1846), 136 [first published in 1839].

75 Knox, *The Races of Men*, 7.

76 *Din scrierile și cuvântarile lui Ion C. Brătianu, 1821–1891* (Bucharest: Inst. de Arte Grafice 'Carol Göbl, 1903), 61.

77 Hans Kohn, "The Eve of German Nationalism," *Journal of the History of Ideas* 12, 2 (1951): 56–84.

78 "Max Weber, Dr. Alfred Ploetz, and W. E. B. Du Bois (Max Weber on Race and Society II)," *Sociological Analysis* 34, 4 (1973): 310.

79 Marius Turda, *Modernism and Eugenics* (Basingstoke: Palgrave, 2010), 6–8.

80 See the discussion in Anthony D. Smith, *The Ethnic Origins of Nations* (Oxford: Basil Blackwell, 1983).

81 Quoted in Federico Chabod, "The Idea of Nation" (1961), in Stuart Woolf, ed., *Nationalism in Europe, 1815 to the Present: A Reader* (London: Routledge, 1996), 133.

82 Kohn, *Nationalism*, 110–12.

83 *Hegel's Philosophy of Right,* translated with notes by T. M. Knox (Oxford: Clarendon Press, 1942), v and sub-section 3 on "The State," 155–223.

84 *Hegel's Philosophy of Right,* 155–6.

85 L. L. Snyder, *Encyclopedia of Nationalism* (London: St James Press, 1990), 134.

86 On Fichte and Romanticism see Hans S. Reiss, *The Political Thought of the German Romantics, 1793–1815* (Oxford: Basil Blackwell, 1955) and Frederick C. Beiser, *The Fate of Reason: German Philosophy from Kant to Fichte* (Cambridge, MA.: Harvard University Press, 1987).

87   David James, *Fichte's Republic: Idealism, History and Nationalism* (Cambridge: Cambridge University Press, 2015).

88   Johann. G. Fichte, *Addresses to the German Nation*, translated by R. F. Jones and G. H. Turnbull (Chicago: Open Court Publishing, 1922), 141 and 152.

89   See Peter F. Sugar and Ivo. J. Lederer, eds., *Nationalism in Eastern Europe* (Seattle: University of Washington Press, 1969).

90   See *Songs of the Serbian People. From the Collections of Vuk Karadžić*, translated and edited by Milne Holton and Vasa D. Mihailovich (Pittsburgh: University of Pittsburgh Press, 1997).

91   Jovan Cvijić, *Remarks on the Ethnography of the Macedonian Slavs* (London: Horace Cox, 1906).

92   See Roger Griffin, *Modernism and Fascism: The Sense of a Beginning under Mussolini and Hitler* (Basingstoke: Palgrave, 2007).

93   According to Gellner, "A marked feature of the nineteenth and twentieth centuries is the political salience of ethnic feeling." See Ernest Gellner, *Encounters with Nationalism* (Oxford: Blackwell, 1994), 35.

94   For good overviews see George M. Fredrickson, *White Supremacy: A Comparative Study of American and South African History* (New York: Oxford University Press, 1981) and Saul Dubow, *Scientific Racism in Modern South Africa* (Cambridge: Cambridge University Press, 1995).

95   See Christoph Marx, "Hendrik Verwoerd's Long March to Apartheid: Nationalism and Racism in South Africa," in Berg and Wendt, eds., *Racism in the Modern World*, 281–302.

96   See Nancy L. Clark and William H. Worger, *South Africa: The Rise and Fall of Apartheid*, 2nd edn (London: Routledge, 2013).

97   See, for example, T. Dunbar Moodie, *The Rise of Afrikanerdom: Power, Apartheid, and the Afrikaner Civil Religion* (Berkeley: University of California Press, 1975).

98   Quoted in Moodie, *The Rise of Afrikanerdom*, 1.

99   C. Bloomberg, *Christian-Nationalism and the Rise of the Afrikaner Broederbond in South Africa, 1918–48*, ed. by Saul Dubow (Basingstoke: Macmillan, 1990), xxii.

100   Donald Harman Akenson, *God's Peoples: Covenant and Land in South Africa, Israel, and Ulster* (Ithaca: Cornell University Press, 1992), 74–5.

101   Brian Bunting, *The Rise of the South African Reich* (Harmondsworth: Penguin, 1964), introduction and chs. 5–6.

102   Ever since President F. W. De Klerk announced his decision in February 1991 to dismantle Apartheid, the neo-Nazi, militant, right-wing organization, *The Afrikaner Resistance Movement* (AWB, *Afrikaner Weerstandsbeweging*), has been dedicated to the cause of secession and the creation of an independent Boer-Afrikaner republic or "*Volkstaat*" ("People's State") or "*Boerestaat*" ("Boer State"). See Elizabeth Wood, *Forging Democracy from Below: Insurgent Traditions in South Africa and El Salvador* (Cambridge: Cambridge University Press, 2000, chs. 5–7.

103 Jean-Piere Lehmann, "Themes and Theories in Modern Japanese History," in Sue Henny and Jean-Pierre Lehmann, eds., *Themes and Theories in Modern Japanese History: Essays in Memory of Richard Storry* (London: Bloomsbury, 2014), 3–24.

104 See Hoi-Eun Kim, *Doctors of Empire: Medical and Cultural Encounters between Imperial Germany and Meiji Japan* (Toronto: University of Toronto Press, 2014).

105 William G. Beasley, "Modern Japan: An Historian's View," in idem, ed., *Modern Japan: Aspects of History, Literature, and Society* (Berkeley: University of California Press, 1975), 13–23.

106 Richard Storry, *The Double Patriots: A Study of Japanese Nationalism* (London: Chatto and Windus, 1957), 1–3.

107 See John S. Brownlee, *Japanese Historians and the National Myths, 1600–1945: The Age of Gods and Emperor Jinmu* (Vancouver: University of British Columbia, 1997).

108 Bruce Armstrong, "Racialisation and Nationalist Ideology: The Japanese Case," *International Sociology* 4, 3 (1989): 329–43.

109 Storry, *The Double Patriots*, 2.

110 Carol Gluck, *Japan's Modern Myths: Ideology in Late Meiji Period* (Princeton: Princeton University Pres, 1985), 112.

111 See Masako Gavin, *Shiga Shigetaka, 1863–1927: The Forgotten Enlightener* (London: Curzon Press, 2001).

112 Kosaku Yoshino, *Cultural Nationalism in Contemporary Japan: A Sociological Inquiry* (London: Routledge, 1992), 26–7.

113 Richard Siddle, *Race, Resistance and the Ainu of Japan* (London: Routledge, 1996); Leo T. S. Ching, *Becoming "Japanese": Colonial Taiwan and the Politics of Identity Formation* (Berkeley: University of California Press, 2001); and Michele M. Mason, *Dominant Narratives of Colonial Hokkaido and Imperial Japan: Envisioning the Periphery and the Modern Nation-State* (New York: Palgrave, 2012).

114 Quoted in David G. Goodman, "Anti-Semitism in Japan: Its History and Current Implications," in Frank Dikötter, ed., *Racial Identities in China and Japan* (London: Hurst, 1997), 180.

115 Sven Saaler, "The Kokuryūkai (Black Dragon Society) and the Rise of Nationalism, Pan-Asianism, and Militarism in Japan, 1901–1925," *International Journal of Asian Studies* 11, 2 (2014): 125–60.

116 Eric Hobsbawm, "Introduction: Inventing Traditions," in Eric Hobsbawm and Terence Ranger, eds., *The Invention of Tradition* (Cambridge: Cambridge University Press, 1983), 4–5.

4 Genealogy

1 Georges Vacher de Lapouge, "Old and New Aspects of the Aryan Question," trans. by Carlos C. Closson, *The American Journal of Sociology* 5, 3 (1899): 346.

2   Michael Burleigh and Wolfgang Wippermann, *The Racial State, Germany, 1933–1945* (Cambridge: Cambridge University Press, 1991). For a recent discussion, see Dan Stone, "Nazi Race Ideologues," *Patterns of Prejudice 50*, 4–5 (2016): 445–57.

3   Thomas Trautmann, *Aryans and British India* (Berkeley: University of California Press, 1997).

4   See Maria Sophia Quine, "Making Italians: Aryanism and Anthropology in Italy during the *Risorgimento*," in Marius Turda, ed., *Crafting Humans: From Genesis to Eugenics and Beyond* (Göttingen: V&R Unipress, 2013), 127–52. See also Bruce Baum, *The Rise and Fall of the Caucasian Race: A Political History of Racial Identity* (New York: New York University Press, 2006).

5   James G. Frazer, *The Golden Bough. The Roots of Religion and Folklore* (New York: Avenel Books, 1981), x [original, in two volumes, published in 1890 as *The Golden Bough: A Study in Comparative Religion*].

6   Athena S. Leoussi, *Nationalism and Classicism: The Classical Body as National Symbol in Nineteenth-Century England and France* (Basingstoke: Macmillan, 1998), 93.

7   David Cesarani, ed., *The Holocaust: Critical Concepts and Historical Studies*, 6 vols. (London: Routledge, 2004).

8   See Joan Leopold, "The Aryan Theory of Race," *The Indian Economic and Social History Review* 7 (1970): 271–97. See also Thomas Trautmann, ed., *The Aryan Debate* (Delhi: Oxford University Press, 2005).

9   Friedrich Nietzsche, *The Birth of Tragedy. Out of the Spirit of Music*, trans. by Shaun Whiteside (London: Penguin Books, 1993), 49.

10   Joan Leopold, "British Applications of the Aryan Theory of Race to India, 1850–1870," *The English Historical Review* 89, 352 (1974): 578–603.

11   Léon Poliakov, *Le mythe aryen. Essai sur les sources du racisme et des nationalismes* (Paris: Calmann-Lévy, 1971).

12   Quoted in Leopold, "British Applications of the Aryan Theory," 591.

13   V. Gordon Childe, *The Aryans: A Study of Indo-European Origins* (London: Kegan Paul, 1926), 211–12.

14   Joan Leopold, ed., *The Prix Volney. Contributions to Comparative Indo-European, African, and Chinese Linguistics: Max Müller and Steinthal*, vol. 3 (Dordrecht: Kluwer Academic, 1999), 11–22, 24–6, 30–3; and Müller's 1849 award-winning essay in the volume, "Comparative Philology of the Indo-European Languages in Its Bearing on the Early Civilization of Mankind," 107–90.

15   Earl of Beaconsfield [Benjamin Disraeli] *Lothair* (London: Longmans, 1901), 136–9 [first published in 1870].

16   Adolphe Pictet, *Les origines Indo-européennes, ou les Aryas primitives: Essai de paléontologie linguistique* (Paris: Joël Cherbuliez, 1859 and 1863).

17   Edwin F. Bryant and Laurie L. Patton, eds., *The Indo-Aryan Controversy: Evidence and Inference in Indian History* (Abingdon: Routledge, 2005).

18 Stephen G. Alter, *Darwinism and the Linguistic Image: Language, Race, and Natural Theology in the Nineteenth Century* (Baltimore: The Johns Hopkins University Press, 1999), 8.

19 Quoted in Alter, *Darwinism and the Linguistic Image*, 8.

20 Friedrich Schlegel, *Ueber die Sprache und Weisheit der Indier: Ein Beitrag zur Begründung der Alterthumskunde* (Heidelberg: Mohr und Zimmer, 1808).

21 Bill Ashcroft, "Language and Race," in Roxy Harris and Ben Rampton, eds., *The Language, Ethnicity and Race Reader* (London: Routledge, 2003), 42.

22 For the British perspective, which assigned a racial identity to the Aryans, see, for example, W. B. Winning, *A Manual of Comparative Philology, in Which the Affinity of the Indo-European Languages is Illustrated and Applied to the Primeval History of Europe, Italy, and Rome* (London: J. G. & F. Rivington, 1838).

23 Maurice Olender, *The Languages of Paradise: Race, Religion, and Philology in the Nineteenth Century*, trans. by Arthur Goldhammer (Cambridge, MA: Harvard University Press, 1992), 1–20.

24 August Schleicher, *Die Sprachen Europas in systematischer Übersicht* (Bonn: H. B. König, 1850). By mid-century, belief in the existence of a group of related "Indo-European" languages which derived from some unknown ancient ancestor of Sanskrit had become orthodoxy. Schleicher also produced definitive grammars of the "family-tree" of Indo-European languages. Amongst many other works which he also co-edited (with A. Kuhn), the journal *Beiträge zur vergleichenden Sprachforschung auf dem Gebiete der arischen, celtischen und slawischen Sprachen* (Berlin, 1858–1876).

25 Léon Poliakov, *The Aryan Myth: A History of Racist and Nationalistic Ideas in Europe*, trans. by Edmund Howard (New York: Basic Books, 1974), 190–2. German students of classical languages, like Müller himself, began to study Sanskrit as appointments and chairs in this field grew in number. Franz Bopp, whose lectures Müller attended at the University of Berlin, published a widely-translated *Comparative Grammar* in 1816.

26 Arie L. Molendijk, *Friedrich Max Muller and the Sacred Books of the East* (New York: Oxford University Press, 2016), 1.

27 His translations of the sacred texts found at Sacred Books of the East (SBE) complete series, at Internet Sacred Text Archive, found at http://www.sacred-texts.com and http://www.holybooks.com [accessed 17 November 2016].

28 Quoted in Martin Maw, *Visions of India: Fulfilment Theology, the Aryan Race Theory, and the Work of British Protestant Missionaries in Victorian India* (Frankfurt am Main: Peter Lang, 1990), 20.

29 See A. Leslie Willson, *A Mythical Image: The Ideal of India in German Romanticism* (Durham, NC: Duke University Press, 1964).

30 See Mircea Eliade, *India* (Bucharest: Cugetarea, 1934).

31 Maw, *Visions of India*, 30–1; see also Edwin Bryant, *The Quest for the Origins of Vedic Culture: The Indo-Aryan Migration Debate* (New York: Oxford University Press, 2001), 283–91.

32 Robert Cowan, *Indo-German Identification: Reconciling South Asian Origins and European Destinies, 1765–1885* (Rochester, NY: Camden House, 2010), 61–2.

33 F. Max Müller, *Biographies of Words and the Home of the Aryas* (London: Macmillan, 1887), 128–32.

34 Max Müller, *The Languages of the Seat of War in the East with a Survey of the Three Families of Language, Semitic, Arian, and Turanian*, 2nd. ed. (London: Williams and Norgate, 1855), 27–8. It is unclear when the first edition was published, but it was probably published earlier in the Crimean War (1853–1856), as Müller explains that one of his aims was to simplify rules of grammar in order to help conquering English soldiers acquire a foreign language easily.

35 Stefan Arvidsson, *Aryan Idols: Indo-European Mythology as Ideology and Science*, trans. by Sonia Wichmann (Chicago: The University of Chicago Press, 2006), 124–76.

36 Quoted in Dorothy Matilda Figueira, *Aryans, Jews, Brahmins: Theorizing Authority through Myths of Identity* (New York: State University of New York Press, 2002), 34.

37 Founded by the prophet Zarathustra, known to the Greeks as Zoroaster, Zoroastrianism was the dominant world religion during the Persian empires (559 BCE to 651 CE). Espousing a belief in a single supreme being or god and heaven and hell, Zoroastrianism flourished in the West during the late Roman Empire and had a major influence upon Christianity, as well as Judaism and Islam. The Avestan canon originally comprised 22 books on liturgy, history, medicine, and law, as well as commentaries. See Mary Boyce, *Zoroastrians: Their Religious Beliefs and Practices* (London: Routledge, 1979).

38 Müller first presented this thesis in 1851 in the *Edinburgh Review*. See Müller, *The Languages of the Seat of War in the East*, 27–8.

39 Bodleian Library, Oxford, Papers of Friedrich Max Müller (1823–1900), Oxford Lectures (1851–1892), MSS.Eng.C.2811, d.2353–5, in manuscript form, in 184 leaves; n. 1.1 [henceforth Papers of Friedrich Max Müller].

40 Papers of Friedrich Max Müller, n. 1.2.

41 This is also the argument put forward by the Austrian anthropologist Karl Penka [1847–1912] in his *Die Herkunft der Arier. Neue Beiträge zur historischen Anthropologie der europäischen Völker* (Vienna: K. Prochaska, 1886).

42 Papers of Friedrich Max Müller, n. 1.5; n. 1.6; n. iv.3

43 Quoted in Figueira, *Aryans, Jews, Brahmins*, 34.

44 Papers of Friedrich Max Müller, n.vi.4, in which he explicitly refers to the Indo-European Arian family as the progenitor of the national races of Europe.

45 The scriptural canon of Hinduism comprised a core of four main Vedas and over one hundred Upanishads. "Veda" (strictly "Ved" in the singular) is the Sanskrit word for truth or knowledge. Produced much later than the Vedas, the Upanishads were essential teachings written in prose and poetry rather than in hymns. See Müller "Lecture on the Vedas, or the Sacred Books of the

Brahmans," (1865) in *The Essential Max Müller: On Language, Mythology, and Religion*, ed. J. Stone (Basingstoke: Palgrave, 2002), 43–67.

46 David Frawley, *The Myth of the Aryan Invasion of India* (New Delhi: Voice of India, 1994), 6–24.

47 Marianne Keppens and Jakob de Roover, "Orientalism and the Puzzle of the Aryan Invasion Theory," *Journal of Human Sciences* 2, 2 (2014): 51–76.

48 Current scholarship does not support the existence of an Aryan invasion of India at any pre-historic time. By the 1980s, there was consensus that there was no archaeological evidence of any kind to support the notion of an Aryan invasion of India. The scientific foundations of the theory came crashing down when the work of population geneticists demonstrated that the people of India are not biologically divided into dark-skinned Southern Dravidians and light-skinned Northern Aryans. They are genetically one people. See Maw, *Visions of India*, 30–1; and Sumit Guhu, *Environment and Ethnicity in India, 1200–1991* (Cambridge: Cambridge University Press, 1999), ch. 1.

49 Figueira, *Aryans, Jews, Brahmins*, 161–2.

50 Quoted in Thomas F. Gossett, *Race: The History of an Idea in America*, new edition (New York: Oxford University Press, 1997), 124 [first published in 1963].

51 S. N. Balagangadhara, "The Future of the Present: Thinking Through Orientalism," *Cultural Dynamics* 10, 2 (1998): 101–21.

52 Joseph P. Widney, *Race Life of the Aryan Peoples*, vol. 1 (New York: Funk & Wagnalls, 1907), iii.

53 See the discussion in Jon Røyne Kyllingstad, *Measuring the Master Race: Physical Anthropology in Norway, 1890–1945* (Cambridge: Open Book Publishers, 2014).

54 Joseph B. Davis and John Thurnman, *Crania Britannica: Delineations and Descriptions of the Skulls of the Aboriginal and Early Inhabitants of the British Isles with Notices of their Remains* (London: Printed for the Subscribers, 1856–1865).

55 Gustaf Retzius and Carl M. Fürst, *Anthropologica Suecica. Beiträge zur Anthropologie der Schweden* (Stockholm: Aftonbladets Druckerei, 1902).

56 Gustaf Retzius, *The So-Called North European Race of Mankind* (London: Royal Anthropological Institute of Great Britain and Ireland, 1909), 277–8.

57 See, for example, one of the foundation texts of Romanian ethnogenesis, *Getica: O protoistorie a Daciei*, written by archaeologist Vasile Pârvan, and published in Bucharest in 1926 in which he argued for the Aryan ancestry of the Getae and the Dacians.

58 Kyllingstad, *Measuring the Master Race*, 54–5.

59 Alfred Fouillée, "Le caractère des races humaines et l'avenir de la race blanche," *Revue des Deux Mondes* 124, 4 (1894): 76–107.

60 Alfred Ploetz, *Grundlinien einer Rassen-Hygiene* (Berlin: S. Fischer, 1895), 5.

61 Karl Pearson, *National Life from the Standpoint of Science*, 2nd edn (London: Adam and Charles Black, 1905), 21 [first edition 1901].

62 G. Vacher de Lapouge, *L'Aryen. Son role social* (Paris: Albert Fontemoing, 1899). See also Sean Quinlan, "The Racial Imagery of Degeneration and Depopulation: Georges Vacher de Lapouge and 'Anthroposociology' in Fin-de-Siècle France," *History of European Ideas* 24, 6 (1998): 393–413.

63 For a recent discussion, see Thomas Etzemüller, *Auf der Suche nach dem Nordischen Menschen: Die deutsche Rassenanthropologie in der modernen Welt* (Bielefeld: Transcript Verlag, 2015).

64 For the purposes of comparison, see Dale T. Knobel, *America for the Americans: The Nativist Movements in the United States* (New York: Twayne Publishers, 1984).

65 Hans F. K. Günther, "The Nordic Race as 'Ideal Type,'" in George L. Mosse, ed., *Nazi Culture: Intellectual, Cultural and Social Life in the Third Reich* (London: W. H. Allen, 1966), 64–5.

66 Chamberlain, *Foundations*, vol. 1, note on p. 93, where he addresses the critics and affirms the existence of the Aryan race.

67 Chamberlain, *Foundations*, vol. 1, 253.

68 Alexandru C. Cuza, *Naţionalitatea în artă. Principii, fapte, concluzii* (Bucharest: Minerva, 1908), 33–5.

69 Cuza, *Naţionalitatea în artă*, 70 [emphasis in the original].

70 Cuza, *Naţionalitatea în artă*, 143 and 217.

71 See William Z. Ripley, *The Races of Europe: A Sociological Study* (London: Kegan Paul, 1900), 55–6.

72 Quoted in Ripley, *The Races of Europe*, 455.

73 Müller, *Biographies of Words*, 154.

74 See Nicholas Goodrick-Clarke, *Black Sun: Aryan Cults, Esoteric Nazism and the Politics of Identity* (New York: New York University Press, 2002).

75 Jane Clare Jones, "Anders Breivik's Chilling Anti-Feminism," *The Guardian* (27 July 2011). Available at https://www.theguardian.com/commentisfree/2011/jul/27/breivik-anti-feminism [accessed 21 October 2016] and "Anders Behring Breivik: The Indictment," *The Guardian* (16 April 2012). Available at https://www.theguardian.com/world/2012/apr/16/anders-behring-breivik-indictment [accessed 22 October 2016].

5 Science

1 John Hooper, "Petrarch – The Poet Who Lost His Head", *The Guardian*, 6 April 2004. Available at https://www.theguardian.com/world/2004/apr/06/research.italy [accessed 7 February 2016]. The story was widely reported in Europe, as well as in America, India, and Japan.

2 Bruce Johnston, "Putting a Face to Humanist Petrarch," *The Telegraph*, 2 November 2003. Available at http://www.telegraph.co.uk/news/worldnews/europe/italy/1445831/Putting-a-face-to-humanist-Petrarch.html [accessed 7 February 2016].

3   D. Caramelli et al., "Genetic Analysis of the Skeletal Remains Attributed to Francesco Petrarca," *Forensic Science International* 173, 1 (2007): 36–40.

4   Roberto Bianchin, "Quel Cranio non é di Petrarca Giallo sui Resti del Grande Poeta", *La Repubblica*, 5 April 2004. Available at http://ricerca.repubblica.it/repubblica/archivio/repubblica/2004/04/05/quel-cranio-non-di-petrarca-giallo-sui.html [accessed 25 July 2016].

5   What became of the brain is not stated. See G. Canestrini, *Le ossa di Francesco Petrarca: Studio antropologico* (Padua: Prosperini, 1874), 6.

6   Canestrini, *Le ossa di Francesco Petrarca*, 9.

7   Carlo Darwin, *Sull'origine delle specie per elezione naturale, ovvero conservazione delle razze perfezionate nella lotta per l'esistenza*, trans. G. Canestrini and L. Salimbeni (Modena: Nicola Zanichelli, 1864) was published with Darwin's approval.

8   Canestrini, *Le ossa di Francesco Petrarca*, 14–16.

9   Canestrini, *Le ossa di Francesco Petrarca*, 19.

10 Etruscans are an ancient, pre-Roman population from Etruria, in central Italy. The American racial theorist William Z. Ripley (1867–1941) believed them to be the "real founders of the Eternal City." See Ripley, *The Races of Europe*, 265.

11 Canestrini, *Le ossa di Francesco Petrarca*, 81–2.

12 A similar controversy surrounded Descartes' skull, currently held in the collections of the Musée de L'Homme in Paris. See Russell Shorto, *Descartes' Bones: A Skeletal History of the Conflict between Faith and Reason* (New York: Knopf Doubleday, 2008).

13 Canestrini, *Le ossa di Francesco Petrarca*, 54–7 and 77.

14 Bronwen Douglas, "Climate to Crania: Science and the Racialization of Human Difference," in Bronwen Douglas and Chris Ballard, eds., *Foreign Bodies: Oceania and the Science of Race 1750–1940* (Canberra: The Australian National University, 2008), 33–96.

15 See Christine Ferguson, *Determined Spirits: Eugenics, Heredity and Racial Regeneration in Anglo-American Spiritualist Writing, 1848–1930* (Edinburgh: Edinburgh University Press, 2012).

16 Britt Rusert, *Fugitive Science: Empiricism and Freedom in Early African American Culture* (New York: New York University Press, 2017), 126.

17 See Charles Colbert, *A Measure of Perfection: Phrenology and the Fine Arts in America* (Chapel Hill: The University of North Carolina Press, 1997).

18 See Stephen Tomlinson, *Head Masters. Phrenology, Secular Education, and Nineteenth-Century Social Thought* (Tuscaloosa: The University of Alabama Press, 2005).

19 See, for example, the article published by the Romanian Dimitrie Anănescu [1831–1885] "Despre originea sau rassele speciei umane," *Jurnal pentru răspândirea ştiinţelor naturale şi exacte în România* 5, 26 and 27 (1862): 201–5 and 209–12.

20   Bindman, *Ape to Apollo*, 190. See also Nicolaas Rupke and Gerhard Lauer, eds., *Johann Friedrich Blumenbach: Race and Natural History, 1750–1850* (Abingdon: Routledge, 2017).

21   Efram Sera-Shriar, "Race," in Mark Bevir, ed., *Historicism and the Human Sciences in Victorian Britain* (Cambridge: Cambridge University Press, 2017), 49.

22   In 1813, Prichard published *Researchers into the Physical History of Mankind*, initially in 2 volumes. By the time of its 4th edition in 1847 it reached 5 volumes.

23   Paul Stock, "'Almost a Separate Race': Racial Thought and the Idea of Europe in British Encyclopaedias and Histories, 1771–1830," *Modern Intellectual History* 8, 1 (2011): 12.

24   Hannah F. Augstein, *James Cowles Prichard's Anthropology: Remaking the Science of Man in Early Nineteenth-Century Britain* (Amsterdam: Rodopi, 1999).

25   For the French version of his 1842 article see Anders Retzius, "De la forme du crane des habitans du Nord," *Annales des sciences naturelles* 5 (1846): 133–72.

26   See Richard McMahon, *The Races of Europe Construction of National Identities in the Social Sciences, 1839–1939* (Basingstoke: Palgrave, 2016).

27   J. Lenhossék, *Az emberi koponyaisme. Cranioscopia* (Budapest: Magyar Tudományos Akadémia, 1875).

28   A. Török, "Adatok az Erdélyi románok koponyáinak jellemzéséhez," *Anthropologiai füzetek* 1 (1882): 50–66.

29   A. Török, *Grundzüge einer Systematischen Kraniometrie* (Stuttgart: Enke, 1890), 422.

30   Benoit Massin, "From Virchow to Fischer: Physical Anthropology and 'Modern Race Theories' in Wilhelmine Germany," in George W. Stocking, Jr., *Volksgeist as Method and Ethic: Essays on Boasian Ethnography and the German Anthropological Tradition* (Madison: The University of Wisconsin Press, 1996), 110.

31   See George W. Stocking, Jr., *Race, Culture, and Evolution: Essays in the History of Anthropology* (New York: Free Press, 1968).

32   See Francis Schiller, *Paul Broca: Founder of French Anthropology, Explorer of the Brain* (Berkeley: University of California Press, 1979).

33   See Alphonse Bertillon, *Identification anthropométrique. Instructions signalétiques*, new edition (Melun: Imprimerie Administrative, 1893).

34   See the discussion in Veronika Lipphardt, "Traditions and Innovations: Visualizations of Human Variation, c. 1900–38," *History of the Human Sciences* 28, 5 (2015): 49–79.

35   See J. Deniker, *The Races of Man: An Outline of Anthropology and Ethnography* (London: Walter Scott, 1900).

36   See Hans F. K. Günther, *Rassenkunde Europas*, 2nd. ed. (München: F. Lehnmans, 1926). See also Amos Morris-Reich, "Race, Ideas, and Ideals: A Comparison of Franz Boas and Hans F. K. Günther," *History of European Ideas* 32 (2006): 313–32.

37 For a description see Carlos C. Closson, "The Hierarchy of European Races," *The American Journal of Sociology* 3, 3 (1897): 314–27. For how ideas of racial classification were used in different institutional contexts, see Frederik Barth et al., *One Discipline, Four Ways: British, German, French, and American Anthropology* (Chicago: University of Chicago Press, 2005).

38 For the French case, see Carole Reynaud-Paligot, *La République Raciale: Paradigme Racial et Idéologie Républicaine, 1830–1930* (Paris: Presses Universitaires de France, 2006).

39 See Betsy L. Nies, *Eugenic Fantasies: Racial Ideology in the Literature and Popular Culture of the 1920's* (Abingdon: Routledge, 2002).

40 Laura Tabili, "Race and Ethnicity," in Michael Seler, ed., *The Fin-de-Siècle World* (Abingdon: Routledge, 2015), 522.

41 See Caroline Bressey, *Empire, Race and the Politics of Anti-Caste* (London: Bloomsbury, 2013).

42 José Martí, "Our America," in Aviva Chomsky et al., eds., *The Cuba Reader: History, Culture, Politics* (Durham, NC: Duke University Press, 2003), 127.

43 For a recent appraisal of Boas's work see Regna Darnell et al., eds., *The Franz Boas Papers, Vol. 1: Franz Boas as Public Intellectual—Theory, Ethnography, Activism* (Lincoln: University of Nebraska Press, 2015).

44 See Franz Boas, *Changes in Bodily Form of Descendants of Immigrants* (Washington: U.S. Government Printing Office, 1910), 5. See also his "The History of the American Race," *Annals of the New York Academy of Sciences* 21 (1912): 177–83 and his *Race, Language and Culture* (New York: The Macmillan Company, 1940), 60–75.

45 Clarence C. Gravlee et al., "Heredity, Environment, and Cranial Form: A Reanalysis of Boas's Immigrant Data," *American Anthropologist* 105, 1 (2003): 125–38.

46 John S. Allen, "Franz Boas's Physical Anthropology: The Critique of Racial Formalism Revisited," *Current Anthropology* 30, 1 (1989): 79–84.

47 Vernon J. Williams, *Rethinking Race: Franz Boas and His Contemporaries* (Lexington: University of Kentucky Press, 1996), 4–6.

48 J. Huxley and A. C. Haddon, *We Europeans: A Survey of 'Racial' Problems* (London: Jonathan Cape, 1935), 91. See also Elazar Barkan, *The Retreat of Scientific Racism*, 296–302 and Gavin Schaffer, *Racial Science and British Society, 1930–1962* (Basingstoke: Palgrave, 2008), 32–9.

49 See Karel Weigner, ed., *Die Gleichwertigkeit der europäischen Rassen und die Wege zu ihrer Vervollkommnung* (Prague: Tschechische Akademie der Wissenschaften, 1935).

50 See Ygrec (Iosif Glicsman), *Rasa și rasismul cea mai mare escrocherie științifică a secolului* (Bucharest: Ed. Adam, 1935).

51 Ruth Benedict, *Patterns of Culture* (Boston: Houghton Mifflin, 1934) and idem, *Race: Science and Politics* (New York: Modern Age Books, 1940).

52 See Ashley Montagu, *Man's Most Dangerous Myth: The Fallacy of Race* (New York: Columbia University Press, 1942). He also strove to combat prejudice

based on gender stereotypes in his *The Natural Superiority of Women* (New York: Macmillan, 1953).

53 Theodosius Dobzhansky, "The Race Concept in Biology," *The Scientific Monthly* 52, 2 (1941): 161.

54 Schaffer, *Racial Science and British Society*, 132–47.

55 For this argument, see L. Luca Cavalli-Sforza et al., *The History and Geography of Human Genes* (Princeton: Princeton University Press, 1994).

56 R. C. Lewontin, "The Apportionment of Human Diversity," in T. Dobzhansky et al., eds., *Evolutionary Biology*, vol. 6 (New York: Plenum Press, 1972), 381–98; see the critique by A. W. F. Edwards, "Human Genetic Diversity: Lewontin's Fallacy," *BioEssays* 25 (2003) 798–801. The alleged 'fallacy' refers to Lewontin's claim that racial classification is "of virtually no genetic or taxonomic significance." Edwards agrees with Lewontin's belief that racial classification is "of no social value and is positively destructive of social and human relations," but disputes the contention that it has no taxonomical relevance.

57 See R. C. Lewontin, *Biology as Ideology: The Doctrine of DNA* (New York: Anansi Press, 1991); and idem, *The Triple Helix: Gene, Organism, and Environment* (Cambridge, MA: Harvard University Press, 2000).

58 See, for example, Nicolas Lahovary, *Les peuples européens. Leur passé ethnologique et leurs parentés réciproques d'après les dernières recherches sanguines et anthropologiques* (Neuchatel: Editions de la Baconnière, 1946).

59 Ilse Schwidetzky, ed., *Die neue Rassenkunde* (Stuttgart: Gustav Fischer Verlag, 1962).

60 O. Necrasov and P. Boev collaborated closely during the 1960s, as documented by their long correspondence. Arhiva Olga Necrasov. Laboratorul de Anatomie și Bioarheologie, Facultatea de Biologie, Universitatea "Alexandru Ioan Cuza" Iași. Marius Turda would like to thank Professor Luminița Bejenaru and Dr Angela Simalcsik for their assistance with this material.

61 Francine Hirsch, *Empires of Nations: Ethnographic Knowledge and the Making of the Soviet Union* (Ithaca, NY: Cornell University Press, 2005), 7.

62 Lydia T. Black, "The Concept of Race in Soviet Anthropology," *Studies in Soviet Thought* 17, 1 (1977): 1–27.

63 Katarzyna A. Kaszycka et al., "Current Views of European Anthropologists on Race: Influence of Educational and Ideological Background," *American Anthropologist* 111, 1 (2009): 50.

64 S. Foltiny and F. Ivaniček, "Bulgaria, Czechoslovakia, Hungary, Poland, Roumania. An Anthropological Review for 1952–1954," *Yearbook of Anthropology* 1 (1955): 678.

65 In East-Central Europe, social and cultural anthropology was subsumed to ethnology. See Bozo Skerlj, "Yugoslavia: An Anthropological Review for 1952–1954," *Yearbook of Anthropology* 1 (1955): 651–70.

66 Milan Dokládal and Josef Brožek, "Physical Anthropology in Czechoslovakia: Recent Developments," *Current Anthropology* 2, 5 (1961): 455.

67 W. W. Howells, *Skull Shapes and the Map: Craniometric Analyses in the Dispersion of Modern Homo* (Cambridge, MA: Harvard University Press, 1989).

68 M. Pietrusewsky, *Metric and Non-Metric Cranial Variation in Australian Aboriginal Populations, Compared with Populations from the Pacific and Asia* (Canberra: Australian Institute of Aboriginal Studies, 1984).

69 Raghavan Pathmanathan, et al., "Indian Craniometric Variability and Affinities," *International Journal of Evolutionary Biology* (2013): 1–25.

70 See Lauren Kallenberger and Varsha Pilbrow, "Using CRANID to Test the Population Affinity of Known Crania," *Journal of Anatomy* 221, 5 (2012): 459–64.

71 R. Wright, *Guide to Using the CRANID Programs CR6LDA.EXE and CR6NN.EXE* (2007), 4. Maria Sophia Quine would like to thank Rob Kruszynski, Vertebrate Curator, the Department of Palaeontology, The Natural History Museum, London, for sending her an electronic version of the CRANID 6 Manual.

72 Three kinds of calliper (a sliding, spreading, and coordinate type) are now commonly used to obtain cranial measurements. These instruments can be the relatively costly anthropometric devices used in forensic science; but the researcher can also improvise with plastic callipers and rulers readily available in hardware stores. Plastic sliding callipers become blunt with wear, so they must be replaced frequently. Measurements become awkward or difficult when only bone fragments are available. Precision is highly important, so the risk of human error must be kept as low as possible. Obviously, the accuracy, consistency, and comparability of results depend upon the skill of the measurer. Even the most serious and methodical scientist can make mistakes in taking and recording numerical data, however, as Stephen Jay Gould so famously discovered, when he painstakingly reconstructed Samuel Morton's experiments. See his *The Mismeasure of Man*, 97–101.

73 D. H. Ubelaker et al., "Application of Forensic Discriminant Functions to a Spanish Cranial Sample," *Forensic Science Communications* 4, 3 (2002): 1–6.

74 Frank L'Engle Williams et al., "Forensic Misclassification of Ancient Nubian Crania: Implications for Assumptions about Human Variation," *Current Anthropology* 46, 2 (2005): 341.

75 Wright, *Guide to Using the* CRANID *Programs*, 27.

76 Williams et al., "Forensic Misclassification of Ancient Nubian Crania," 345.

77 For a discussion of this collection, see Quine, "Making Italians: Aryanism and Anthropology in Italy during the *Risorgimento*," 127–52.

78 Katalin Wolff et al., "Anthropological Examination of the Chronologically Separated Groups of the 11th–13th Century Zalavár-Chapel (Zalavár-Kápolna) Cemetery from Hungary," *Anthropological Anzeiger* 69, 4 (2012): 473–90.

79 Wright, *Guide to Using the CRANID programs*, 29.

80 See Giuseppe Sergi, *The Mediterranean Race: A Study of the Origins of European Peoples* (London: Walter Scott, 1901).

81 Royal College of Surgeons of England, Hunterian Museum, section C on "Ancient Italian Skulls" in 275.h.6 (10), J. B. Davis, *Catalogue of a Collection of Modern and Ancient Greek and Italian Sculls, The Property of Giustiniano Nicolucci in Isola di Lora (Naples, Italy)* and 275.h.6 (11), G. Nicolucci, *Catalogo di una collezione di crani Greci ed Italiani, antichi e moderni, posseduta da Giustiniano Nicolucci, in Isola di Sora, (Napoli)*; skulls 12–51 of his collection were identified as "ancient Italian ones."

82 The only notation which he makes as to the origins of any of the "modern"' skulls pertains to number 159, which Nicolucci says is from a sixteenth-century tomb.

83 Royal College of Surgeons of England, Hunterian Museum, Museum Letter Book, Series 2 (1868–1906), serial no. 5949, letter of 18 January 1870 from Davis to Flower.

84 Rob Kruszinski at the Natural History Museum kindly shared his ideas about the usefulness of the new craniometry with Maria Sophia Quine, but refused to answer challenging questions about it or his procedures in compiling the data which comprises the Nicolucci sample base within CRANID.

85 Wright, *Guide to Using the Cranid Programs*, note 18 on p. 27, in which he simply states that his critics are wrong and that "numerous studies" prove him right, but he fails to mention a single one.

86 George J. Armelagos and Dennis P. van Gerven, "A Century of Skeletal Biology and Paleopathology: Contrasts, Contradictions, and Conflicts," *American Anthropologist* 105, 1 (2003): 53.

87 Claude Lévi-Strauss, "Claude Lévi-Strauss Reconsiders: From Rousseau to Burke," Interview with Jean-Marie Benoist, *Encounter* 53 (1979): 19–26.

Conclusion

1 Widney, *Race Life of the Aryan Peoples*, vol. 1, iii.

2 Quoted from Donald Trump's Inauguration Speech. Available at https://www. theguardian.com/world/2017/jan/20/donald-trump-inauguration-speech-full-text [accessed 21 January 2017].

3 For the connection between radical-conservative movements in Russia and Western Europe, see Mark Bassin, "Lev Gumilev and the European New Right," *Nationalities Papers* 43, 6 (2015): 840–65.

4 Lucian Tudor, "The Philosophy of Identity: Ethnicity, Culture, and Race in Identitarian Thought," *The Occidental Quarterly* 14, 3 (2014): 85.

5 Tudor, "The Philosophy of Identity," 85.

6 Tomislav Sunic, *Against Democracy and Equality: The European New Right* (New York: Peter Lang, 1990); Alain de Benoist, "What is Racism"? trans. by Francis Greene, *Telos* 114 (1999): 11–48 and Michael O'Meara, *New Culture, New Right: Anti-Liberalism in Postmodern Europe* (Bloomington, IN: 1stBooks, 2004).

7   Quoted in Kate Connolly, "After the US, far right says 2017 will be the year Europe wakes up," *The Guardian*, 21 January 2007. Available at https://www.theguardian.com/world/2017/jan/21/koblenz-far-right-european-political-leaders-meeting-brexit-donald-trump [accessed 22 January 2017].

8   Quoted in Atika Shubert, "Europe's Far-Right Leaders Speak on Trump at Conference," *CNN Politics*, 21 January 2007. Available at http://edition.cnn.com/2017/01/21/politics/europe-far-right-conference/index.html [accessed 22 January 2017].

9   At the Dutch general elections held in March 2017 Geert Wilders' party lost to Mark Rutte's People's Party for Freedom and Democracy. In the second round of the French presidential elections held in May 2017 Marine Le Pen received 33.94%, losing to the current president, Emmanuel Macron, who won 66.06% of the votes.

10 According to data released by the Community Security Trust, which monitors anti-Semitism in the UK, 1,309 incidents of anti-Jewish hate occurred in 2016, compared with 960 in 2015; in total a rise of 36%. See Harriet Sherwood, "Reports of Antisemitic Incidents Increase to Record Levels in the UK," *The Guardian*, 2 February 2017. Available at https://www.theguardian.com/world/2017/feb/02/reports-of-antisemitic-incidents-increase-to-record-levels-in-uk [accessed 2 February 2017].

11 See Akwasi Owusu-Bempah, "Race and Policing in Historical Context: Dehumanization and the Policing of Black People in the 21st Century," *Theoretical Criminology* 20, 4 (2016): 1–12.

12 See the discussions and statements associated with the movement in Christopher J. Lebron, *The Making of Black Lives Matter: A Brief History of An Idea* (New York: Oxford University Press, 2017).

13 "Racial Profiling: Definition." Available at https://www.aclu.org/other/racial-profiling-definition?redirect=racial-profiling-definition [accessed 2 July 2016].

14 See Bryan Fanning, *Racism and Social Change in the Republic of Ireland* (Manchester: Manchester University Press, 2002) and Anthony W. Marx, *Making Race and Nation: A Comparison of the United States, South Africa, and Brazil* (New York: Cambridge University Press, 1998).

15 Michael Ignatieff, *Blood and Belonging: Journeys into the New Nationalism* (New York: Farrar, Straus, and Giroux, 1993), 4.

16 UNESCO, *Roadmap: The Rapprochement of Cultures* (2016), 5. Available at http://unesdoc.unesco.org/images/0024/002443/244334e.pdf [accessed 9 November 2016].

17 Walter R. Duncan and G. Paul Holman, Jr., eds., *Ethnic Nationalism and Regional Conflict: The Former Soviet Union and Yugoslavia* (Boulder, CO: Westview Press, 1994).

18 "Address by ICTY President Theodor Meron, at Potocari Memorial Cemetery," The Hague, 23 June 2004. Available at http://www.icty.org/; and see the organization's 'Documents' section on the same website [accessed 26 October 2016].

19 See Eric D. Weitz, *A Century of Genocide: Utopias of Race and Nation*, with a new preface by the author (Princeton: Princeton University Press, 2015) [first published 2003].

20 Thomas C. Holt, *The Problem of Race in the Twenty-First Century* (Cambridge, MA: Harvard University Press, 2000), 5.

21 M'Charek, "Beyond Fact or Fiction," 424.

22 Michael Kenny and Nick Pearce, "The Empire Strikes Back," *The New Statesman*, 24 January 2017. Available at http://www.newstatesman.com/politics/uk/2017/01/empire-strikes-back [accessed 25 January 2017].

23 Manuel Valls, "In France, Women are Free", *The Huffington Post*, 6 September 2016. Available at http://www.huffingtonpost.com/manuel-valls/in-france-women-are-free_b_11867242.html [accessed 9 November 2016].

24 See Crystal Marie Fleming, *Resurrecting Slavery: Racial Legacies and White Supremacy in France* (Philadelphia: Temple University Press, 2017).

25 Ben Collins, "Alt-Right Declares Total Victory: 'We're the Establishment Now'," *The Daily Beast*. Available at http://www.thedailybeast.com, posted on 9 November 2016 [accessed 9 November 2016].

26 Aryn Baker, "Between the Devil and the Deep Blue Sea", *Time*, 12–19 September 2016. Available at http://www.magzter.com/article/News/Time/Between-the-Devil-and-the-Deep-Blue-Sea [accessed 15 November 2016].

27 Dan Merica, "Trump signs executive order to keep out 'radical Islamic terrorists'," *CNN Politics* (29 January 2017). Available at http://edition.cnn.com/2017/01/27/politics/trump-plans-to-sign-executive-action-on-refugees-extreme-vetting [accessed 30 January 2017].

28 Brattain, "Race, Racism, and Anti-Racism," 1413.

29 See Frank Dikötter, *The Discourse of Race in Modern China*, fully revised and expanded second edition (Oxford: Oxford University Press, 2015) [first published in 1992]; idem, ed., *The Construction of Racial Identities in China and Japan* (London: Hurst, 1997); and Edward E. Telles, *Race in Another America: The Significance of Skin Color in Brazil* (Princeton: Princeton University Press, 2006).

30 Michael Banton, *What We Know about Race and Ethnicity* (New York: Berghahn, 2015), 3.

31 Snait B. Gissis, "When is 'Race" a Race? 1946–2003," *Studies in History and Philosophy of Science* 29, 4 (2008): 437–50.

32 Katharina Schramm et al., eds., *Identity Politics and the New Genetics: Re/Creating Categories of Difference and Belonging* (New York: Berghahn, 2012).

33 Cressida Fforde et al., eds., *The Dead and their Possessions: Repatriation in Principle, Policy, and Practice* (London: Routledge, 2002).

34 Department of Culture, Media, and Sport, *The Report of the Working Group on Human Remains* (Published 14 November 2003), 14 and 164. Available at http://webarchive.nationalarchives.gov.uk/+/http:/www.culture.gov.uk/reference_library/publications/4553.aspx [accessed 2 November 2016].

35   Quoted in Douglas Cole, *Captured Heritage: The Scramble for Northwest Coast Artefacts* (Vancouver: University of British Columbia, 1995), 308 [first published 1985].

36   See Ricardo Roque, *Headhunting and Colonialism: Anthropology and the Circulation of Human Skulls in the Portuguese Empire, 1870–1930* (Basingstoke: Palgrave, 2010).

37   Claire Wintle, "Decolonizing the Smithsonian: Museums as Microcosms of Political Encounter," *The American Historical Review* 121, 5 (2016): 1492–1520.

38   Tony Platt, "Bitter Legacies: A War of Extermination, Grave Looting, and Culture Wars in the American West," in Élisabeth Anstett and Jean-Marc Dreyfus, eds., *Human Remains and Identification: Mass Violence, Genocide, and the 'Forensic Turn'* (Manchester: Manchester University Press, 2015), 14–33.

39   Cornelia Dean, "James Watson Retires after Racial Remarks," *The New York Times*, 25 October 2007. Available at http://www.nytimes.com/2007/10/25/science/25cnd-watson.html [accessed 2 January 2017].

40   Alexander G. Weheliye, *Habeas Viscus: Racializing Assemblages, Biopolitics, and Black Feminist Theories of the Human* (Durham, NC: Duke University Press, 2014), 4.

41   Gould, *The Mismeasure of Man*, 28–9.

BIBLIOGRAPHY

Archives

Hunterian Museum, Royal College of Surgeons of England, London
Section C on "Ancient Italian Skulls".
275.h.6 (10), J. B. Davis, *Catalogue of a Collection of Modern and Ancient Greek and Italian Sculls, The Property of Giustiniano Nicolucci in Isola di Lora (Naples, Italy)*.
275.h.6 (11), G. Nicolucci, *Catalogo di una collezione di crani Greci ed Italiani, antichi e moderni, posseduta da Giustiniano Nicolucci, in Isola di Sora, (Napoli)*.
Museum Letter Book, Series 2 (1868–1906), serial no. 5949, letter of 18 January 1870 from Davis to Flower.
Bodleian Library, Oxford.
Papers of Friedrich Max Müller (1823–1900), Oxford Lectures (1851–1892), MSS.Eng.C.2811, d.2353–5, in manuscript form, in 184 leaves; n. 1.1; 1.2; n. 1.5; n. 1.6; n. iv.3; n.vi.4.
Arhiva Olga Necrasov, Laboratorul de Anatomie și Bioarheologie, Facultatea de Biologie, Universitatea "Alexandru Ioan Cuza" Iași, Romania.

Online sources

"Address by ICTY President Theodor Meron, at Potocari Memorial Cemetery," The Hague, 23 June 2004. Available at http://www.icty.org/; and see the organization's 'Documents' section on the same website [accessed 26 October 2016].
"Anders Behring Breivik: The Indictment," *The Guardian* (16 April 2012). Available at https://www.theguardian.com/world/2012/apr/16/anders-behring-breivik-indictment [accessed 22 October 2016].
Baker, A. "Between the Devil and the Deep Blue Sea", *Time*, 12–19 September 2016. Available at http://www.magzter.com/article/News/Time/Between-the-Devil-and-the-Deep-Blue-Sea [accessed 15 November 2016].
Bianchin, R. "Quel Cranio non é di Petrarca Giallo sui Resti del Grande Poeta", *La Repubblica*, 5 April 2004. Available at http://ricerca.repubblica.it/repubblica/archivio/repubblica/2004/04/05/quel-cranio-non-di-petrarca-giallo-sui.html [accessed 25 July 2016].
Collins, B. "Alt-Right Declares Total Victory: 'We're the Establishment Now'," *The Daily Beast*; available at http://www.thedailybeast.com, posted on 9 November 2016 [accessed 9 November 2016].

Connolly, K. "After the US, far right says 2017 will be the year Europe wakes up," *The Guardian*, 21 January 2007. Available at https://www.theguardian.com/world/2017/jan/21/koblenz-far-right-european-political-leaders-meeting-brexit-donald-trump [accessed 22 January 2017].

Dean, C. "James Watson Retires after Racial Remarks," *The New York Times*, 25 October 2007. Available at http://www.nytimes.com/2007/10/25/science/25cnd-watson.html [accessed 2 January 2017].

Department of Culture, Media, and Sport, *The Report of the Working Group on Human Remains* (Published 14 November 2003). Available at http://webarchive.nationalarchives.gov.uk/+/http:/www.culture.gov.uk/reference_library/publications/4553.aspx [accessed 2 November 2016].

Donald Trump's Inauguration Speech. Available at https://www.theguardian.com/world/2017/jan/20/donald-trump-inauguration-speech-full-text [accessed 21 January 2017].

Hooper, J. "Petrarch – The Poet Who Lost His Head", *The Guardian*, 6 April 2004. Available at https://www.theguardian.com/world/2004/apr/06/research.italy [accessed 7 February 2016].

Johnston, B. "Putting a Face to Humanist Petrarch," *The Telegraph*, 2 November 2003. Available at http://www.telegraph.co.uk/news/worldnews/europe/italy/1445831/Putting-a-face-to-humanist-Petrarch.html [accessed 7 February 2016].

Jones, J. C. "Anders Breivik's Chilling Anti-Feminism," *The Guardian* (27 July 2011). Available at https://www.theguardian.com/commentisfree/2011/jul/27/breivik-anti-feminism [accessed 21 October 2016].

Kenny, M. and Pearce, N. "The Empire Strikes Back," *The New Statesman*, 24 January 2017. Available at http://www.newstatesman.com/politics/uk/2017/01/empire-strikes-back [accessed 25 January 2017].

Merica, D. "Trump signs executive order to keep out 'radical Islamic terrorists'," *CNN Politics*, 29 January 2017. Available at http://edition.cnn.com/2017/01/27/politics/trump-plans-to-sign-executive-action-on-refugees-extreme-vetting [accessed 30 January 2017].

"President Obama's Farewell Address," Chicago, 10 January 2017. Available at https://www.nytimes.com/2017/01/10/us/politics/obama-farewell-address-speech.html?_r=0 [accessed 11 January 2017].

"Racial Profiling: Definition." Available at https://www.aclu.org/other/racial-profiling-definition?redirect=racial-profiling-definition [accessed 2 July 2016].

Sacred Books of the East (SBE) complete series, Internet Sacred Text Archive. Available at http://www.sacred-texts.com and http://www.holybooks.com [accessed 17 November 2016].

Sherwood, H. "Reports of antisemitic incidents increase to record levels in the UK," *The Guardian*, 2 February 2017. Available at https://www.theguardian.com/world/2017/feb/02/reports-of-antisemitic-incidents-increase-to-record-levels-in-uk [accessed 2 February 2017].

Shubert, A. "Europe's far-right leaders speak on trump at conference," *CNN Politics*, 21 January 2007. Available at http://edition.cnn.com/2017/01/21/politics/europe-far-right-conference/index.html [accessed 22 January 2017].

Smith, C. S. "Poor and Muslim? Jewish? Soup Kitchen is not for you," *The New York Times*, 28 February 2006. Available at http://www.nytimes.com/2006/02/28/world/europe/poor-and-muslim-jewish-soup-kitchen-is-not-for-you.html [accessed 24 January 2016].

The Casey Review. Available at https://www.gov.uk/government/publications/the-casey-review-a-review-into-opportunity-and-integration [accessed 5 December 2016].

Traynor, I. "Migration crisis: Hungary PM says Europe in grip of madness," *The Guardian*, 3 September 2015. Available at https://www.theguardian.com/world/2015/sep/03/migration-crisis-hungary-pm-victor-orban-europe-response-madness [accessed 22 January 2016].

TV programme "Things We Won't Say about Race are True," 15 March 2015, British Channel 4. Available athttp://www.channel4.com/programmes/things-we-wont-say-about-race-that-are-true [accessed 22 December 2016].

TV programme Newsnight with Emily Maitlis on 9 January 2017, BBC 2. Available at http://www.bbc.co.uk/iplayer/episode/b088k00m/newsnight–09012017

UNESCO, *Roadmap: The Rapprochement of Cultures* (2016). Available at http://unesdoc.unesco.org/images/0024/002443/244334e.pdf, [accessed 9 November 2016].

Valls, M. "In France, Women are Free", *The Huffington Post*, 6 September 2016. Available at http://www.huffingtonpost.com/manuel-valls/in-france-women-are-free_b_11867242.html [accessed 9 November 2016].

Primary sources

Acton, *Essays on Freedom and Power* (Boston: The Beacon Press, 1949).

Anănescu, D. "Despre originea sau rassele speciei umane," *Jurnal pentru răspândirea ştiinţelor naturale şi exacte în România* 5, 26 and 27 (1862): 201–5 and 209–12.

Angel, J. L. "A Racial Analysis of the Ancient Greeks," *American Journal of Physical Anthropology* 2, 4 (1944): 329–76.

Angel, J. L. "Social Biology of Greek Culture Growth," *American Anthropologist* 48, 4 (1946): 493–533.

Barzun, J. *The French Race* (New York: Columbia University Press, 1932).

Benedict, R. *Race: Science and Politics* (New York: Modern Age Books, 1940).

Benedict, R. *Patterns of Culture* (Boston: Houghton Mifflin, 1934)

Benoist, A. de "What is Racism"? trans. by Francis Greene, *Telos* 114 (1999): 11–48.

Beöthy, Z. *A magyar irodalom kis-tükre* (Budapest: Athenaeum, 1896).

Bertillon, A. *Identification anthropométrique. Instructions signalétiques*, new edition (Melun: Imprimerie Administrative, 1893).

Blache, P. V. de la. *Principes de géographie humaine* (Paris: Librairie Armand Colin, 1922).

Boas, F. *Race, Language and Culture* (New York: The Macmillan Company, 1940).

Boas, F. "The History of the American Race," *Annals of the New York Academy of Sciences* 21 (1912): 177–83.

Boas, F. *Changes in Bodily Form of Descendants of Immigrants* (Washington: U.S. Government Printing Office, 1910).

Boev, P. "Anthropological Data on the Ethnogenesis of the Ancient Thracians," *Mankind Quarterly* 16 (1975): 68–73.

Boev, P. *Die Rassentypen der Balkanhalbinsel und der Ostägäischen Inselvelt und deren Bedeutung für die Herkunft ihrer Bevölkerung* (Sofia: Verlag der Bulgarischen Akademie der Wissenschaften, 1972).

Bovio, G. *Il diritto pubblico e le razze umane* (Naples: A. Morano, 1887).

Buricescu, I. F. "Rasa şi sufletul românesc," *Revista de Filosofie* 26, 1–2 (1941): 56–84.

Canestrini, G. *Le ossa di Francesco Petrarca: Studio antropologico* (Padua: Prosperini, 1874).

Chamberlain, H. S. *Foundations of the Nineteenth Century*, vol. I, trans. by John Lees (London: John Lane, 1910)

Chamberlain, H. S. *The Wagnerian Drama: An Attempt to Inspire a Better Appreciation of Wagner as a Dramatic Poet* (London: John Lane, 1923), trans. by John Lees [first published in German in 1892].

Childe, V. G. *The Aryans: A Study of Indo-European Origins* (London: Kegan Paul, 1926).

Closson, C. C. "The Hierarchy of European Races," *American Journal of Sociology* 3, 3 (1897): 314–27.

Courtet (de l'Isle), V. *Tableau ethnographique du genre humain* (Paris: Arthus Bertrand, 1849).

Crainic, N. "Rasă şi religiune," *Gândirea* 14, 2 (1933): 57–66.

Croce, B. *Teoria e storia della storiografia*, 2nd rev. edn (Bari: G. Laterza, 1920).

Cuza, A. C. *Naţionalitatea în artă. Principii, fapte, concluzii* (Bucharest: Minerva, 1908).

Cvijić, J. *Remarks on the Ethnography of the Macedonian Slavs* (London: Horace Cox, 1906).

Cvijić, J. *La Péninsule Balkanique. Géographie humaine* (Paris: Armand Colin, 1918).

Darwin, C. *The Descent of Man and Selection in Relation to Sex*, 2 vols. (London: John Murray, 1871).

Darwin, C. *Sull'origine delle specie per elezione naturale, ovvero conservazione delle razze perfezionate nella lotta per l'esistenza*, trans. by G. Canestrini and L. Salimbeni (Modena: Nicola Zanichelli, 1864).

Davis, J. B. and Thurnman, J. *Crania Britannica: Delineations and Descriptions of the Skulls of the Aboriginal and Early Inhabitants of the British Isles with Notices of their Remains* (London: Printed for the Subscribers, 1856–1865).

Deniker, J. *The Races of Man: An Outline of Anthropology and Ethnography* (London: Walter Scott, 1900).

Densuşianu, N. *Dacia preistorică* (Bucharest: Inst. de Arte Grafice 'Carol Göbl', 1913).

Dictionary of Races or Peoples. Reports of the Immigration Commission (Washington: Government Printing Office, 1911).

Dilke, C. W. *Greater Britain: A Record of Travel in English-speaking Countries during 1866–7* (London: Macmillan, 1869).

Din scrierile şi cuvântarile lui Ion C. Brătianu, 1821–1891 (Bucharest: Inst. de Arte Grafice 'Carol Göbl', 1903).

Disraeli, B. *Tancred: or, the New Crusade*, vol. 1 (New York: Walter Dunne, 1904).

Disraeli, B. [Earl of Beaconsfield] *Lothair* (London: Longmans, 1901) [first published in 1870].

Dobzhansky, T. "The Race Concept in Biology," *The Scientific Monthly* 52, 2 (1941): 161–5.

Dragoumis, I. *Ελληνικός πολιτισμός* (Alexandria: Grammata, 1914).

Dragoumis, I. *Ο Ελληνσμός μου και οι Έλληνες* (Athens: Estia, 1927).

Du Bois, W. E. B. "The Conservation of Races" (1897), in W. E. B du Bois, *On Sociology and the Black Community*, eds. Dan S. Green and Edwin D. Driver (Chicago: University of Chicago Press, 1978), 238–49.

Eliade, M. *Myths, Dreams and Mysteries* (London: Collins, 1968).

Eliade, M. *Myth and Reality*, trans. Willard R. Trask (New York: Harper Torchbooks, 1963).

Eliade, M. *India* (Bucharest: Cugetarea, 1934).

Elsenhans, T. *Kants Rassentheorie und ihre bleibende Bedeutung* (Leipzig: Verlag von Wilhelm Engelmann, 1904).

Fallmerayer, J. P. *Welchen Einfluss hatte die Besetzung Griechelands durch die Slaven auf das Schicksal der Stadt Athen und der Landschaft Attika?* (Stuttgart: J. G. Cotta'che Buchhandlung, 1835).

Fanon, F. *Black Skins, White Masks*, trans. by Richard Philcox (New York: Grove Press, 2008) [first published in French in 1952].

Febvre, L. "Zur Entwiklung des Wortes und der Vorstellung von 'Civilisation,'" (1930), in Lucien Febvre, *Das Gewissen des Historikers*, ed. Ulrich Raulff (Berlin: Wagenbach, 1988), 39–79.

Fichte, J. G. *Addresses to the German Nation*, translated by R. F. Jones and G. H. Turnbull (Chicago: Open Court Publishing, 1922).

Fouillée, A. "Le caractère des races humaines et l'avenir de la race blanche," *Revue des Deux Mondes* 124, 4 (1894): 76–107.

Frazer, J. G. *The Golden Bough. The Roots of Religion and Folklore* (New York: Avenel Books, 1981).

Freeman, E. A. *Historical Essays* (London: Macmillan, 1879).

Frobenius, L. *Histoire de la civlisation africaine* (Paris: Gallimard, 1936).

Four Statements on the Race Question (Paris: UNESCO, 1969).

Gobineau, A. de. *The Inequality of Human Races* (New York: Howard Fertig, 1999).

Gobineau, A. de. *Deux études sur la Grèce moderne: Capodistrias. Le Royaume des Hellènes* (Paris: Librairie Plon, 1905).

Gobineau, A. de. *The Moral and Intellectual Diversity of Races, with Particular Reference to their Respective Influence in the Civil and Political History of Mankind* (Philadelphia: J. B. Lippincott, 1856).

Günther, H. F. K. "The Nordic Race as 'Ideal Type'," in George L. Mosse, ed., *Nazi Culture: Intellectual, Cultural and Social Life in the Third Reich* (London: W. H. Allen, 1966), 61–5.

Günther, H. F. K. *Rassenkunde Europas*, 2nd edn (München: F. Lehnmans, 1926).

Hankins, F. H. *The Racial Basis of Civilization. A Critique of the Nordic Doctrine* (New York: Alfred A. Knopf, 1926).

Harmand, J. *Domination et colonisation* (Paris: Ernest Flammarion, 1910).

Hayes, C. J. H. *Essays on Nationalism* (New York: Macmillan, 1926).

Hegel's Philosophy of Right, translated with notes by T. M. Knox (Oxford: Clarendon Press, 1942).

Herder, J. G. *Another Philosophy of History and Selected Political Writings*, trans. with introd. and notes by Ioannis D. Evrigenis and Daniel Pellerin (Indianapolis, IN: Hackett Publishing, 2004).

Herder on Social and Political Culture, selected, trans. and ed. F. M Barnard (Cambridge: Cambridge University Press, 1969).

Herodotus, *The Histories*, trans. and intro. by Aubrey de Selincourt (Harmondsworth: Penguin Classics, 1954).

Hobson, J. A. *Imperialism: A Study* (London: James Nisbet, 1902).

Hume, D. *Selected Essays* (Oxford: Oxford University Press, 1996).

Huxley, J. and Haddon, A. C. *We Europeans: A Survey of 'Racial' Problems* (London: Jonathan Cape, 1935).

Kant, I. "Of the Different Human Races," trans. by Jon Mark Mikkelsen, in Robert Bernasconi and Tommy L. Lott, eds., *The Idea of Race* (Indianapolis, IN: Hackett, 2000), 8–22.

Kant's Critique of Judgement, trans. with introd. and notes by J. H Bernard, 2nd edn revised (London: Macmillan, 1914).

Karr, J.-B. A. *Les guêpes (sixième série)* (Paris: Michel Lévy, 1862).

Keyserling, H. *Europe*, trans. by Maurice Samuel (London: Jonathan Cape, 1928).

Knox, R. *The Races of Men: A Fragment* (Philadelphia: Lea & Blanchard, 1850).

Kohn, H. *Nationalism: Its Meaning and History* (1955); rev. edn (Princeton: Princeton University Press, 1965) [first published in 1955].

Kohn, H. "The Eve of German Nationalism," *Journal of the History of Ideas* 12, 2 (1951): 56–84.

Koumaris, J. "On the Morphological Variety of Modern Greeks," *Man* 48 (1948): 126–7.

Kozáry, G. "Az Eugenics kérdése," *Athenaeum* 16, 1 (1907): 59–69.

Lahovary, N. *Les peuples européens. Leur passé ethnologique et leurs parentés réciproques d'après les dernières recherches sanguines et anthropologiques* (Neuchatel: Editions de la Baconnière, 1946).

Lapouge, G. V. de. "Old and New Aspects of the Aryan Question," trans. by Carlos C. Closson, *The American Journal of Sociology* 5, 3 (1899): 329–46.

Lapouge, G. V. de. *L'Aryen. Son role social* (Paris: Albert Fontemoing, 1899).

Le Bon, G. *Lois psychologiques de l'évolution des peuples* (Paris: Félix Alcan, 1895).

Lenhossék, J. *Az emberi koponyaisme. Cranioscopia* (Budapest: Magyar Tudományos Akadémia, 1875).

Lévi-Strauss, C. "Claude Lévi-Strauss Reconsiders: From Rousseau to Burke," Interview with Jean-Marie Benoist, *Encounter* 53 (1979): 19–26.

Lewontin, R. C. *The Triple Helix: Gene, Organism, and Environment* (Cambridge, MA: Harvard University Press, 2000).

Lewontin, R. C. *Biology as Ideology: The Doctrine of DNA* (New York: Anansi Press, 1991).

Lewontin, R. C. "The Apportionment of Human Diversity," in T. Dobzhansky et al., eds., *Evolutionary Biology*, vol. 6 (New York: Plenum Press, 1972), 381–98.

Lipták, P. *Avars and Ancient Hungarians* (Budapest: Akadémiai Kiadó, 1983).

Martí, J. "Our America," in Aviva Chomsky et al., eds., *The Cuba Reader: History, Culture, Politics* (Durham, NC: Duke University Press, 2003), 122–7.

"Max Weber, Dr. Alfred Ploetz, and W. E. B. Du Bois (Max Weber on Race and Society II)," *Sociological Analysis* 34, 4 (1973): 308–12.

Mazzini, G. "Europe: its Condition and Prospects," in *Essays: Selected from the Writings, Literary, Political and Religious of Joseph Mazzini*, ed. William Clark (London: Walter Scott, 1880), 261–98.

Mehedinţi, M. *Vechimea poporului român şi legătura cu elementele alogene* (Bucharest: Cartea Românească, 1925).

Méhely, L. "Blut und Rasse," *Zeitschrift für Morphologie und Anthropologie*, Festband Eugen Fischer, 34 (1934): 244–57.

Meyer, H. *Houston Stewart Chamberlain als Völkischer Denker* (Munich: H. Bruckmann, 1939).

Michaut, G. *Le génie latine: la race, le milieu, le moment* (Paris: A. Fontemoing, 1900).

Michelet, J. *Le Peuple* (Paris: Hachette, 1846).

Mill, J. S. *Principles of Political Economy. Collected Works*, vol. 2 (Toronto: Toronto University Press, 1965).

Mill on Bentham and Coleridge (London: Chatto & Windus, 1950).

Montagu, A. *The Natural Superiority of Women* (New York: Macmillan, 1953).

Montagu, A. *Man's Most Dangerous Myth: The Fallacy of Race* (New York: Columbia University Press, 1942).

Müller, M. "Lecture on the Vedas, or the Sacred Books of the Brahmans," (1865) in *The Essential Max Müller: On Language, Mythology, and Religion*, ed. J. Stone (Basingstoke: Palgrave, 2002), 43–67.

Müller, M. "Comparative Philology of the Indo-European Languages in Its Bearing on the Early Civilization of Mankind," in Joan Leopold, ed., *The Prix Volney. Contributions to Comparative Indo-European, African, and Chinese Linguistics: Max Müller and Steinthal*, vol. 3 (Dordrecht: Kluwer Academic, 1999), 107–90.

Müller, F. M. *Biographies of Words and the Home of the Aryas* (London: Macmillan, 1887).

Müller, M. *The Languages of the Seat of War in the East with a Survey of the Three Families of Language, Semitic, Arian, and Turanian*, 2nd. ed. (London: Williams and Norgate, 1855), 27–8.

Neele, H. "Survey of the Greek, the Roman, and the Modern Historians," *The Edinburg Review* 47, 94 (1828): 117–45.

Nietzsche, F. *The Birth of Tragedy. Out of the Spirit of Music*, trans. by Shaun Whiteside (London: Penguin Books, 1993).

Obédénare, M. "Presentation de quelques cranes roumains," *Bulletins de la Société d'Anthropologie de Paris* 9 (1874): 725–6.

Orwell, G. *In Defence of English Cooking* (London: Penguin Books, 2005).

Panaitescu, P. P. "Noi suntem de aici," *Cuvântul* 17, 38 (20 November 1940): 1.

Pârvan, V. *Getica: O protoistorie a Daciei* (Bucharest: Cultura naţională, 1926).

Pearson, K. "The Application of the Coefficient of Racial Likeness to Test the Character of Samples," *Biometrika* 20B, 3–4 (1928): 294–300.

Pearson, K. "On the Coefficient of Racial Likeness," *Biometrika* 18, 1–2 (1926): 105–17

Pearson, K. *The Academic Aspect of the Science of National Eugenics* (London: Dulau, 1911).

Pearson, K. *National Life from the Standpoint of Science*, 2nd edn (London: Adam and Charles Black, 1905).

Penka, K. Die *Herkunft der Arier. Neue Beiträge zur historischen Anthropologie der europäischen Völker* (Vienna: K. Prochaska, 1886).

Pictet, A. *Les origines Indo-européennes, ou les Aryas primitives: Essai de paléontologie linguistique* (Paris: Joël Cherbuliez, 1859 and 1863).

Pliny the Elder, "Natural Histories," in Rebecca F. Kennedy et al., eds., *Race and Ethnicity in the Classical World: An Anthology of Primary Sources in Translation* (Indianapolis, IN: Hackett Publishing, 2013), 48–9.

Ploetz, A. *Grundlinien einer Rassen-Hygiene* (Berlin: S. Fischer, 1895).

Race and the Enlightenment: A Reader, ed. Emmanuel C. Eze (Oxford: Blackwell, 1997).

Radić, R. *Živo hrvatsko pravo na Bosnu i Hercegovinu* (Zagreb: Hrvatski dnevnik, 1907).

Rădulescu-Motru, C. "Filosofia lui Houston Stewart Chamberlain asupra raselor," *Noua Revistă Română pentru politică, literatură, ştiinţă şi artă* 2, 17 (1900): 165–74.

Ranke, L. von. *History of the Latin and Teutonic Nations, from 1494 to 1514*, trans. by Philip A. Ashworth (London: George Bell and Sons, 1887).

Retzius, A. "De la forme du crane des habitans du Nord," *Annales des sciences naturelles* 5 (1846): 133–72.

Retzius, G. *The So-Called North European Race of Mankind* (London: Royal Anthropological Institute of Great Britain and Ireland, 1909).

Retzius, G. and Fürst, C. M. *Anthropologica Suecica. Beiträge zur Anthropologie der Schweden* (Stockholm: Aftonbladets Druckerei, 1902).

Ripley, W. Z. *The Races of Europe: A Sociological Study* (London: Kegan Paul, 1900).

Ritter, C. "Attempt at a General Comparative Geography," trans. by Daniel Theisen, in *German Essays on Science in the 19th Century*, ed. Wolfgang Schirmacher (New York: Continuum, 1996), 31–6.

Rosenberg, A. *Houston Stewart Chamberlain als Verkünder und Begründer einder Deutscher Zukunft* (Munich: H. Bruckmann, 1927).

Rota, E. *Il Giansenismo in Lombardia e le origini del Risorgimento italiano* (Pavia: Fusi, 1907).

Rousseau, J.-J. *The Plan for Perpetual Peace, On the Government of Poland, and Other Writings on History and Politics*, trans. by Christopher Kelly and Judith Bush (Hanover, NH: University of New England, 2005).

Rousseau, J.-J. *The Government of Poland*, trans. by Willmoore Kendall (Indianapolis, IN: Hackett Publishing, 1985).

Royce, J. *Race Questions: Provincialism and Other American Problems* (New York: The Macmillan Company, 1908).

Schemann, K. L. *Gobineau und die deutsche Kultur* (Leipzig: Eckardt, 1910).

Schlegel, F. *Ueber die Sprache und Weisheit der Indier: Ein Beitrag zur Begründung der Alterthumskunde* (Heidelberg: Mohr und Zimmer, 1808).

Schleicher, A. *Die Sprachen Europas in systematischer Übersicht* (Bonn: H. B. König, 1850).

Schwidetzky, I. ed., *Die neue Rassenkunde* (Stuttgart: Gustav Fischer Verlag, 1962).

Seeley, J. R. *The Expansion of England* (London: Macmillan, 1914).

Šegvić, K. *Die gotische Abstammung der Kroaten* (Berlin: Verlag Klinkhardt & Biermann, 1936).

Šegvić, K. *Die Kroaten und ihre Mission während dreizehn Jahrhunderte der Geschichte* (Zagreb: Kugli, 1942).

Seltzer, C. C. "A Critique of the Coefficient of Racial Likeness," *American Journal of Physical Anthropology* 23, 1 (1937): 101–9.

Sergi, G. *The Mediterranean Race: A Study of the Origins of European Peoples* (London: Walter Scott, 1901).

Sheytanov, N. "Bulgarian Worldview," trans. by Zornitsa Dimova-Hristova, in Diana Mishkova, Marius Turda and Balázs Trencsényi, eds., *Anti-Modernism: Radical Revisions of Collective Identity*, vol. 4 (Budapest: Central European University Press, 2014), 229–32.

Skerlj, B. "Yugoslavia: An Anthropological Review for 1952–1954," *Yearbook of Anthropology* 1 (1955): 651–70.

Siemens, H. W. *Race Hygiene and Heredity* (New York: D. Appleton, 1924).

Songs of the Serbian People. From the Collections of Vuk Karadžić, translated and
    edited by Milne Holton and Vasa D. Mihailovich (Pittsburgh: University of
    Pittsburgh Press, 1997).
Spiller, G. ed., *Papers on Inter-Racial Problems* (London: P. S. King & Son, 1911).
Stan, L. *Rasă și religiune* (Sibiu: Tiparul Tipografiei Arhidiecezane, 1942).
Taine, H. A. *Histoire de la littérature anglaise*, 5 vols. (Paris: L. Hachette, 1866–1878).
Taylor, E. B. *Primitive Culture: Researches into the Development of Mythology,
    Philosophy, Religion, Art, and Custom*, 2. vols. (London: John Murray, 1871).
The Essential Writings of Rousseau, ed. by L. Damrosch and trans. by P.
    Constantine (New York: Random House, 2013).
*The Future of Multi-Ethnic Britain. Report of the Commission of Multi-Ethnic
    Britain* (London: Profile Books, 2000).
The Politics of Aristotle, trans. by E. Barker, with intro. and notes by R. F. Stalley
    (Oxford: Oxford University Press, 1995).
Thierry, A. *Dix ans d'études historiques*, 5th edn (Paris: Furne, 1846).
This is Race: An Anthology from the International Literature on the Races of Man,
    ed. Earl W. Count (New York: Henry Schuman, 1950).
Török, A. "Adatok az Erdélyi románok koponyáinak jellemzéséhez,"
    Anthropologiai füzetek 1 (1882): 50–66.
Török, A. *Grundzüge einer Systematischen Kraniometrie* (Stuttgart: Enke, 1890).
Treitschke, H. von. *Das deutsche Ordensland Preußen* (Leipzig: Insel Verlag, 1862).
Voegelin, E. "The Growth of the Race Idea," *The Review of Politics* 2, 3 (1940):
    283–317.
Weigner, K. ed., *Die Gleichwertigkeit der europäischen Rassen und die Wege zu ihrer
    Vervollkommnung* (Prague: Tschechische Akademie der Wissenschaften, 1935).
White, C. *An Account of the Regular Gradation in Man, and in Different Animals
    and Vegetables; and from the Former to the Latter* (London: C. Dilly, 1799).
Widney, J. P. *Race Life of the Aryan Peoples*, vol. 1 (New York: Funk & Wagnalls, 1907).
Winning, W. B. *A Manual of Comparative Philology, in Which the Affinity of the
    Indo-European Languages is Illustrated and Applied to the Primeval History of
    Europe, Italy, and Rome* (London: J. G. & F. Rivington, 1838).
Ygrec (Iosif Glicsman), *Rasa și rasismul cea mai mare escrocherie științifică a
    secolului* (Bucharest: Ed. Adam, 1935).
Ypsilantis, A. "Fight for Faith and Motherland!", trans. by Mary Kitroeff, in Balázs
    Trencsényi and Michal Kopeček, eds., *Discourses of Collective Identity in
    Central and Southeast Europe*, vol. 2 National Romanticism (Budapest: CEU
    Press, 2007), 399–402.
Zollschan, I. *The Significance of the Racial Factor as a Basis in Cultural
    Development* (London: Le Play House Press, 1934).

Secondary sources

Akenson, D. H. *God's Peoples: Covenant and Land in South Africa, Israel, and
    Ulster* (Ithaca: Cornell University Press, 1992).
Alcoff, L. M. *The Future of Whiteness* (Cambridge: Polity Press, 2015).
Alcoff, L. M. *Visible Identities: Race, Gender, and the Self* (New York: Oxford
    University Press, 2005).

Alim, H. S. et al., eds., *Raciolinguistics: How Language Shapes our Ideas about Race* (New York: Oxford University Press, 2016).

Allen, J. S. "Franz Boas's Physical Anthropology: The Critique of Racial Formalism Revisited," *Current Anthropology* 30, 1 (1989): 79–84.

Almeida, M. V. de. *An Earth-Colored Sea 'Race', Culture and the Politics of Identity in the Post-Colonial Portuguese-Speaking World* (New York: Berghahn, 2004).

Alter, S. G. *Darwinism and the Linguistic Image: Language, Race, and Natural Theology in the Nineteenth Century* (Baltimore: The Johns Hopkins University Press, 1999).

Aly, R. M. K. *Becoming Arab in London: Performativity and the Undoing of Identity* (London: Pluto Press, 2015).

Ambler, W. "Aristotle on Nature and Politics: The Case of Slavery," *Political Theory* 15, 3 (1987): 390–410.

Anderson, B. *Imagined Communities: Reflections on the Origin and Spread of Nationalism*, revised edn (London: Verso, 2006) [first published 1983].

Anderson, E. *The Cosmopolitan Canopy: Race and Civility in Everyday Life* (New York: W. W. Norton, 2011).

Anstett, È and Dreyfus, J-M eds., *Human Remains and Identification: Mass Violence, Genocide, and the 'Forensic Turn'* (Manchester: Manchester University Press, 2015)

Armelagos G. J. and Gerven, D. P. van. "A Century of Skeletal Biology and Paleopathology: Contrasts, Contradictions, and Conflicts," *American Anthropologist* 105, 1 (2003): 53–64.

Armstrong, B. "Racialisation and Nationalist Ideology: The Japanese Case," *International Sociology* 4, 3 (1989): 329–43.

Arvidsson, S. *Aryan Idols: Indo-European Mythology as Ideology and Science*, trans. by Sonia Wichmann (Chicago: The University of Chicago Press, 2006).

Ashcroft, B. "Language and Race," in Roxy Harris and Ben Rampton, eds., *The Language, Ethnicity and Race Reader* (London: Routledge, 2003), 37–53.

Atkin, A. *The Philosophy of Race* (Abingdon: Routledge, 2014).

Augstein, H. F. *James Cowles Prichard's Anthropology: Remaking the Science of Man in Early Nineteenth-Century Britain* (Amsterdam: Rodopi, 1999).

Baker, L. D. *From Savage to Negro: Anthropology and the Construction of Race, 1896–1954* (Berkeley: University of California Press, 1998).

Balagangadhara, S. N. "The Future of the Present: Thinking Through Orientalism," *Cultural Dynamics* 10, 2 (1998): 101–21.

Banac, I. and Verdery, K. eds., *National Character and National Ideology in Interwar Eastern Europe* (New Haven: Yale Center for International Studies, 1995).

Bangham, J. "*What is Race*? UNESCO, Mass Communication and Human Genetics in the early 1950s," *History of the Human Sciences* 25, 5 (2015): 80–107.

Banton, M. *What We Know about Race and Ethnicity* (New York: Berghahn, 2015).

Barber, T. *Oriental Identities in Super-Diverse Britain: Young Vietnamese in London* (Basingstoke: Palgrave, 2015).

Barkan, E. *The Retreat of Scientific Racism: Changing Concepts of Race in Britain and the United States between the World Wars* (New York: Cambridge University Press, 1992).

Barker, F. et al., eds., *Europe and its Others: Proceedings of the Essex Conference on the Sociology of Literature, July 1984*, 2. vols. (Colchester: University of Essex, 1985).

Barnard, F. M. *Herder's Social and Political Thought: From Enlightenment to Nationalism* (Oxford: Clarendon Press, 1965).

Bar-On, T. *Rethinking the French New Right: Alternatives to Modernity* (Abingdon: Routledge, 2013).

Barth, F. *Ethnic Groups and Boundaries: the Social Organization of Culture Difference* (Boston: Little, Brown, 1969).

Barth, F. et al., *One Discipline, Four Ways: British, German, French, and American Anthropology* (Chicago: University of Chicago Press, 2005).

Bartulin, N. *The Racial Idea in the Independent State of Croatia: Origins and Theory* (Leiden: Brill, 2014).

Bassin, M. *The Gumilev Mystique: Biopolitics, Eurasianism, and the construction of community in modern Russia* (Ithaca, NY: Cornell University Press, 2016).

Bassin, M. "Lev Gumilev and the European New Right," *Nationalities Papers* 43, 6 (2015): 840–65.

Bassin, M. "Nurture *is* Nature: Lev Gumilev and the Ecology of Ethnicity," *Slavic Review* 68, 4 (2009): 872–97.

Bassin, M. "Imperialism and the Nation-State in Friedrich Ratzel's Political Geography," *Progress in Human Geography* 11 (1987): 473–95.

Bates, A. *The Anatomy of Robert Knox: Murder, Mad Science and Medical Regulation in Nineteenth-Century Edinburgh* (Brighton: Sussex Academic Press, 2010).

Baum, B. *The Rise and Fall of the Caucasian Race: A Political History of Racial Identity* (New York: New York University Press, 2006).

Beasley, W. G. "Modern Japan: An Historian's View," in idem, ed., *Modern Japan: Aspects of History, Literature, and Society* (Berkeley: University of California Press, 1975), 13–23.

Bell, D. *Reordering the World: Essays on Liberalism and Empire* (Princeton: Princeton University Press, 2016).

Beiser, F. C. *The Fate of Reason: German Philosophy from Kant to Fichte* (Cambridge, MA.: Harvard University Press, 1987).

Berger, P. L. and Luckmann, T. *The Social Construction of Reality* (New York: Doubleday, 1966).

Berger, S. and Lorenz, C. eds., *Nationalizing the Past: Historians as Nation Builders* (Basingstoke: Palgrave, 2015).

Berghe, P. L. van den. "Does Race Matter?" *Nations and Nationalism* 1, 3 (1995): 357–68.

Berlin, I. *Vico and Herder: Two Studies in the History of Ideas* (London: Hogarth Press, 1976).

Bernal, M. *Black Athena. The Afroasiatic Roots of Classical Civilization*, vol. 1. *The Fabrication of Ancient Greece, 1785–1985* (London: Vintage, 1991) [first published in 1987].

Bernasconi, R. "Kant as an Unfamiliar Source of Racism," in Julie K. Ward and Tommy L. Lott, eds., *Philosophers on Race: Critical Essays* (Oxford: Blackwell, 2002), 145–66.

Bernasconi, R. *Race and Racism in Continental Philosophy* (Bloomington, IN: Indiana University Press, 2003).

Bernasconi, R. "On Needing Not to Know and Forgetting What One Never Knew: The Epistemology of Ignorance in Fanon's Critique of Sartre," in Shannon Sullivan and Nancy Tuana, eds., *Race and Epistemologies of Ignorance* (Albany, NY: State University of New York Press, 2007), 231–40.

Bernstein, R. B. *Thomas Jefferson: The Revolution of Ideas* (Oxford: Oxford University Press, 2004).

Bethencourt, F. *Racisms: From the Crusades to the Twentieth Century* (Princeton: Princeton University Press, 2013).

Biddiss, M. D. *Father of Racist Ideology: The Social and Political Thought of Count Gobineau* (London: Weidenfeld, 1970).

Biddiss, M. D. "Prophecy and Pragmatism: Gobineau's Confrontation with Tocqueville," *The Historical Journal* 13, 4 (1970): 611–33.

Biddiss, M. "History as Destiny: Gobineau, H. S. Chamberlain and Spengler," *Transactions of the Royal Historical Society* 7 (1997): 73–100.

Bindman, D. *Ape to Apollo: Aesthetics and the Idea of Race in the 18th Century* (London: Reaktion Books, 2002).

Black, L. T. "The Concept of Race in Soviet Anthropology," *Studies in Soviet Thought* 17, 1 (1977): 1–27.

Blaut, J. M. *The Colonizer's Model of the World: Geographical Diffusionism and Eurocentric History* (New York: The Guilford Press, 1993).

Bleich, E. *Race Politics in Britain and France: Ideas and Policymaking since the 1960s* (New York: Cambridge University Press, 2003).

Bliss, C. *Race Decoded: The Genomic Fight for Social Justice* (Stanford: Stanford University Press, 2012).

Bloomberg, C. *Christian-Nationalism and the Rise of the Afrikaner Broederbond in South Africa, 1918–48*, ed. by Saul Dubow (Basingstoke: Macmillan, 1990).

Boaz, R. E. *In Search of 'Aryan Blood': Serology in Interwar and National Socialist Germany* (Budapest: Central European University Press 2012).

Boia, L. *History and Myth in Romanian Consciousness*, trans. James Christian Brown (Budapest: CEU Press, 2001).

Boissel, J. *Victor Courtet (1813–1867), premier théoricien de la hiérarchie des races. Contribution à l'histoire de la philosophie politique du romantisme* (Paris: Presses Universitaires de France, 1972).

Bolt, C. *Victorian Attitudes to Race* (London: Routledge and Kegan Paul, 1971).

Bonilla-Silva, E. *Racism without Racists: Color-Blind Racism and the Persistence of Racial Inequality in America*, 4th edn (Lanham, MD: Rowman & Littlefield, 2014).

Borgstede, S. B. *'All is Race': Benjamin Disraeli on Race, Nation and Empire* (Münster: LIT Verlag, 2011).

Bouchard, G. ed., *National Myths: Constructed Pasts, Contested Presents* (Abingdon: Routledge, 2013).

Boulle, P. H. "François Bernier and the Origins of the Modern Concept of Race," in Sue Peabody and Tyler Stovall, eds., *The Color of Liberty: Histories of Race in France* (Durham, NC: Duke University Press, 2003), 11–27.

Bowden, B. *The Empire of Civilization: The Evolution of An Imperial Idea* (Chicago: University of Chicago Press, 2009).

Boxill, B. "Kantian Racism and Kantian Theology," in Naomi Zack, ed., *The Oxford Handbook of Philosophy and Race* (Oxford: Oxford University Press, 2017), 44–53.

Boyce, M. *Zoroastrians: Their Religious Beliefs and Practices* (London: Routledge, 1979).

Brantlinger, P. *Dark Vanishings: Discourse on the Extension of Primitive Races, 1800–1930* (Ithaca, NY: Cornell University Press, 2003).

Brattain, M. "Race, Racism, and Anti-Racism: UNESCO and the Politics of Presenting Science to the Postwar Public," *The American Historical Review* 112, 5 (2007): 1386–413.

Bressey, C. *Empire, Race and the Politics of Anti-Caste* (London: Bloomsbury, 2013).

Brownlee, J. S. *Japanese Historians and the National Myths, 1600–1945: The Age of Gods and Emperor Jinmu* (Vancouver: University of British Columbia, 1997).

Brubaker, R. *Grounds for Difference* (Cambridge, MA: Harvard University Press, 2015).

Brubaker, R. *Ethnicity without Groups* (Cambridge, MA: Harvard University Press, 2004).

Brubaker, R. *Citizenship and Nationhood in France and Germany* (Cambridge, MA: Harvard University Press, 1992).

Bryant, E. *The Quest for the Origins of Vedic Culture: The Indo-Aryan Migration Debate* (New York: Oxford University Press, 2001).

Bryant, E. F. and Patton, L. L., eds., *The Indo-Aryan Controversy: Evidence and Inference in Indian History* (Abingdon: Routledge, 2005).

Buenzod, J. *La formation de la pensée de Gobineau et 'L'Essai sur l'inégalité des races humaines'* (Paris: A. G. Nizet, 1967).

Bunting, B. *The Rise of the South African Reich* (Harmondsworth: Penguin, 1964).

Burkholder, Z. *Color in the Classroom: How American Schools Taught Race, 1900–1954* (Oxford: Oxford University Press, 2011).

Burleigh, M. and Wippermann, W. *The Racial State, Germany, 1933–1945* (Cambridge: Cambridge University Press, 1991).

Butler, J. *Bodies that Matter: On the Discursive Limits of "Sex"* (London: Routledge, 1993).

Caramelli, D. et al., "Genetic Analysis of the Skeletal Remains Attributed to Francesco Petrarca", *Forensic Science International*, 173, 1 (2007): 36–40.

Cavalli-Sforza, L. L. *Genes, Peoples and Languages*, trans. by Mark Seielstad (London: Penguin Books, 2001).

Cavalli-Sforza, L. L. et al. *The History and Geography of Human Genes* (Princeton: Princeton University Press, 1994).

Cesarani, C. ed., *The Holocaust: Critical Concepts and Historical Studies*, 6. vols. (London: Routledge, 2004).

Chabod, F. "The Idea of Nation" (1961), trans. by Kathy Wolff, in Stuart Woolf, ed., *Nationalism in Europe, 1815 to the Present: A Reader* (London: Routledge, 1996), 124–34.

Chartier, R. *Cultural History: Between Practices and Representations* (Oxford: Polity Press, 1993) [first published in 1988].

Chatterjee, P. *The Nation and Its Fragments: Colonial and Postcolonial Histories*, (Princeton, Princeton University Press, 1993).

Chin, R. et al., *After the Nazi Racial State: Difference and Democracy in Germany and Europe* (Ann Arbor: The University of Michigan Press, 2009).

Ching, L. T. S. *Becoming "Japanese": Colonial Taiwan and the Politics of Identity Formation* (Berkeley: University of California Press, 2001).

Clark, N. L. and Worger, W. H. *South Africa: The Rise and Fall of Apartheid*, 2nd edn (London: Routledge, 2013).

Colbert, C. *A Measure of Perfection: Phrenology and the Fine Arts in America* (Chapel Hill: The University of North Carolina Press, 1997).

Cole, D. *Captured Heritage: The Scramble for Northwest Coast Artefacts* (Vancouver: University of British Columbia, 1995) [first published 1985].

Collini, S. "The Idea of 'Character' in Victorian Political Thought," *Transactions of the Royal Historical Society* 35 (1985): 29–50.

Conklin, A. L. *A Mission to Civilize: The Republican Idea of Empire in France and West Africa, 1895–1930* (Stanford: Stanford University Press, 1997).

Cowan, R. *Indo-German Identification: Reconciling South Asian Origins and European Destinies, 1765–1885* (Rochester, NY: Camden House, 2010).

Darnell, R. et al., eds., *The Franz Boas Papers, Vol. 1: Franz Boas as Public Intellectual—Theory, Ethnography, Activism* (Lincoln: University of Nebraska Press, 2015).

Darwin, J. *The Empire Project: The Rise and Fall of the British World System, 1830–1970* (Cambridge: Cambridge University Press, 2009).

Davies, S. *Renaissance Ethnography and the Invention of the Human: New Worlds, Maps and Monsters* (Cambridge: Cambridge University Press, 2016).

Dávila, J. *Diploma of Whiteness, Race and Social Policy in Brazil, 1917–1945* (Durham, NC: Duke University Press, 2003).

De la Fuente, A. *A Nation for All: Race, Inequality, and Politics in Twentieth-Century Cuba* (Chapel Hill: The University of North Carolina Press, 2001),

Desmond, A. and Moore, J. *Darwin's Sacred Cause: How a Hatred of Slavery shaped Darwin's Views on Human Evolution* (New York: Houghton Mifflin Harcourt, 2009).

Diggins, J. P. "Slavery, Race and Equality: Jefferson and the Pathos of the Enlightenment," *American Quarterly* 28, 2 (1976): 206–28.

Dikötter, F. *The Discourse of Race in Modern China*, fully revised and expanded second edition (Oxford: Oxford University Press, 2015) [first published in 1992].

Dikötter, F. ed., *The Construction of Racial Identities in China and Japan* (London: Hurst, 1997).

Dikötter, F. "The Racialization of the Globe: Historical Perspective," in Manfred Berg and Simon Wendt, eds., *Racism in the Modern World: Historical Perspectives on Cultural Transfer and Adaptation* (New York: Berghahn, 2011), 20–40.

Dokládal, M and Brožek, J. "Physical Anthropology in Czechoslovakia: Recent Developments," *Current Anthropology* 2, 5 (1961): 445–77.

Douglas, B. "Climate to Crania: Science and the Racialization of Human Difference," in Bronwen Douglas and Chris Ballard, eds., *Foreign Bodies: Oceania and the Science of Race 1750–1940* (Canberra: The Australian National University, 2008), 33–96.

Drace-Francis, A. *The Traditions of Invention. Romanian Ethnic and Social Stereotypes in Historical Context* (Leiden: Brill Publishers, 2013).

Dubow, S. *Scientific Racism in Modern South Africa* (Cambridge: Cambridge University Press, 1995).

Duncan, W. R. and G. Paul Holman, Jr., G. P. eds. *Ethnic Nationalism and Regional Conflict: The Former Soviet Union and Yugoslavia* (Boulder, CO: Westview Press, 1994).

Edwards, A. W. F. "Human Genetic Diversity: Lewontin's Fallacy," *BioEssays* 25 (2003) 798–801.

Ehlers, N. *Racial Imperatives: Disciplines, Performativity, and Struggles against Subjection* (Bloomington, IN: Indiana University Press, 2012).

Eliav-Feldon, M. et al., eds., *The Origins of Racism in the West* (Cambridge: Cambridge University Press, 2009).

El-Tayeb, F. *European Others: Queering Ethnicity in Postnational Europe* (Minneapolis: University of Minnesota Press, 2011).

Ergin, M. *"Is the Turk a White Man?": Race and Modernity in the Making of Turkish Identity* (Leiden: Brill, 2016).

Ersoy, A. et al., eds., 4 vols., *Discourses of Collective Identity in Central and Southeast Europe 1770–1945: Texts and Commentaries* (Budapest: CEU Press, 2006–2014).

Etkind, A. *Internal Colonization: Russia's Imperial Experience* (Cambridge: Polity Press, 2011).

Etzemüller, T. *Auf der Suche nach dem Nordischen Menschen: Die deutsche Rassenanthropologie in der modernen Welt* (Bielefeld: Transcript Verlag, 2015).

Evans, A. D. *Anthropology at War: World War I and the Science of Race in Germany* (Chicago: University of Chicago Press, 2010).

Fanning, B. *Racism and Social Change in the Republic of Ireland* (Manchester: Manchester University Press, 2002)

Ferguson, C. *Determined Spirits: Eugenics, Heredity and Racial Regeneration in Anglo-American Spiritualist Writing, 1848–1930* (Edinburgh: Edinburgh University Press, 2012).

Fforde, C. et al., eds., *The Dead and their Possessions: Repatriation in Principle, Policy, and Practice* (London: Routledge, 2002).

Field, G. G. *Evangelist of Race: The Germanic Vision of Houston Stewart Chamberlain* (New York: Columbia University Press, 1981).

Figueira, D. M. *Aryans, Jews, Brahmins: Theorizing Authority through Myths of Identity* (New York: State University of New York Press, 2002).

Fisch, J. "Zivilisation, Kultur," in Otto Brunner, Werner Conze and Reinhart Koselleck, eds., *Geschichtliche Grundbegriffe: Historisches Lexikon zur politisch-sozialen Sprache in Deutschland* vol. 7 (Stuttgart: Klett-Cotta, 1992), 679–774.

Fleming, Crystal Marie. *Resurrecting Slavery: Racial Legacies and White Supremacy in France* (Philadelphia: Temple University Press, 2017).

Flint, J. E. *Cecil Rhodes* (London: Hutchinson, 1976).

Floyd-Wilson, M. *English Ethnicity and Race in Early Modern Drama* (Cambridge: Cambridge University Press, 2003).

Foltiny, S. and Ivaniček, F. "Bulgaria, Czechoslovakia, Hungary, Poland, Roumania. An anthropological review for 1952–1954," *Yearbook of Anthropology* 1 (1955): 671–92.

Fortier, P. A. "Gobineau and German Racism," *Comparative Literature* 19, 4 (1967): 341–50.

Francesco, A. de. *Mito e storiografia della 'Grande rivoluzione'. La Rivoluzione francese nella cultura politica italiana del '900* (Naples: Alfredo Guida, 2006).

Frawley, D. *The Myth of the Aryan Invasion of India* (New Delhi: Voice of India, 1994).

Fredrickson, G. M. *Racism: A Short History* (Princeton: Princeton University Press, 2012).

Fredrickson, G. M. *White Supremacy: A Comparative Study of American and South African History* (New York: Oxford University Press, 1981).

Gavin, M. *Shiga Shigetaka, 1863–1927: The Forgotten Enlightener* (London: Curzon Press, 2001).

Gellner, E. *Encounters with Nationalism* (Oxford: Blackwell, 1994).

Gentile, E. *La Grande Italia: The Myth of the Nation in the Twentieth Century*, trans. by Suzanne Dingee and Jennifer Pudney (Madison: The University of Wisconsin Press, 2009) [first published in Italian in 1997].

Gifford, P. and Hauswedell, T. eds., *Europe and Its Others: Essays on Interpretation and Identity* (Bern: Peter Lang, 2010).

Gilman, S. C. "Degeneracy and Race in the Nineteenth Century," *Journal of Ethnic Studies* 10, 4 (1983): 27–50.

Gilroy, P. *Between Camps: Nations, Cultures and the Allure of Race* (London: Penguin Books, 2000).

Girard, R. "The Scapegoat as Historical Referent," *The Girard Reader*, ed. James G. Williams (New York: The Crossroad Publishing, 2003), 97–106.

Gissis, S. B. "When is 'Race' a Race? 1946–2003," *Studies in History and Philosophy of Science* 29, 4 (2008): 437–50.

Gluck, C. *Japan's Modern Myths: Ideology in Late Meiji Period* (Princeton: Princeton University Pres, 1985).

Golash-Boza, T. "A Critical and Comprehensive Sociological Theory of Race and Racism," *Sociology of Race and Racism* 2, 2 (2016): 129–41.

Goldberg, D. T. *Racist Culture: Philosophy and the Politics of Meaning* (Malden, MA: Blackwell, 1993).

Goodman, D. G. "Anti-Semitism in Japan: Its History and Current Implications," in Frank Dikötter, ed., *Racial Identities in China and Japan* (London: Hurst, 1997), 177–98.

Goodrick-Clarke, N. *Black Sun: Aryan Cults, Esoteric Nazism and the Politics of Identity* (New York: New York University Press, 2002).

Gossett, T. F. *Race: The History of an Idea in America*, new edition (New York: Oxford University Press, 1997) [first published in 1963].

Gould, S. J. *The Mismeasure of Man*, rev. and exp. edn, with a new intro. (New York: W. W. Norton, 1996) [first published 1981].

Gourgouris, S. *Dream Nation: Enlightenment, Colonization and the Institution of Modern Greece* (Stanford: Stanford University Press, 1996).

Graham, R. ed., *The Idea of Race in Latin America, 1870–1940* (Austin, TX: University of Texas Press, 1990).

Gravlee, C. C. et al., "Heredity, Environment, and Cranial Form: A Reanalysis of Boas's Immigrant Data," *American Anthropologist* 105, 1 (2003): 125–38.

Green, S. K. *Inventing a Christian America: The Myth of the Religious Funding* (New York: Oxford University Press, 2015).

Griffin, R. *Fascism* (Cambridge: Polity Press, 2018).

Griffin, R. *Modernism and Fascism: The Sense of a Beginning under Mussolini and Hitler* (Basingstoke: Palgrave, 2007).

Guhu, S. *Environment and Ethnicity in India, 1200–1991* (Cambridge: Cambridge University Press, 1999).

Hall, B. S. *A History of Race in Muslim West Africa, 1600–1960* (Cambridge: Cambridge University Press, 2014).

Hall, K. F. *Things of Darkness: Economies of Race and Gender in Early Modern England* (Ithaca, NY: Cornell University Press, 1995).

Hanebrink, P. A. *In Defense of Christian Hungary: Religion, Nationalism, and Antisemitism, 1890–1944* (Ithaca, NY: Cornell University Press, 2006).

Harootunian, H. D. *Things Seen and Unseen: Discourse and Ideology in Tokugawa Nativism* (Chicago: University of Chicago Press, 1988).

Harris, M. *The Rise of Anthropological Theory: A History of Theories of Culture*, updated edition (Lanham, MD: AltaMira Press, 2001) [first published 1968].

Hartog, F. *Regimes of Historicity: Presentism and Experiences of Time*, trans. by Saskia Brown (New York: Columbia University Press, 2015) [first published in French in 2003].

Heath, M. "Aristotle on Natural Slavery," *Phronesis: A Journal for Ancient Philosophy* 53, 3 (2008): 243–70.

Hendricks, M. "Race: A Renaissance Category?" in Michael Hattaway, ed., *A Companion to English Renaissance Literature and Culture* (Oxford: Blackwell, 2003), 690–8.

Herman, A. *The Idea of Decline in Western History* (New York: The Free Press, 1997).

Heusser, M. and Grabher, G. eds., *American Foundational Myths* (Tübingen: Narr, 2002).

Hirsch, F. *Empires of Nations: Ethnographic Knowledge and the Making of the Soviet Union* (Ithaca, NY: Cornell University Press, 2005).

Hobsbawm, E. and Ranger, T., eds., *The Invention of Tradition* (Cambridge: Cambridge University Press, 1983).

Holt, T. C. *The Problem of Race in the Twenty-First Century* (Cambridge, MA: Harvard University Press, 2000).

Holt, T. C. "Marking: Race, Race-Making, and the Writing of History," *The American Historical Review* 100, 1 (1995): 1–20.

Horsman, R. *Race and Manifest Destiny: The Origins of American Racial Anglo-Saxonism* (Cambridge, MA: Harvard University Press, 1981).

Horsman, R. "Origins of Racial Anglo-Saxonism in Great Britain before 1850," *Journal of the History of Ideas* 37, 3 (1976): 387–410.

Howell, D. L. "Civilization and Enlightenment: Markers of Identity in Nineteenth-Century Japan," in Joshua A. Fogel, ed., *The Teleology of the Modern Nation-State* (Philadelphia: University of Pennsylvania Press, 2005), 117–37.

Howells, W. W. *Skull Shapes and the Map: Craniometric Analyses in the Dispersion of Modern Homo* (Cambridge, MA: Harvard University Press, 1989).

Iggers, G. G. *The German Conception of History: The National Tradition of Historical Thought from Herder to the Present*, revised edn (Middletown, CN: Wesleyan University Press, 1983) [first published 1968].

Ignatieff, M. *Blood and Belonging: Journeys into the New Nationalism* (New York: Farrar, Straus, and Giroux, 1993).

Israel, J. *Revolutionary Ideas: An Intellectual History of the French Revolution from the Rights of Man to Robespierre* (Oxford and Princeton: Princeton University Press, 2014).

Issac, B. *The Invention of Racism in Classical Antiquity* (Princeton: Princeton University Press, 2004).

Isyar, B. "The Origins of Turkish Republican Citizenship: The Birth of Race," *Nations and Nationalism* 11, 3 (2005): 343–60.

James, D. *Fichte's Republic: Idealism, History and Nationalism* (Cambridge: Cambridge University Press, 2015).

Jordheim, H. "The Nature of Civilization: The Semantics of Civilization and Civility in Scandinavia," in Helge Jordheim and Margrit Pernau, eds., *Civilizing Emotions. Concepts in Nineteenth-Century Asia and Europe* (Oxford: Oxford University Press, 2015), 25–44.

Kaliakatsos, M. "Ion Dragoumis and 'Machiavelli': Armed Struggle, Propaganda, and Hellenization in Macedonia and Thrace, 1903–1908," *Journal of Modern Greek Studies* 31, 1 (2013): 53–84.

Kallenberger, L. and Pilbrow, V. "Using CRANID to Test the Population Affinity of Known Crania," *Journal of Anatomy* 221, 5 (2012): 459–64.

Karpat, K. H. *The Politicization of Islam: Reconstructing Identity, State, Faith, and Community in the Late Ottoman State* (New York: Oxford University Press, 2001).

Kaszycka K. A. et al. "Current Views of European Anthropologists on Race: Influence of Educational and Ideological Background," *American Anthropologist* 111, 1 (2009): 43–56.

Kendi, I. X. *Stamped from the Beginning: The Definite History of Racist Ideas in America* (New York: Nation Books, 2016).

Kent, M. and Wade, P. "Genetics against Race: Science, Politics and Affirmative Action in Brazil," *Social Studies of Science* 45, 6 (2015): 816–38.

Keppens, M. and Roover, J. de. "Orientalism and the Puzzle of the Aryan Invasion Theory," *Journal of Human Sciences* 2, 2 (2014): 51–76.

Kerr, A. "From Savagery to Sovereignty: Identity, Politics, and International Expositions of Argentine Anthropology (1878–1892)," *Isis* 108, 1 (2017): 62–81.

Kidd, C. *The Forging of Races: Race and Scripture in the Protestant Atlantic World, 1600–2000* (Cambridge: Cambridge University Press, 2000).

Kim, H.-E. *Doctors of Empire: Medical and Cultural Encounters between Imperial Germany and Meiji Japan* (Toronto: University of Toronto Press, 2014).

King, D. *Making Americans: Immigration, Race, and the Origins of the Diverse Democracy* (Cambridge, MA: Harvard University Press, 2000).

Knobel, D. T. *America for the Americans: The Nativist Movements in the United States* (New York: Twayne Publishers, 1984).

Koepping, K.-P. *Adolf Bastian and the Psychic Unity of Mankind: Foundations of Anthropology in Nineteenth Century Germany* (St. Lucia, Qld.: University of Queensland Press, 1983).

Kra, P. "Rousseau et la politique du caractère national," in Robert Thiéry, ed., *Jean-Jacques Rousseau, politique et nation* (Paris: Champion, 2001), 813–22.

Kundnani, A. *Muslims are Coming! Islamophobia, Extremism, and the Domestic War on Terror* (London: Verso, 2014).

Kyllingstad, J. R. *Measuring the Master Race: Physical Anthropology in Norway, 1890–1945* (Cambridge: Open Book Publishers, 2014).

Laqueur, W. *Fascism: Past, Present, Future* (Oxford: Oxford University Press, 1996).

Laski, G. *Untimely Democracy: The Politics of Progress after Slavery* (New York: Oxford University Press, 2017).

Lebron, C. J *The Making of Black Lives Matter: A Brief History of An Idea* (New York: Oxford University Press, 2017).

Lehmann, J.-P. "Themes and Theories in Modern Japanese History," in Sue Henny and Jean-Pierre Lehmann, eds., *Themes and Theories in Modern Japanese History: Essays in Memory of Richard Storry* (London: Bloomsbury, 2014), 3–24.

Leopold, J. ed., *The Prix Volney. Contributions to Comparative Indo-European, African, and Chinese Linguistics: Max Müller and Steinthal*, vol. 3 (Dordrecht: Kluwer Academic, 1999).

Leopold, J. "British Applications of the Aryan Theory of Race to India, 1850–1870," *The English Historical Review* 89, 352 (1974): 578–603.

Leopold, J. "The Aryan Theory of Race," *The Indian Economic and Social History Review* 7 (1970): 271–97.

Leoussi, A. S. *Nationalism and Classicism: The Classical Body as National Symbol in Nineteenth-Century England and France* (Basingstoke: Macmillan, 1998).

Levtzion, N. and Pouwels, R. L. eds., *The History of Islam in Africa* (Athens, OH: Ohio University Press, 2000).

Lindquist, M. A. *Race, Social Science and the Crisis of Manhood, 1890–1970: We are the Supermen* (New York: Routledge, 2012).

Lipphardt, L. "Traditions and Innovations: Visualizations of Human Variation, c.1900–38," *History of the Human Sciences* 28, 5 (2015): 49–79.

Loomba, A. and Burton, J. eds., *Race in Early Modern England: A Documentary Companion* (New York: Palgrave, 2007).

Lorimer, D. *Science, Race Relations and Resistance. Britain, 1870–1914* (Manchester: Manchester University Press, 2013).

Lorimer, D. *Colour, Class, and the Victorians: English Attitudes to the Negro in the Mid-Nineteenth Century* (Leicester: Leicester University Press, 1978).

MacMaster, N. *Racism in Europe: 1870–2000* (Basingstoke: Palgrave, 2001).

Maio, M. C. and Santos, R. V. "Antiracism and the Uses of Science in the Post-World War II: An Analysis of UNESCO's First Statements on Race (1950–1951)," *Vibrant: Virtual Brazilian Anthropology* 12, 2 (2015): 1–26.

Makdisi, S. *Making England Western: Occidentalism, Race and Imperial Culture* (Chicago: Chicago University Press, 2014).

Maksudyan, N. "The *Turkish Review of Anthropology* and the Racist Face of Turkish Nationalism," *Cultural Dynamics* 17, 3 (2005): 291–322.

Malik K., *The Meaning of Race: Race, History, and Culture in Western Society* (New York: New York University Press, 1996).

Mandler, P. *The English National Character: The History of an Idea from Edmund Burke to Tony Blair* (New Haven: Yale University Press, 2006).

Manias, C. "The Growth of Race and Culture in Nineteenth-Century Germany: Gustav Klemm and the Universal History of Humanity," *Modern Intellectual History* 9, 1 (2012): 1–31.

Marchand, S. L. *German Orientalism in the Age of Empire: Religion, Race, and Scholarship* (New York: Cambridge University Press, 2009).

Marchand, S. L. *Down From Olympus: Archaeology and Philhellenism in Germany, 1750–1970* (Princeton: Princeton University Press, 1996).

Marsden, W. "Rooting Racism into the Educational Experience of Childhood and Youth in the Nineteenth- and Twentieth-Centuries," *History of Education* 19, 4 (1990): 333–53.

Marx, A. W. *Faith in Nation: Exclusionary Origins of Nationalism* (Oxford: Oxford University Press, 2003).

Marx, A. W. *Making Race and Nation: A Comparison of the United States, South Africa, and Brazil* (New York: Cambridge University Press, 1998).

Marx, C. "Hendrik Verwoerd's Long March to Apartheid: Nationalism and Racism in South Africa," in Berg and Wendt, eds., *Racism in the Modern World*, 281–302.

Mason, M. M. *Dominant Narratives of Colonial Hokkaido and Imperial Japan: Envisioning the Periphery and the Modern Nation-State* (New York: Palgrave, 2012).

Massin, B. "From Virchow to Fischer: Physical Anthropology and 'Modern Race Theories' in Wilhelmine Germany," in George W. Stocking, Jr., *Volksgeist as Method and Ethic: Essays on Boasian Ethnography and the German Anthropological Tradition* (Madison: The University of Wisconsin Press, 1996), 79–154.

Matos, P. F. de. "Anthropology in Portugal: The Case of the Portuguese Society of Anthropology and Ethnology (SPACE), 1918," in Regna Darnell and Frederic

W. Gleach, eds., *Local Knowledge, Global Stage* (Lincoln: University of Nebraska Press, 2016), 53–97.

Matos, P. F. de. *The Colours of the Empire Racialized Representations during Portuguese Colonialism*, trans. by Mark Ayton (New York: Berghahn, 2013).

Maw, M. *Visions of India: Fulfilment Theology, the Aryan Race Theory, and the Work of British Protestant Missionaries in Victorian India* (Frankfurt am Main: Peter Lang, 1990).

McCarthy, T. *Race, Empire and the Idea of Human Development* (Cambridge: Cambridge University Press, 2009).

McGirr, L. *Suburban Warriors: The Origins of the American New Right*, with a new preface (Princeton: Princeton University Press, 2015) [first published 2001].

McMahon, R. *The Races of Europe Construction of National Identities in the Social Sciences, 1839–1939* (Basingstoke: Palgrave, 2016).

M'Charek, A. et al., "Topologies of Race: Doing Territory, Population and Identity in Europe," *Science, Technology & Human Values* 39, 4 (2014): 468–87.

M'Charek, A. "Beyond Fact or Fiction: On the Materiality of Race in Practice," *Cultural Anthropology* 28, 3 (2013): 420–42.

Mikkelsen, J. M. ed., *Kant and the Concept of Race. Late Eighteenth-Century Writings* (New York: State University of New York Press, 2013).

Miller, C. L. *Black Darkness: Africanist Discourse in French* (Chicago: University of Chicago Press, 1985).

Mills, C. W. *Blackness Visible* (Ithaca, NY: Cornell University Press, 1998).

Minawi, M. *The Ottoman Scramble for Africa: Empire and Diplomacy in the Sahara and the Hijaz* (Stanford: Stanford University Press, 2016).

Mishkova, D. et al., eds., *Anti-Modernism: Radical Revisions of Collective Identity* (Budapest: CEU Press, 2014).

Mishkova, M. ed., *We, The People: Politics of National Peculiarity in Southeastern Europe* (Budapest: CEU Press, 2009).

Mogilner, M. "Beyond, Against, and with Ethnography: Physical Anthropology as Science of Russian Modernity," in Roland Cvetkovksi and Alexis Hofmeister, eds., *An Empire of Others: Creating Ethnographic Knowledge in Imperial Russia and the USSR* (Budapest: CEU Press, 2014), 81–120.

Molendijk, A. L. *Friedrich Max Muller and the Sacred Books of the East* (New York: Oxford University Press, 2016).

Mommsen, W. J. ed., *Leopold von Ranke und die moderne Geschichtswissenschaft* (Stuttgart: Klett-Cotta, 1988).

Moodie, T. D. *The Rise of Afrikanerdom: Power, Apartheid, and the Afrikaner Civil Religion* (Berkeley: University of California Press, 1975).

Morning, A. *The Nature of Race: How Scientists Think and Teach about Human Difference* (Berkeley: University of California Press, 2011).

Morris-Reich, A., Rupnow, D. eds., *Ideas of 'Race' in the History of the Humanities* (Basingstoke: Palgrave, 2017).

Morris-Reich, A. *Race and Photography: Racial Photography as Scientific Evidence, 1876–1980* (Chicago: The University of Chicago Press, 2016).

Morris-Reich, A. "Race, Ideas, and Ideals: A Comparison of Franz Boas and Hans F. K. Günther," *History of European Ideas* 32 (2006): 313–32.

Mosse, G. L. *The Crisis of German Ideology: Intellectual Origins of the Third Reich* (New York: Grosset and Dunlap Publishers, 1965).

Mosse, G. L. *The Nationalization of the Masses: Political Symbolism and Mass Movements in Germany from the Napoleonic Wars through the Third Reich* (New York: Howard Fertig, 1974).

Mudde, C. ed., *The Populist Radical Right: A Reader* (London: Routledge, 2017).

Murji, K. and Solomos, J. eds., *Theories of Race and Ethnicity: Contemporary Debates and Perspectives* (Cambridge: Cambridge University Press, 2015).

Murray, D. *The Strange Death of Europe: Immigration, Identity and Islam* (London: Bloomsbury, 2017).

Nale, J. "Arthur de Gobineau on Blood and Race," *Critical Philosophy of Race* 2, 1 (2014): 106–24.

Napoli, O. de. "Race and Empire: The Legitimation of Italian Colonialism in Juridical Thought," *The Journal of Modern History* 85, 4 (2013): 801–32.

Nies, B. L. *Eugenic Fantasies: Racial Ideology in the Literature and Popular Culture of the 1920's* (Abingdon: Routledge, 2002).

Nirenberg, D. "Race and the Middle Ages: The Case of Spain and Its Jews," in Margaret R. Greer et al., eds, *Rereading The Black Legend: The Discourses of Religious and Racial Difference in the Renaissance Empires* (Chicago: The University of Chicago University Press, 2007), 71–87.

Olender, M. *The Languages of Paradise: Race, Religion, and Philology in the Nineteenth Century*, trans. by Arthur Goldhammer (Cambridge, MA: Harvard University Press, 1992).

O'Meara, M. *New Culture, New Right: Anti-Liberalism in Postmodern Europe* (Bloomington, IN: 1stBooks, 2004).

Onuf, P. S. *Jefferson's Empire: The Language of American Nationhood,* (Charlottesville: University Press of Virginia, 2000).

Owusu-Bempah, A. "Race and Policing in Historical Context: Dehumanization and the Policing of Black People in the 21st Century," *Theoretical Criminology* 20, 4 (2016): 1–12.

Panayi, P. *Immigration, Ethnicity and Racism in Britain, 1815–1914* (Manchester: Manchester University Press, 1994).

Park, P. K. J. *Africa, Asia, and the History of Philosophy: Racism in the Formation of the Philosophical Canon, 1780–1830* (New York: SUNY Press, 2013).

Pathmanathan, R. et al., "Indian Craniometric Variability and Affinities," *International Journal of Evolutionary Biology* (2013): 1–25.

Patriarca, S. and Riall, L. eds., *The Risorgimento Revisited: Nationalism and Culture in Nineteenth-Century Italy* (Basingstoke: Palgrave Macmillan, 2012).

Peckham, R. S. *National Histories, Natural States: Nationalism and the Politics of Place in Greece* (London: I. B. Tauris, 2001).

Pick, D. *Faces of Degeneration: A European Disorder, c. 1848-c. 1918* (Cambridge: Cambridge University Press, 1989).

Pietrusewsky, M. *Metric and Non-Metric Cranial Variation in Australian Aboriginal Populations, Compared with Populations from the Pacific and Asia* (Canberra: Australian Institute of Aboriginal Studies, 1984).

Platt, T. "Bitter Legacies: A War of Extermination, Grave Looting, and Culture Wars in the American West," in Élisabeth Anstett and Jean-Marc Dreyfus, eds., *Human Remains and Identification: Mass Violence, Genocide, and the 'Forensic Turn'* (Manchester: Manchester University Press, 2015), 14–33.

Poliakov, L. *Le mythe aryen. Essai sur les sources du racisme et des nationalismes* (Paris: Calmann-Lévy, 1971).

Poliakov, L. *The Aryan Myth: A History of Racist and Nationalistic Ideas in Europe*, trans. by Edmund Howard (New York: Basic Books, 1974).

Pollard, F. *The Literary Quest for an American National Character* (New York: Routledge, 2009).

Porter, B. *The Absent-Minded Imperialists: Empire, Society and Culture in Britain* (Oxford: Oxford University Press, 2004).

Prodan, D. *Supplex Libellus Valachorum or the Political Struggle of the Romanians in Transylvania during the 18th Century* (Bucharest: Publishing House of the Academy, 1971).

Quine, M. S. "The Destiny of Races 'Not Yet Called to Civilization': Giustiniano Nicolucci's Critique of American Polygenism and Defense of Liberal Racism," in Richard McMahon, ed., *National Races: Transnational Power Struggles in Science and Politics, 1840s–1940s* (Lincoln, NE: University of Nebraska Press, forthcoming).

Quine, M. S. "Making Italians: Aryanism and Anthropology in Italy during the *Risorgimento*," in Marius Turda, ed., *Crafting Humans: From Genesis to Eugenics and Beyond* (Göttingen: V&R Unipress, 2013), 127–52.

Quinlan, S. "The Racial Imagery of Degeneration and Depopulation: Georges Vacher de Lapouge and 'Anthroposocioloy' in Fin-de-Siècle France," *History of European Ideas* 24, 6 (1998): 393–413.

Qureshi, S. "Displaying Sarah Baartman: The 'Venus Hottentot,'" *History of Science* 42, 136 (2004): 233–57.

Rasmussen, K. S. "Foucault's Genealogy of Racism," *Theory, Culture & Society* 28, 5 (2011): 34–51.

Reiss, H. S. *The Political Thought of the German Romantics, 1793–1815* (Oxford: Basil Blackwell, 1955).

Reynaud-Paligot, C. *La République Raciale: Paradigme Racial et Idéologie Républicaine, 1830–1930* (Paris: Presses Universitaires de France, 2006).

Rich, P. P. *Race and Empire in British Politics*, 2nd edn (Cambridge: Cambridge University Press, 1990) [first edition 1986].

Richards, E. "The 'Moral Anatomy' of Robert Knox: The Interplay between Biological and Social Thought in Victorian Scientific Naturalism," *Journal of the History of Biology* 22, 3 (1989): 373–436.

Romani, R. *National Character and Public Spirit in Britain and France, 1750–1914* (Cambridge: Cambridge University Press, 2002).

Roque, R. *Headhunting and Colonialism: Anthropology and the Circulation of Human Skulls in the Portuguese Empire, 1870–1930* (Basingstoke: Palgrave, 2010).

Rosemblatt, K. A. "Sexuality and Biopower in Chile and Latin America," *Political Power and Social Theory* 15 (2002): 229–62.

Roth, W. D. "The Multiple Dimensions of Race," *Ethnic and Racial Studies* 39, 8 (2016): 1310–38.

Ruehl, M. A. *The Italian Renaissance in the German Historical Imagination, 1860–1930* (Cambridge: Cambridge University Press, 2015).

Rupke, N. and Lauer, G. eds., *Johann Friedrich Blumenbach: Race and Natural History, 1750–1850* (Abingdon: Routledge, 2017).

Rusert, B. *Fugitive Science: Empiricism and Freedom in Early African American Culture* (New York: New York University Press, 2017).

Saaler, S. "The Kokuryūkai (Black Dragon Society) and the Rise of Nationalism, Pan-Asianism, and Militarism in Japan, 1901–1925," *International Journal of Asian Studies* 11, 2 (2014): 125–60.

Said, E. *Orientalism: Western Conceptions of the Orient* (London: Penguin Books, 1995) [first edition 1978].

Said, E. *Culture and Imperialism* (New York: Vintage Books, 1994).

Schaffer, G. *Racial Science and British Society, 1930–62* (Basingstoke: Palgrave Macmillan, 2008).

Schiller, F. *Paul Broca: Founder of French Anthropology, Explorer of the Brain* (Berkeley: University of California Press, 1979).

Schramm, K. et al., eds., *Identity Politics and the New Genetics: Re/Creating Categories of Difference and Belonging* (New York: Berghahn, 2012).

Sera-Shriar, E. "Race," in Mark Bevir, ed., *Historicism and the Human Sciences in Victorian Britain* (Cambridge: Cambridge University Press, 2017), 48–76.

Serequeberhan, T. "The Critique of Eurocentrism and the Practice of African Philosophy," in Emmanuel C. Eze, ed., *Post-Colonial African Philosophy: A Critical Reader* (Oxford: Blackwell, 1997), 141–60.

Shorto, R. *Descartes' Bones: A Skeletal History of the Conflict between Faith and Reason* (New York: Knopf Doubleday, 2008).

Siddle, R. *Race, Resistance and the Ainu of Japan* (London: Routledge, 1996).

Siedentop, L. *Inventing the Individual: The Origins of Western Liberalism* (London: Allen Lane, 2014).

Sieg, U. *Germany's Prophet: Paul de Lagarde and the Origins of Modern Antisemitism* (Waltham, MD: Brandeis University Press, 2013).

Silva, D. F. da. *Toward a Global History of Race* (Minneapolis: University of Minnesota Press, 2007).

Skey, M. *National Belonging and Everyday Life: The Significance of Nationhood in an Uncertain World* (Basingstoke: Palgrave, 2011).

Slotkin, R. *Regeneration through Violence: The Mythology of the American Frontier, 1600–1860* (Norman, OK: University of Oklahoma Press, 1973).

Smith, A. D. *The Ethnic Origins of Nations* (Oxford: Basil Blackwell, 1983).

Smith, J. A. "Nationalism, Virtue, and the Spirit of Liberty in Rousseau's 'Government of Poland'," *The Review of Politics* 65, 3 (2003): 409–37.

Smith, J. E. H. *Nature, Human Nature, & Human Difference: Race in Early Modern Philosophy* (Princeton: Princeton University Press, 2015).

Smith, W. D. *Politics and the Science of Culture in Germany, 1840–1920* (New York: Oxford University Press, 1991).

Snyder, L. L. *Encyclopedia of Nationalism* (London: St James Press, 1990).

Solonari, V. *Purifying the Nation: Population Exchange and Ethnic Cleansing in Nazi-Allied Romania* (Baltimore: Johns Hopkins University Press, 2010).

Sontag, S. *Styles of Radical Will* (London: Penguin Books, 2009) [first published in 1966].

Spencer, V. A. *Herder's Political Thought: A Study of Language, Culture, and Community* (Toronto: Toronto University Press, 2012).

Stackelberg, R. *Idealism Debased: From Völkisch Ideology to National Socialism* (Kent, OH: Kent State University Press, 1981).

Steffen, K. "Ludwik Hirszfeld, the Great War, and Seroanthropology: Expectations and Unfulfilled Promises," *Ab Imperio* 2 (2016): 125–52.

Stepan, N. *The Idea of Race in Science: Great Britain, 1800–1960* (London: Macmillan, 1982).

Sternhell, Z. *The Anti-Enlightenment Tradition*, trans. David Maisel (New Haven: Yale University Press, 2010) 21 [originally published 2006].

Stock, P. "'Almost a Separate Race': Racial Thought and the Idea of Europe in British Encyclopaedias and Histories, 1771–1830," *Modern Intellectual History* 8, 1 (2011): 3–29.

Stocking, G. W. Jr. ed., *Bones, Bodies, Behavior: Essays on Biological Anthropology* (Madison: University of Wisconsin Press, 1988).

Stocking, G. W. Jr. *Victorian Anthropology* (New York: The Free Press, 1987).

Stocking, G. W. Jr. *Race, Culture, and Evolution: Essays in the History of Anthropology* (New York: Free Press, 1968).

Stoler, A. L. *Carnal Knowledge and Imperial Power: Race and the Intimate in Colonial Rule* (Berkeley: University of California Press, 2002).

Stone, D. "Nazi Race Ideologues," *Patterns of Prejudice* 50, 4–5 (2016): 445–57.

Storry, R. *The Double Patriots: A Study of Japanese Nationalism* (London: Chatto and Windus, 1957).

Stuchtey, B. ed., *Science across the European Empires* (Oxford: Oxford University Press, 2005).

Sugar, P. F. and Lederer, I. J. eds., *Nationalism in Eastern Europe* (Seattle: University of Washington Press, 1969).

Sun, L.-K. *The Chinese National Character: From Nationhood to Individuality* (New York: M. E. Sharpe, 2002).

Sunic, T. *Against Democracy and Equality: The European New Right* (New York: Peter Lang, 1990).

Tabili, L. "Race and Ethnicity," in Michael Seler, ed., *The Fin-de-Siècle World* (Abingdon: Routledge, 2015), 518–34.

Tabili, L. "Race is a Relationship not a Thing," *Journal of Social History* 37, 1 (2003): 125–30.

Talbot, P. A. and Mulhall, H. *The Physical Anthropology of Southern Nigeria: A Biometric Study in Statistical Method* (New York: Cambridge University Press, 1962).

Tamanoi, M. A. "Knowledge, Power, and Racial Classification: The 'Japanese' in 'Manchuria,'" *The Journal of Asian Studies* 59, 2 (2000): 248–76.

Taylor, W. R. *Cavalier and Yankee: The Old South and American National Character* (New York: Oxford University Press, 1993) [first published 1961].

Telles, E. E. *Race in Another America: The Significance of Skin Color in Brazil* (Princeton: Princeton University Press, 2006).

Tierney, T. R. *Tropics of Savagery: The Culture of Japanese Empire in Comparative Frame* (Berkeley: University of California Press, 2010).

Tilley, H. *Africa as a Living Laboratory: Empire, Development, and the Problem of Scientific Knowledge, 1870–1950* (Chicago: The University of Chicago Press, 2011).

Thornton, J. *Africa and Africans in the Making of the Atlantic World, 1400–1800*, 2nd edn (Cambridge: Cambridge University Press, 1998).

Todorov, T. *On Human Diversity: Nationalism, Racism, and Exoticism in French Thought* (Cambridge, MA.: Harvard University Press, 1993).

Tomlinson, S. *Head Masters. Phrenology, Secular Education, and Nineteenth-Century Social Thought* (Tuscaloosa: The University of Alabama Press, 2005).

Trautmann, T. ed., *The Aryan Debate* (Delhi: Oxford University Press, 2005).

Trautmann, T. *Aryans and British India* (Berkeley: University of California Press, 1997).

Trencsényi, B. et al., *A History of Modern Political Thought in East Central Europe*. Volume I: Negotiating Modernity in the 'Long Nineteenth Century' (Oxford: Oxford University Press, 2016).

Trencsényi, T. *The Politics of 'National Character': A Study in Interwar East European Thought* (Abingdon: Routledge, 2012).

Tucker, W. H. *The Science and Politics of Racial Research* (Urbana, IL: University of Illinois Press, 1994).

Tudor, L. "The Philosophy of Identity: Ethnicity, Culture, and Race in Identitarian Thought," *The Occidental Quarterly* 14, 3 (2014): 83–112.

Turda, M. *Modernism and Eugenics* (Basingstoke: Palgrave, 2010).

Turda, M. "Entangled Traditions of Race: Physical Anthropology in Hungary and Romania, 1900–1940," *Focaal* 58 (2010): 32–46.

Turda, M. "Conservative Palingenesis and Cultural Modernism in Early Twentieth-Century Romania," *Totalitarian Movements and Political Religions* 9, 4 (2008): 437–53.

Turda, M. "The Nation as Object: Race, Blood, and Biopolitics in Interwar Romania," *Slavic Review* 66 (2007): 413–41.

Ubelaker D. H. et al. "Application of Forensic Discriminant Functions to a Spanish Cranial Sample," *Forensic Science Communications* 4, 3 (2002): 1–6.

Varga, B. *The Monumental Nation: Magyar Nationalism and Symbolic Politics in Fin-de-siècle Hungary* (New York: Berghahn, 2016).

Vasilopoulou, S. and Halikiopoulou, D. *The Golden Dawn's 'Nationalist Solution': Explaining the Rise of the Far Right in Greece* (New York: Palgrave Macmillan, 2015).

Verdery, K. *National Ideology under Socialism: Identity and Cultural Politics in Ceausescu's Romania* (Berkeley: University of California Press, 1995).

Verdery, K. "The Production and Defense of 'the Romanian Nation', 1900 to World War II," in Richard D. Fox, ed., *National Ideologies and the Production of National Culture* (Washington, DC: American Anthropological Association, 1990), 81–111.

Viroli, M. *For Love of Country. An Essay on Patriotism and Nationalism* (Oxford: Clarendon Press, 1995).

Wade, P. *Race: An Introduction* (Cambridge: Cambridge University Press, 2015).

Wade, P. "'Race', Nature and Culture," *Man* 28, 1 (1993): 17–34.

Weber, E. *Peasants into Frenchmen: The Modernization of Rural France, 1870–1914* (Stanford: Stanford University Press, 1976).

Weheliye, A. G. *Habeas Viscus: Racializing Assemblages, Biopolitics, and Black Feminist Theories of the Human* (Durham, NC: Duke University Press, 2014).

Weitz, E. D. *A Century of Genocide: Utopias of Race and Nation*, with a new preface by the author (Princeton: Princeton University Press, 2015) [first published 2003].

Wekker, G. *White Innocence: Paradoxes of Colonialism and Race* (Durham, NC: Duke University Press, 2016).

White, H. *Tropics of Discourse: Essays in Cultural Criticism* (Baltimore: The Johns Hopkins University Press, 1978).

Williams, R. *Keywords: A Vocabulary of Culture and Society* (London: HarperCollins, 2014) [first published in 1976].

Williams, D. L. *Rousseau's 'The Social Contract': An Introduction* (New York: Cambridge University Press, 2014).

Williams, F. L. et al., "Forensic Misclassification of Ancient Nubian Crania: Implications for Assumptions about Human Variation," *Current Anthropology* 46, 2 (2005): 341.

Williams, V. J. *Rethinking Race: Franz Boas and His Contemporaries* (Lexington: University of Kentucky Press, 1996), 4–6.

Willson, A. L. *A Mythical Image: The Ideal of India in German Romanticism* (Durham, NC: Duke University Press, 1964).

Wimmer, A. *Ethnic Boundary Making: Institutions, Power, Networks* (New York: Oxford University Press, 2013).

Wintle, C. "Decolonizing the Smithsonian: Museums as Microcosms of Political Encounter," *The American Historical Review* 121, 5 (2016): 1492–520.

Wolff, K. et al., "Anthropological Examination of the Chronologically Separated Groups of the 11th–13th Century Zalavár-Chapel (Zalavár-Kápolna) Cemetery from Hungary," *Anthropological Anzeiger* 69, 4 (2012): 473–90.

Wolff, L. and Cipolloni, C. eds., *The Anthropology of the Enlightenment* (Stanford: Stanford University Press, 2007).

Wood, E. *Forging Democracy from Below: Insurgent Traditions in South Africa and El Salvador* (Cambridge: Cambridge University Press, 2000).

Woodroffe, M. "Racial Theories of History and Politics: The Example of Houston Stewart Chamberlain," in Paul Kennedy and Anthony Nicholls, eds., *Nationalist and Racialist Movements in Britain and Germany before 1914* (London: Macmillan, 1981), 143–53.

Woolf, S. J. *The Italian Risorgimento: Problems and Perspectives in History* (London: Longmans, 1969).

Wormell, D. *Sir John Seeley and the Uses of History* (Cambridge: Cambridge University Press, 1980).

Wright, R. *Guide to Using the CRANID Programs CR6LDA.EXE and CR6NN. EXE* (2007).

Yancy, G. *Black Bodies, White Gazes: The Continuous Significance of Race* (Lanham, MD: Rowman & Littlefield, 2008).

Yeomans, R. *Visions of Annihilation: The Ustasha Regime and the Cultural Politics of Fascism, 1941–1945* (Pittsburgh: Pittsburgh University Press, 2013).

Yilmaz, H. *Becoming Turkish: Nationalist Reforms and Cultural Negotiations in Early Republican Turkey, 1923–1945* (Syracuse, NY: Syracuse University Press, 2013)

Yōichi, K. "Rule in the Name of 'Protection': The Vocabulary of Colonialism," in Michele M. Mason and Helen J. S. Lee, eds., *Reading Colonial Japan: Text, Context, and Critique* (Stanford: Stanford University Press, 2012), 60–76.

Yoshino, K. *Cultural Nationalism in Contemporary Japan: A Sociological Inquiry* (London: Routledge, 1992).

Yudell, M. *Race Unmasked: Biology and Race in the Twentieth Century* (New York: Columbia University Press, 2014).

Zack, N. ed., *The Oxford Handbook of Philosophy and Race* (Oxford: Oxford University Press, 2017).

Zeidel, R. F. *Immigrants, Progressives, and the Exclusion Politics: The Dillingham Commission, 1900–1927* (DeKalb, IL: Northern Illinois University Press, 2004).

Zimmerman, A. *Anthropology and Antihumanism in Imperial Germany* (Chicago: Chicago University Press, 2001).

Zimmermann, M. *Wilhelm Marr: The Patriarch of Anti-Semitism* (New York: Oxford University Press, 1986).

INDEX